15th International Conference e-Learning (EL2021)

Held at the 15th Multi-Conference on Computer Science and Information Systems (MCCSIS 2021)

Online
20 - 23 July 2021

ISBN: 978-1-7138-3579-0

Printed from e-media with permission by:

Curran Associates, Inc.
57 Morehouse Lane
Red Hook, NY 12571

International Association for Development of the Information Society (IADIS)
Rua Sao Sebastiao Da Pedreira
No. 100, 30, 1050-209
Lisbon, Portugal

Phone: 351 21 3151373
Fax: 351 21 3151244

secretariat@iadis.org

Additional copies of this publication are available from:

Curran Associates, Inc.
57 Morehouse Lane
Red Hook, NY 12571 USA
Phone: 845-758-0400
Fax: 845-758-2633
Email: curran@proceedings.com
Web: www.proceedings.com

TABLE OF CONTENTS

E-SKILLS AND DIGITAL LITERACY FOR FOREIGN LANGUAGES EDUCATION: STUDENT CASE STUDY IN UKRAINE

Rusudan Makhachashvili and Ivan Semenist
Borys Grinchenko Kyiv University, Bulvarno-Kudryavska-st., 18/2, Kyiv, Ukraine

ABSTRACT

The COVID-19 pandemic induced amplified digitalization measures in the higher education sphere, informed by the need to take quick comprehensive action to achieve the overarching result to transform educational scenarios into interdisciplinary digital, remote, and hybrid frameworks. The consequent functional tasks to meet this challenge are estimated as 1) to activate comprehensive complex skillsets, otherwise latent or underutilized in the educational process; 2) to boost ICT competence and digital literacy of all participants of the educational process, relocated to the computer realm. The study objective is to diagnose and critically review the empirical case of digital skills viral development and application to construe interdisciplinary competencies of students of European and Oriental Languages major programs in Ukraine, employed in the years 2020-2021 due to quarantine measures. The study premise is the identification of various competency principles, derivative of twenty-first-century skills, and projected digital literacy requirements. The survey method and diagnostic analysis of different digital literacy components and e-skills implementation are used to assess the parameters of efficiency of transforming real-life linguistic education practices into the digital and hybrid format. The investigation novelty is in the identification of the interoperability between various groups of applied e-skills and soft skills, instrumental to develop interdisciplinary professional awareness of Foreign Languages students in Ukraine. The study allows detection of challenges for actual and underdeveloped skills (hard, technical, and soft), that participants of the educational process encountered through digital format adaptation in programs of European and Oriental Languages.

KEYWORDS

Digital Literacy, Viral Digital Skills, e-Skills, e-Learning, Foreign Languages Education (FLE)

1. INTRODUCTION

Transformative shifts in the knowledge economy of the XXI century, Industry 4.0 development and elaboration of the networked society, emergency digitization due to quarantine measures have imposed pressing revisions onto interdisciplinary and cross-sectorial job market demands of Liberal Arts university graduates' skillsets, upon entering the workforce. This, in turn, stipulates reevaluation of the interdisciplinary approaches to comprehensive professional competencies in foreign languages acquisition, education, and application.

The COVID-19 pandemic induced amplified digitalization measures in the higher education sphere, informed by the need to take quick comprehensive action to achieve the overarching result to transform educational scenarios into interdisciplinary digital, remote, and hybrid frameworks.

The consequent functional tasks to meet this challenge in the educational sphere are estimated as 1) adapt the existent educational scenarios to digital, remote and hybrid formats; 2) to upgrade ICT competence and digital literacy of all participants of the educational process; 3) to activate complex interdisciplinary skillsets, otherwise latent or underutilized in the educational process.

These motivations inform the study **objective** - to diagnose and critically review the empirical case of digital skills development and application to construe interdisciplinary competencies of students of European (English, Spanish, French, Italian, German) and Oriental (Mandarin Chinese, Japanese) Languages major programs at Borys Grinchenko Kyiv University, Ukraine through the span of educational activities in the time-frame of COVID-19 quarantine measures of March 2020 to March 2021.

The inquiry contribution is disclosed through the study **design**, which includes the following elements:

1) The modeling of interoperability between various competency principles, derivative of twenty-first-century skills (Abbott, 2013), (DosReis, 2015), (Davies & Fidler, 2011) and projected digital literacy requirements for Foreign Languages Education (FLE) across core digital literacy frameworks (European e-Competence Framework, UNESCO ICT Competence framework for educators and European Commission Digital Competence Framework: DigComp 2020);
2) The survey method application for diagnostic analysis of different digital literacy components and dimensions, as well as digital skills implementation, was used to assess the parameters of efficiency of transforming real-life linguistic education practices into the digital and hybrid format.
3) The identification of the correlation between various groups of applied digital skills and soft skills, instrumental to develop interdisciplinary professional competence of FLE students.

The following grid of groundwork concepts is applied to profile the Foreign Languages Education (FLE) digitization in the COVID-19 timeframe: INTERDISCIPLINARITY; INTEROPERABILITY; DIGITAL LITERACY; COMPLEX SKILLS; VIRAL DIGITAL SKILLS.

The meaning of INTERDISCIPLINARITY is synthesized for the purpose of this study as an agglomeration of two or more fields of knowledge into one scope/goal of study, inquiry, or activity (Callaos & Marlowe, 2020), (Frodeman, 2017), (Holbrook, 2013), (Jacobs & Frickel, 2009).

The concept of INTEROPERABILITY is disclosed across different lenses (Interoperability Working Group, 2021), (Slater, 2013) as a characteristic of an object, product or system, that allows its interface to be comprehensible, to work with other objects, products, or systems.

As applied to Foreign Languages Education, the concept of interoperability represents the property of functional, dynamic interconnectivity between the source and target domains of linguistic content, linguistic theory content, related areas of scientific and universal knowledge, and domains of professional and social application.

Interoperability for FLE e-skills is ensured by the communicative nature (Hymes, 1972) of interdisciplinary skills in general. The core cross-sectorial domain that is referential for primary skills (social skills, emotional intellect, collaboration, communication, digital literacy), necessary for educational goals achievement, is estimated to be COMMUNICATION. DIGITAL LITERACY in its turn is defined as the ability to use information and communication technologies to find, evaluate, create, and communicate information, requiring both cognitive and technical skills (DQ report, 2019). Digital literacy and e-skills assessment in the educational context has been subject to academic reevaluation due to the objective conditions of the pandemic global lockdown measures and has been approached through a different lens: regional variation in digital literacy level development in education (Gródek-Szostak et al, 2021); technological challenges for the development of soft skills (Liesa Orús et al, 2020; Troussas et al, 2021); challenges and opportunities of e-learning in higher education (Al-Jardani, 2020; Supriyatno et al, 2020).

The fundamental interdisciplinarity, that COVID-19 digital procedural transformations imposed on the educational process in the area of Foreign languages acquisition, is verified by a unified framework of correspondence between the components of communication (Shannon, 1948) and communicative competence (Hymes, 1972), comprising of a diverse skillset, and various aspects of ICT competence in Foreign Languages Education (European Commission, 2020), (European Commission, 2020), (UNESCO, 2018), utilized in the educational process, elaborated for the purposes of this study (Figure 1):

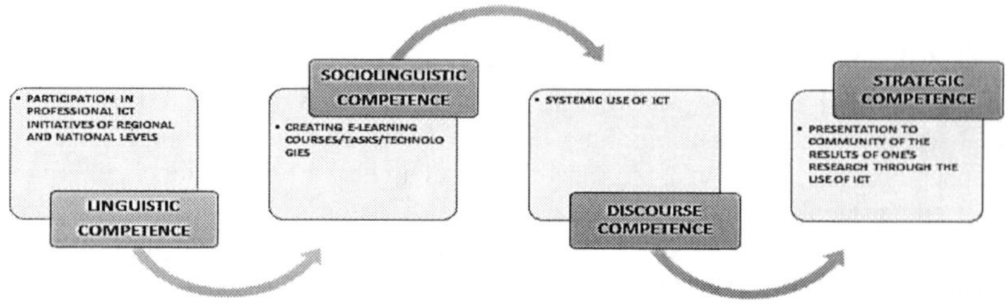

Figure 1. Interdisciplinary Correspondence Between Communicative Competence and ICT Competence in Foreign Languages Education

A COMPLEX SKILL, subsequently, is defined as a skill requiring to process lots of information and make lots of decisions simultaneously (Wulf & Shea, 2002).

VIRAL DIGITAL SKILLS for the purpose of this study are defined as rhizomatic capabilities of interoperable manipulation of digital data, tools, and communication formats, acquired institutionally, intuitively or on a peer-to-peer basis.

Given the nature of the increasingly digitalized context of foreign languages education and communicative application ("the Technospheric shift" (Makhachashvili & Semenist, 2021), it is suggested to consider the different types of information source and information destination (human and machine/computer/program, accordingly) in the structure of the groundwork Communication Model (Shannon, 1948), when communication is approached as the core factor of interoperability of source and target knowledge and application domains in FLE.

Subsequently, a model of soft skills paradigms and digital literacy frameworks INTEROPERABILITY in FLE is developed (Figure 2):

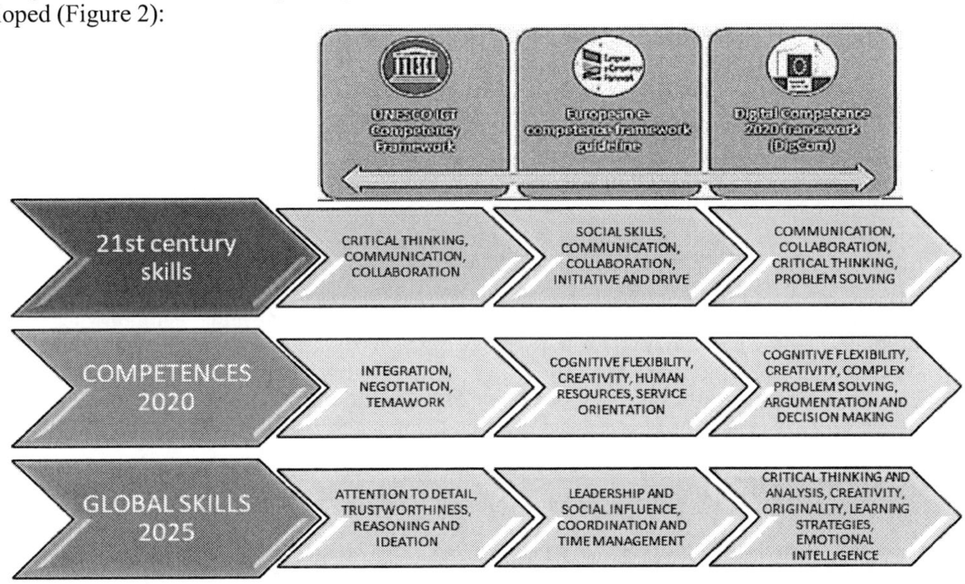

Figure 2. Soft skills paradigms and Digital literacy frameworks interoperability

1) European E-competence Framework Guideline (European Commission, 2020), customized according to European Professional Competence Framework, accommodates the following types of soft skills in terms of digital competence requirements for vocational activity in FLE: service orientation; attention to detail, learning strategies, leadership, and social influence, cognitive creativity and flexibility, coordination and time-management; human resources management;

2) UNESCO ICT Competence framework (UNESCO, 2018), customized for pre-service teachers of foreign languages, accommodates the following types of soft skills in terms of digital competence requirements: collaboration, teamwork, problem-solving, reasoning, and ideation.

3) Digital Competence 2020 framework (European Commission, 2020) for the general public, accommodates the following types of soft skills in terms of digital competence requirements for efficient digital citizenship: Communication and collaboration, creativity and adaptability, learning and innovation, trustworthiness, emotional intelligence, complex problem-solving.

2. E-SKILLS AND DIGITAL LITERACY FOR FOREIGN LANGUAGES EDUCATION: SURVEY RESULTS

2.1 Method Overview

The study employs the combination of mixed methods (Almalki 2016) – a proportional arrangement of quantitative and qualitative inquiry to assess in-depth aspects of subjective and individual quality estimation of digital distance and hybrid learning. The comprehensive study design methodology included the following consecutive steps:

1) The qualitative profiling of various competency principles, derivative of twenty-first-century skills (Abbott, 2013), (DosReis, 2015), (Davies & Fidler, 2011), (Makhachashvili & Semenist 2021), and digital literacy requirements for Foreign Languages Education (FLE) across digital literacy frameworks (European e-Competence Framework, UNESCO ICT Competence framework for educators and European Commission Digital Competence Framework: DigComp 2020);

2) The online survey method - based on D. Dillman's concept of mixed media and mixed-mode surveys (Dillman 2014) - applied to conduct an in-depth assessment of different digital literacy components and dimensions, as well as digital skills implementation, used to assess the parameters of efficiency of transforming real-life linguistic education practices into the digital and hybrid format in Oriental and European Languages university level programs at Borys Grinchenko Kyiv University, Kyiv, Ukraine;

3) The evaluation of interoperability between various groups of applied digital skills and soft skills, instrumental to develop interdisciplinary professional competence of FLE students.

Based on the digital literacy profile of FLE (e-skills frameworks, customized for Foreign Languages Education) an online survey was devised to assess in-depth subjective experiences of e-learning and hybrid learning in the COVID-19 timeframe (March 2020 – March 2021) for students of Oriental languages (Mandarin Chinese and Japanese) and European Languages (French, Italian, Spanish, English, German) major programs.

The survey structure comprised of 16 complex diagnostic questions (multiple-choice, criteria comparison, and Likert scale score types), divided into the *following categories*: 1) questions on the overall assessment of digital literacy level in the framework of COVID-19 lockdown and quarantine measures for university programs of Oriental and European languages; 2) questions on diagnostics of future specialists in FLE according to the established frameworks of digital competencies and e-skills in the professional field; 3) questions on diagnostics of interoperability of linguistic/communicative/soft professional and digital skills for university programs of European and Oriental languages.

2.2 Data Gathering

A sizable sample of 235 respondents total across 7 Foreign Languages Programs - Oriental (Mandarin Chinese, Japanese) and European (English, French, Spanish, Italian, German) languages at Borys Grinchenko Kyiv University took part in the survey. The following groups of stakeholders of the digital distant education in the timespan of COVID-19 pandemic measures were respondents of the survey overall on all three tiers of educational levels according to the legislature of Ukraine (Law OHE 2019): undergraduate, graduate, and post-graduate: 1) students of Bachelor's programs for Oriental (Mandarin Chinese, Japanese) and European (French, Italian, Spanish, English, German) languages (1st, 2nd, 3rd and 4th years of study) – 93.6%; 2) students of Master's programs for Oriental (Mandarin Chinese, Japanese) and European (English, French, Spanish, Italian, German) languages (1st and 2nd years of study) – 4.3%; students of Post-graduate programs for Oriental (Mandarin Chinese, Japanese) and European (French, Italian, Spanish, English, German) languages (1st, 2nd, 3rd and 4th years of study) – 2.1%.

For the purposes of this paper, the survey results were scaled to accommodate the sample of students of Oriental (Mandarin Chinese, Japanese) and European (French, Italian, Spanish, English, German) languages programs of Borys Grinchenko Kyiv University of Ukraine (Kyiv being the capital city). This limitation was adopted to assess the case of best practices of educational digitization to estimate the parameters and challenges of the individual experiences and digital skills development in the framework of COVID-19 lockdown, comprehensively implemented at Borys Grinchenko Kyiv university since the first days of the global lockdown in March of 2020 and thereon, as a parcel of the university overall digital campus and digital literacy implementation policy.

2.3 Survey Results and Discussion

Group 1 of survey questions - *overall assessment of digital literacy level in the framework of COVID-19 lockdown and quarantine measures for university programs of Oriental and European languages* - yielded the following representative results across the board.

Estimation of overall digital literacy level in the framework of COVID-19 lockdown for university programs of Oriental and European languages was conducted according to the 5-Point Likert Scale (a response scale in which responders specify their level of engagement with a statement or a parameter in five points: (1) Strongly disagree; (2) Disagree; (3) Neither agree nor disagree; (4) Agree; (5) Strongly agree (Handbook 2010). The extremum points for evaluation were 1 (maximum negative overall mastery of the given digital literacy level) and 5 (maximum positive overall mastery of the given digital literacy level).

The qualitative dimensions provided for evaluation were: Elementary digital literacy; Medium digital literacy; Advanced digital literacy; No defined digital literacy level.

The quantitative assessment of individual digital level yielded a range of scalable results (Figure 3):

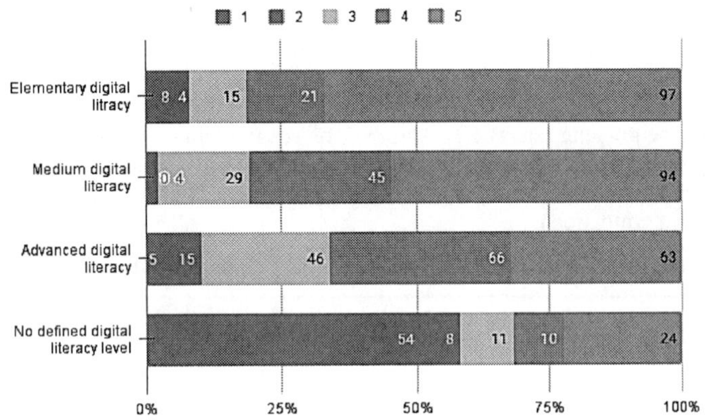

Figure 3. Assessment of Individual Digital Level

Stakeholders of European and Oriental languages programs evaluated their individual digital literacy levels in the COVID-19 timeframe as predominantly *advanced* (83% of respondents) and *medium* (73.2%). However, the elementary and medium digital literacy levels were assessed with the highest standard deviation of score range (SD=34). These levels of digital literacy mastery were assessed as predominantly 5 (maximum positive overall mastery of the given digital literacy level): Elementary level - 41.3%; Medium level – 40% of respondents.

Comparative evaluation of individual digital literacy level for university programs of Oriental and European languages during and prior to the framework of COVID-19 lockdown (Figure 4) allowed to estimate the dynamics of digital literacy from the timespan before the global pandemic measures and through the emergency online education of 2020-2021:

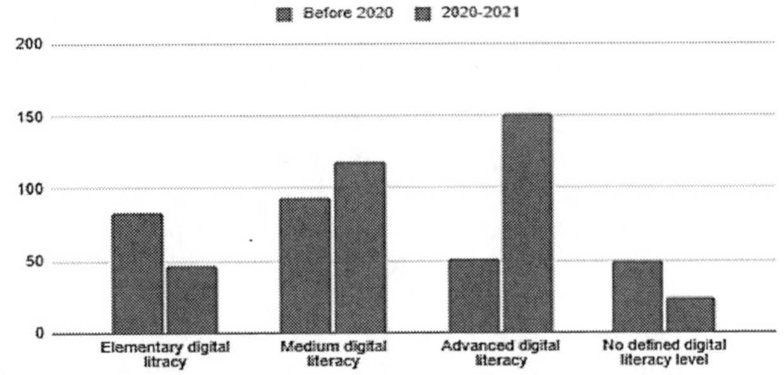

Figure 4. Comparative evaluation of individual digital literacy level

Digital literacy level in the timeframe before 2020 is estimated by the stakeholders of Oriental and European languages university programs as predominantly Elementary (35.3%) to Medium (39.6%). Digital literacy level in the timeframe of Covid-19 quarantine measures of 2020-2021 is estimated by the stakeholders of Oriental and European languages university programs was estimated as predominantly Medium (50.2%) to Advanced (64.3%). The estimated positive dynamics of the digital literacy mastery by Foreign Languages students comprise +10% for the Medium level and +42% for the Advanced level. There's a notable drop in the score for the 'No defined digital literacy level' dimension of assessment between the compared timespans of pre-pandemic and during the pandemic emergency online learning measures (20.8% decreased to 10.2% accordingly).

Group 2 of survey questions - *diagnostics of future specialists in FLE according to the established frameworks of digital competencies and e-skills in the professional field-* yielded the following representative results across the board.

Group 2.1 of questions - *Diagnostics of future specialists in FLE* ***according to European e-Competence Framework*** *and estimation of digital skills of FLE for professional application* - allowed to evaluate of the professional e-competence dimensions for FLE students among the following: A. PLAN, B. BUILD, C. RUN, D. ENABLE, and E. MANAGE professional processes with the help of digital tools and services.

Within the given dimensions the following top-scoring *professional goals* of FLE students were estimated (Figure 5): 1) Planning of professional processes (in the field of or with the help of foreign languages) (A) – 60.8% of respondents; 2) Monitoring of professional activity (in the field of or with the help of foreign languages) (C) – 49.8% of respondents; 3) Provision (facilitation) of professional activity (in the field of or with the help of foreign languages) (D) – 46.3% of respondents. According to the prioritized professional goals, the following dominant professional e-competence dimensions for FLE students are identified (Table 1): 1) to PLAN; 2) to RUN; 3) to ENABLE professional processes in Foreign Languages application (communication and education).

Table 1. FLE to implement digital tools for professional goals

PROFESSIONAL GOAL	% OF RESPONDENTS	DIGITAL COMPETENCE DIMENSION
Planning of professional processes (in the field of foreign languages) (A)	60,8	A. PLAN
Development of professional products (in the field of foreign languages) (B)	39,6	B. BUILD
Monitoring of professional activity (in the field of foreign languages) (C)	49,8	C. RUN
Provision (facilitation) of professional activity (in the field of foreign languages) (D)	46,3	D. ENABLE
Management/governance of professional activities (in the field of foreign languages) (E)	39,6	E. MANAGE

Therefore, the priority *types of dominant digital skills for professional application* of FLE students according to the European e-competence framework are estimated as 1) *ICT user skills* – 74.25% of respondents; 2) *ICT practitioner skills* – 72.75/% of respondents.

According to the Likert Scale, assessment ICT user skills get a top ranking of 4 (46% of respondents) and ICT practitioner skills get a top ranking of 5 (37% of respondents).

The following specific digital skills for Foreign Languages professionals correspond to the prioritized types: 1) ICT PRACTITIONER SKILLS: Skills for language and communication research; Skills for strategic planning of communication; Skills for communicative management; Skills for consulting; 2) ICT USER SKILLS: Skills for the effective application of ICT systems and devices; Skills to apply ICT systems as tools in support of one's work; User skills for common software tools and specialized tools supporting business functions within professional area of foreign languages use.

Highest assessed separate digital skills for Foreign Languages professionals (score 5 – most relevant for Foreign Languages professionals) are determined to be: 1)

The general underperformance of *E-business skills* type in the assessment of stakeholders (41% of respondents) testifies to the lack of entrepreneurial orientation of Foreign Languages Education in Ukraine in general and overall public/state service orientation of the Foreign Languages/Philological jobs market in general.

The comparative assessment of general types of digital skills for professional application of FLE students in the pre- Covid-19 (before 2020) and Covid-19 proper quarantine measures (2020-2021) timeframe yielded the range of quantitative and qualitative results. Three formats of Foreign languages learning were compared: 1) Traditional learning (pre-2020); 2) Online learning (2020-2021); 3) Hybrid learning (2020-2021). Online learning and hybrid learning were the two interchangeable formats, adopted by Borys Grinchenko Kyiv University through the pandemic emergency measures, depending on the week-to-week quarantine assessment.

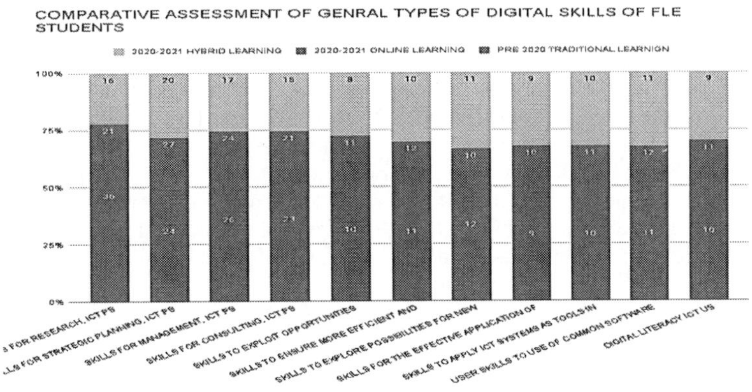

Figure 5. Comparative assessment of digital skills for professional application of FLE students

The comparative assessment of general types of digital skills across different paradigms of learning allowed to identify the following top-scoring digital skills, estimated as significant for Foreign languages education and professional application in the pre-pandemic timeframe (Figure 5): 1) Skills for language and communication research (49.3% of respondents); 2) skills for communicative management (39% of respondents); 3) Skills for consulting (38.2% of respondents).

The top-scoring digital skills, estimated as enhanced for Foreign languages education and professional application in the pandemic timeframe (2020-2021) through the format of *online learning* are as follows: 1) skills for strategic planning (38% of respondents); 2) skills to exploit opportunities, provided by ICT (37.4% of respondents); 3) skills to ensure more efficient and effective performance of different types of organizations (36.4 of respondents); 4) Skills for communicative management (36% of respondents).

As can be concluded, the dynamics of digital skills enhancement and real-life application by FLE professionals in the pandemic paradigm provided for the prominence of E-business skills, otherwise latent or underdeveloped in the Foreign Languages education context and professional field.

Group 2.2 of questions - *Diagnostics of digital skills of FLE for pre-service and in-service teachers* ***according to UNESCO ICT Competence Framework for Educators*** – allowed to identify 1) professional activity goals of FLE pre-service teachers for digital skills application and 2) student-oriente**d** goals of FLE pre-service teachers for digital skills application.

Qualitatively, professional activity goals of FLE pre-service teachers for digital skills application were identified as follows: to develop curricula using digital tools; to develop learning materials using digital tools; to understand the role of digital technologies in language education; to develop strategies and tactics for learning foreign languages at different levels using digital tools; to develop assessment tools and models using digital tools; to choose a pedagogical strategy and implement it with the help of digital tools; to organize and administer the learning process using digital tools; to improve one's teaching skills with digital tools.

Quantitatively, the priority (scoring 5-4 on the evaluation scale) professional activity goals of FLE pre-service teachers for digital skills application are estimated by the stakeholders as: 1) to improve one's teaching skills with digital tools (62.8% of respondents). 2) to develop learning materials using digital tools (58.6% of respondents); 3) to understand the role of digital technologies in language education (58.6% of respondents); 4) to develop curricula using digital tools (51.6% of respondents).

Qualitatively student-oriented goals of FLE pre-service teachers for digital skills application were identified as follows: to teach digital literacy in general; to teach to process language data using digital tools; to teach to implement different types of speech activities via digital tools (oral, written, listening, dialogue, monologue); to identify individual learning needs and gaps in foreign language skills using digital tools; to identify group learning needs and gaps in foreign language skills using digital tools; to teach to work in a team / organize collaboration; to teach to organize communication of different types with the help of digital tools; to teach to think critically using digital tools; to teach to solve problems with digital tools; to help learn independently via digital tools; to help become effective participants in civil society through digital tools.

Quantitatively, priority (scoring 5-4 on the evaluation scale) student-oriented goals of FLE pre-service teachers for digital skills application are estimated as: 1) to help learn independently via digital tools (63% of respondents); 2) to help to become effective participants in civil society through digital tools (60.3% of respondents); 3) to teach to solve problems with digital tools (60% of respondents); 4) to teach to think critically using digital tools (55% of respondents); 5) to teach to implement different types of speech activities (oral, written, listening, dialogue, monologue) – 53.1% of respondents; 6) to teach to work in a team / organize collaboration (52.3% of respondents);

It bears pointing out that the dominant students-oriented goals for digital skills application correspond to the generic soft skills, identified across various frameworks: 1) Learning and innovation; 2) human resources management, social intellect; 3) problem solving and critical thinking; collaboration and communication.

The student-oriented goals for digital skills application, *interoperable* with the professional language acquisition and communication activity are ranked relatively low by the stakeholders: to teach to implement different types of speech activities via digital tools - 53.1% of respondents; to teach to process language data using digital tools – 52% of respondents; to identify individual learning needs and gaps in foreign language skills using digital tools – 51.2% of respondents.

Group 2.3 of questions - *Diagnostics of future specialists in FLE according to* ***European Commission DigComp 2020*** *Framework* - ensured assessment of digital skills of FLE for digital citizenship.

Qualitatively, digital competence dimensions for digital citizenship, enhanced by FLE (foreign languages education) are identified as (Figure 6): 1) Information and data literacy; 2) Communication and collaboration; 3) Digital content creation; 4) Safety; 5) Problem-solving.

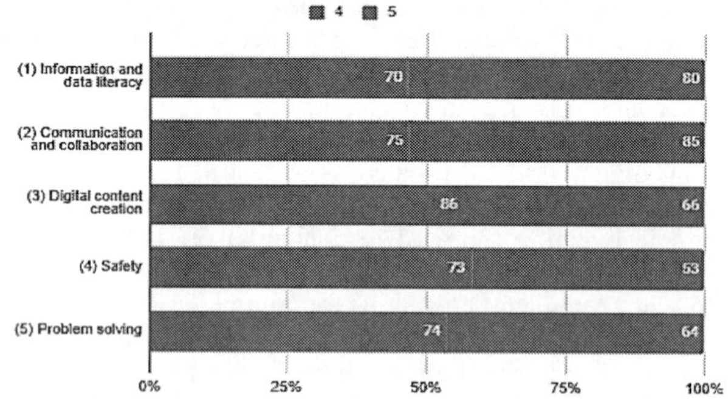

Figure 6. Digital competence dimensions for digital citizenship, enhanced by FLE

Quantitatively, the dominant (scoring 5-4 on the evaluation scale) digital competence dimensions for digital citizenship, enhanced by FLE are estimated by the stakeholders as (Figure 6): 1) Information and data literacy (53.3% of respondents); 2) Communication and collaboration (53.1% of respondents); 3) Problem solving (46.4% of respondents).

Within the identified priority digital competence dimensions for digital citizenship, the dominant (scoring 5-4 on the evaluation scale) digital activities mastery in FLE, enhanced through COVID-19 timeframe was estimated as follows (Figure 7): 1) to keep up-to-date with the digital evolution (62% of respondents); 2) to articulate information needs, to locate and retrieve digital data, information and content (60% of respondents); 3) to interact, communicate and collaborate through digital technologies while being aware of cultural and generational diversity (58.3% of respondents); 4) to create and edit digital content (56.5% of respondents); to judge the relevance of the source and its content (56% of respondents); 5) to store, manage, and organize digital data, information, and content (55% of respondents).

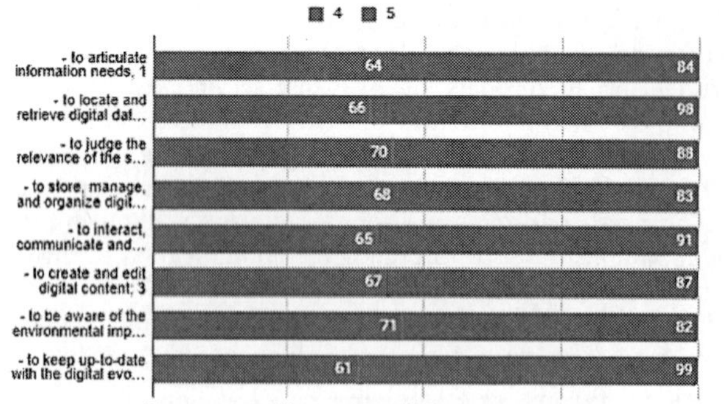

Figure 7. Digital activities mastery in FLE

The majority of digital activities in FLE, estimated as activated through COVID-19 timeframe refer to dimension (1) *Information and data literacy* of the digital competence (to articulate information needs; to locate and retrieve digital data; information and content; to judge the relevance of the source and its content; to store, manage, and organize digital data, information and content. However, the highest-scoring digital activities represent underlying interoperability of FLE through the COVID-19 paradigm with such dimensions of digital competence as (5) *Problem solving* (to keep up-to-date with the digital evolution) and (2) Communication and collaboration (to interact, communicate and collaborate through digital technologies while being aware of cultural and generational diversity).

Group 3 of survey questions - *Diagnostics of interoperability of linguistic/communicative/soft professional and digital skills for university programs of FLE* - yielded the following comprehensive results.

Digital communication elements, instrumental for professional linguistic competence formation were evaluated (Figure 8). Qualitatively, the Linguistic competence components were synthesized as: *Linguistic (Semiotic) Competence; Sociolinguistic Competence; Discoursive Competence; Strategic Competence.* Across different frameworks, digital communication components in FLE were synthesized as: *Participation in group ICT initiatives; Creation of e-learning courses/tasks; Systemic use of ICT; Presentation to the community of the results of one's activity via ICT.*

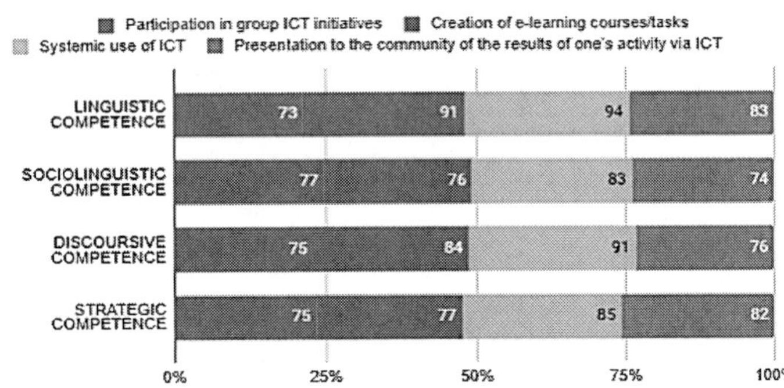

Figure 8. Digital communication elements, instrumental for professional linguistic competence formation

Dominant combinations of digital communication elements, instrumental for professional linguistic competence formation are estimated as follows: 1) linguistic (semiotic) competence is enhanced by such elements of digital communication as the *creation of e-learning content* (26.7%), *systemic use of ICT* (27.6%); 2) sociolinguistic competence is enhanced by such elements of digital communication as *participation in group ICT initiatives* (25%), *systemic use of ICT* (27%); 3) discoursive competence is enhanced by such elements of digital communication as *systemic use of ICT* (28%), *creation of e-learning content* (26%); 4) strategic competence is enhanced by such elements of digital communication as *systemic use of ICT* (27%), presentation to the community of the results of one's activity via ICT (26%).

Professional linguistic competence elements, instrumental for digital communication (Figure 9) were evaluated by the Foreign Languages stakeholders.

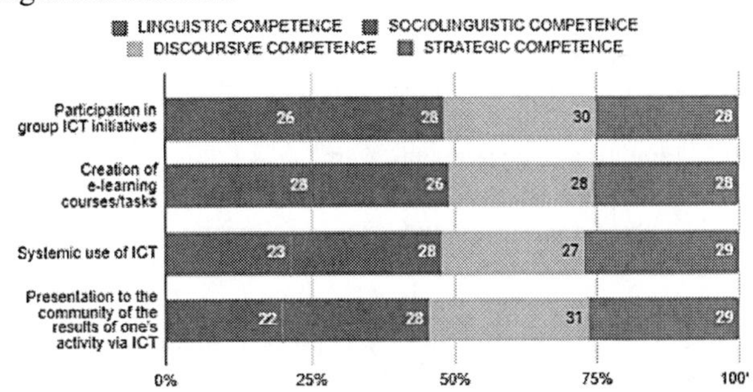

Figure 9. Professional linguistic competence elements, instrumental for digital communication

Dominant linguistic competence elements, instrumental for digital communication (Figure 9) were evaluated as follows: 1) *discoursive competence* is estimated as dominant for participation in group ICT initiatives (27%); 2) *linguistic (semiotic) competence* and *strategic competence* are estimated as dominant for creation of e-learning content (25.5%); 3) *sociolinguistic competence* (26.2%) and *strategic competence* (27.1%) are estimated as dominant for systemic use of ICT; 4) *discoursive competence* is estimated as dominant for presentation to the community of the results of one's activity via ICT (28.2%).

Digital competence dimensions effective for the implementation of foreign language acquisition activities (Figure 10) were assessed by the Foreign Languages programs stakeholders. The following set of foreign language acquisition activities was identified and evaluated: Oral monologue; Oral dialogue; Small group communication; Public speech; Written literary communication; Written business communication; Written private communication; Listening; Active vocabulary; Passive vocabulary; Grammar skills; Phonetic skills; Rhetorical skills; Stylistic skills.

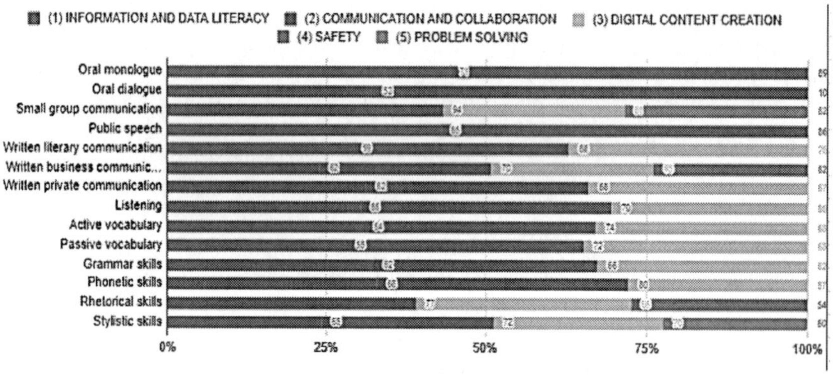

Figure 10. Digital competence dimensions for foreign language acquisition activities

Key digital competencies, effective for the implementation of foreign language acquisition activities, were quantified as follows: 1) for *Oral speech* activities the dominant digital competencies are Information and data literacy (43.1%), Communication and collaboration (61%); 2) for *Written speech* activities the dominant digital competences are Communication and collaboration (33.7%), Digital content creation (32.6%), Safety (24%); 3) For *Audial* activities the dominant digital competences are Information and data literacy (39%), Communication and collaboration (30.6%), Digital content creation (30.6%); 4) For *Vocabulary* acquisition activities the dominant digital competences are Communication and collaboration (36%) and Digital content creation (34.1%); 5) for *Stylistic* acquisition activities the dominant digital competences are Communication and collaboration (39.1%), Digital content creation (32.5%), Problem-solving (27.4%).

3. CONCLUSION

The global pandemic emergency e-learning measures and underlying shift in the digital economy informed the comprehensive modeling of interoperability between various competency principles, derivative of the soft marketable skills, and projected digital literacy requirements for foreign languages education across core digital literacy frameworks. The comprehensive diagnostics of the dimensions of digital competence for foreign languages education across actual frameworks has disclosed the interoperability of soft skills and digital communication skills across contrasting timeframes and stages of foreign languages acquisition by students of European and Oriental Languages programs and early career training.

Various levels of digital literacy have been identified in the inquiry in the sampled university of Ukraine. Across the board, implementation of Foreign Languages Education in the emergency online learning paradigm requires of participants of educational process medium to advanced digital literacy.

Digital domain, digital communication, and digital literacy are assessed as interoperable parameters across different e-competence frameworks, that inform underlying interdisciplinarity of foreign languages education in the timespan of the Covid-19 emergency e-learning measures.

Evaluation of digital skills of FLE for professional application allowed to determine the priority dimensions of professional e-competence as *to plan, to run, and to enable* professional processes in foreign languages application. The types of dominant digital skills for professional application of FLE are identified as ICT *user skills* and ICT *practitioner skills*. The demands of the digital and knowledge economy job market are not met by the liberal arts curriculum design, as the *e-business* skills are evaluated scoring lowest in priority by FLE stakeholders.

Assessment of digital skills of FLE for pre-service and in-service teachers indicated priority professional activity goals and student-oriented goals for digital skills application to be interoperable with such soft skills types as learning and innovation, cognitive flexibility, and service orientation.

Evaluation of digital skills of FLE for digital citizenship allowed to determine the priority e-competence dimensions, activated by formal linguistic training or consistent foreign languages use: Information and data literacy; Communication and collaboration; Problem-solving.

The dominant interoperable skills, acquired through FLE, are: communication, emotional intellect, creativity, problem-solving, and innovation. Digital literacy features as a prominent interoperable skill, facilitating the application of other types of soft skills of a communicative nature.

The study findings helped to detect challenges for actual and underdeveloped skills (hard, technical, and soft), that stakeholders of the European and Oriental languages education encountered through digital format adaptation in the COVID-19 timeframe, such as: 1) Digital literacy challenges: Lack of proficiency in the use of LMS tools for specific purposes; Lack of proficiency in use of specific communicative interface options; Lack of proficiency in use of Google Suite tools for collaboration; Lack of proficiency in the use of mobile versions of e-learning platforms, tools and services, used in FLE workflow; 2) Digital divide in the accessibility of computer and online technologies, necessary for all stages of Foreign Languages Education: Internet bandwidth and stability of connection; Update of PC hardware and software; Access to back-up smart devices to carry out the FLE; 3) Soft skills challenges: Learning and innovation (professional activity outside of the comfort zone); Cognitive flexibility; Entrepreneurial outlook; Time-management; Collaboration and networking via digital media; Emotional intelligence and awareness; Critical thinking and decision making.

The comprehensive study results inform the derivation of the following recommendations for e-skills development in FLE: 1) to critical review of the curriculum content to accommodate the dynamics of digital society input; 2) to review and update the FLE curriculum content interconnectivity and learning outcomes to accommodate the interoperable interface of skills, customized to facilitate professional activity and language application in the intensely digitized world; 3) to devise a flexible model of FLE content upgrade to meet the dynamic transdisciplinary requirements of the job market in the digital economy of the post-pandemic timespan and to enhance the universality of professional application for foreign languages majors in the digital age.

The presented study is limited in scope to the indicative survey results, exemplifying the interoperable dimensions of e-skills development and assessment for Oriental and European languages programs in the capital city university of Ukraine, induced by Covid-19 measures. The study results have the potential to be furthered and elaborated in the assessment of interdisciplinary and interoperable digital skills adaptability for separate groups of FLE stakeholders, according to roles and tasks performed in the language acquisition workflow, as well as according to age and entry digital literacy level. The perspective of the study is in scaling the inquiry to estimate the parameters of digital literacy formation for separate groups of source and target languages acquired, for different types of e-learning tools used for foreign languages acquisition, as well as to diagnose interdisciplinary digitization trends of FLE across countries of Asia and countries of Europe.

ACKNOWLEDGEMENT

Empirical findings and survey procedures have been conducted under the auspices of the Integrated Research framework of Romance Languages and Typology Chair of Borys Grinchenko Kyiv University European Languages And Literatures Development In Cross-Communication Context (0116U006607) and Integrated Research framework of Oriental Languages and Translation Chair of Borys Grinchenko Kyiv University Oriental Studies Development in the framework of Higher Education Internationalization (0116U007073).

REFERENCES

Abbott, S. 2013. *The Glossary of Education Reform.* Retrieved from Edglossary: http://edglossary.org/hidden-curriculum

Al-Jardani, Khalid Salim. 2020. E-Learning in Higher Education: Challenges and Opportunities. *International Journal of Innovation, Creativity and Change*, 14 (11), pp. 58-64.

Almalki, S. 2016. Integrating Quantitative and Qualitative Data in Mixed Methods Research - Challenges and Benefits. *Journal of Education and Learning*, 5(3), pp. 288-296.

Callaos, N., & Marlowe, T. 2020. Inter-Disciplinary Communication Rigor. *Rigor and Inter-Disciplinary Communication: Intellectual Perspectives from Different Disciplinary and Inter-Disciplinary Fields*. TIDC, LLC. pp. 4-29.

Davies, A., & Fidler, D. 2011. *Future Work Skills 2020.* Retrieved from Institute for the Future for University of Phoenix Research Institute: https://www.iftf.org/uploads/media/SR-1382A_UPRI_future_work_skills_sm.pdf

Dillman, D. A., Smyth, J. D., Christian, Leah Melani, 2014. Internet, Phone, Mail and Mixed-Mode Surveys: The Tailored Design Method, 4th edition. John Wiley: Hoboken, NJ.

DosReis, A. 2015. To Be a (Blended) Teacher in the 21st Century - Some Reflections. *International Journal of Research in E-learning, 1*(1), pp. 11-24.

DQ Global Standards. 2019. *World's first global standard for digital literacy, skills and readiness launched by the Coalition for Digital Intelligence.* Retrieved from DQ Global Standards Report: https://www.dqinstitute.org

European Commission. 2020. *Digital Competence 2020.* Retrieved from European Commission: https://ec.europa.eu/jrc/en/digcomp/digital-competence-framework

European Commission. (2020). *European E-Competence Framework Guideline.* Retrieved from European Commission: https://www.ecompetences.eu/

Frodeman, R. (Ed.). 2017. *The Oxford Handbook of Interdisciplinarity* (2 ed.). Oxford: Oxford University Press.

Gródek-Szostak, Z. , Suder, M., Piechaczek, A., Siguencia, L.O. 2021. Assessment and Comparison of Digital Competences in Education for Selected European Countries. *European Research Studies Journal*, 24(1), pp. 348-361.

Holbrook, J. B. (2013). What is interdisciplinary communication. Reflections on the very idea of disciplinary integration. *Synthese, 190*(11), 1865–1879.

Hymes, D. H. 1972. Communicative competence. In *Sociolinguistics: selected readings* (pp. 269–293). Harmondsworth : Penguin.

Interoperability Working Group. 2021. *Definition of Interoperability.* Retrieved from Interoperability Working Group: http://interoperability-definition.info/en/

Jacobs, J., & Frickel, S. 2009. Interdisciplinarity: a critical assessment. *Annual Review of Sociology, 35*, pp. 43–65.

Liesa-Orús M., Latorre-Cosculluela C., Vázquez-Toledo S. and Sierra-Sánchez V. 2020. The Technological Challenge Facing Higher Education Professors: Perceptions of ICT Tools for Developing 21st Century Skills. *Sustainability,* 12 (5339), pp. 2-14.

Makhachashvili, R., & Semenist, I. 2021. Covid-19 Context For Meta Assessment Of Digital Learning On European And Oriental Languages Programs. *Proceedings of the 12th International Multi-Conference on Complexity, Informatics and Cybernetics*, 2, pp. 129-134.

Makhachashvili, R., & Semenist, I. 2021. Interdisciplinary Skills Development Through Final Qualification Assessment: Survey Study for European and Oriental Languages Programs. *Proceedings of the 12th International Multi-Conference on Complexity, Informatics and Cybernetics,* pp. 144-152.

Slater, T. 2013. *Cross-Domain Interoperability.* Retrieved from Network Centric Operations Industry Consortium - NCOIC: https:// www.ncoic.org

Shannon, C. E. 1948. A Mathematical Theory of Communication. *Bell System Technical Journal, 27* (3), pp. 379–423.

Supriyatno T., Kurniawan F. 2020. A New Pedagogy and Online Learning System on Pandemic COVID 19 Era at Islamic Higher Education. *6th International Conference on Education and Technology (ICET)*, pp. 7-10.

Troussas C., Krouska A. and Sgouropoulou C. 2021. A Novel Teaching Strategy Through Adaptive Learning Activities for Computer Programming. *Transactions on Education*, 64 (2), pp. 103-109.

UNESCO. 2018. *ICT Competency Framework for Teachers.* Retrieved from UNESCO: https://unesdoc.unesco.org/ark:/48223/pf0000265721

Wulf, G., & Shea, G. 2002. Principles derived from the study of simple skills do not generalize to complex skill learning". *Psychonomic Bulletin & Review, 9*, pp. 185–211.

World Economic Forum. 2020. *The Future of Jobs Report.* Retrieved from World Economic Forum: http://www3.weforum.org/docs/WEF_Future_of_Jobs_2020.pdf

World's first global standard for digital literacy, skills and readiness launched by the Coalition for Digital Intelligence. 2019. The DQ Global Standards Report. Retrieved from: https://www.dqinstitute.org/

EMERGENCY ELEARNING DURING A PANDEMIC: TALES OF A FORCED TRANSITION

Gerald E. Evans, Daniel C. Evans and Michael V. Harrington
College of Business, University of Montana
32 Campus Dr. Missoula, MT 59812, USA

ABSTRACT

This paper explores the impact on faculty and students of the forced transition to eLearning caused by the COVID-19 pandemic. A review of the literature on eLearning modalities and the issues involved in transitioning from face-to-face instruction is followed by a series of reports on the experiences of 10 faculty in making the change from traditional instruction to various modalities of eLearning. The methodology employed is an adaptation of the grounded theory approach used in sociology. The results indicate that the primary advantages to the transition to eLearning were the flexibility afforded both faculty and students and the ability to continue delivering quality instruction during the pandemic. The primary negatives were the difficulty in engaging students in the new delivery modalities and the significant challenges involved in proctoring exams. Prior experience with online and blended learning on the part of the faculty and students made the transition smoother.

KEYWORDS

Emergency eLearning, Online Education, Proctoring, Engagement, Flexibility

1. INTRODUCTION

The COVID-19 pandemic forced faculty in higher education to adapt quickly and abruptly to an eLearning environment. The question addressed here is how well faculty adapted to this forced transition and what were their positive and negative experiences. For most traditional colleges and universities, the choice was to either move instruction online or shut down. eLearning and the associated platforms became a lifeline for higher education (Müller et al. 2021) and caused much stress and anxiety among faculty. During this transition, educators had to learn how to use instructional technology often with little training or support. They also had to become proficient in previously unused instructional modalities, as face-to-face instruction was abandoned in favor of eLearning. This paper will analyze the experience of 10 university faculty with varying degrees of prior eLearning experience.

The COVID-19 pandemic was a significant disruptive event and affected every institution and the way of life for the general population. Although college-age students were at a lower mortality risk, governments and institutions forced a transition from face-to-face instruction to various modalities of eLearning using the theory of securitization (Murphy, 2020). This transition, termed "emergency eLearning" (Murphy, 2020, p 492), was sudden and caught many members of the faculty unprepared.

Müller et al. (2021) catalogued and analyzed the experiences of 14 faculty in medical disciplines at a large university in Singapore. A high level of stress and anxiety was noted along with the necessity of adjusting expectations. Key opportunities included reduced apprehension toward eLearning, greater flexibility allowing learning independence for students, reflection and examination of the teaching process, and reduction of barriers to faculty-student interaction. The challenges were more psychological than technical and included creating engagement at the social, emotional, and cognitive levels; addressing diverse student needs; and providing a holistic learning experience.

One thing that a crisis does is force change. That can be good given the innate human resistance to it (Shimoni, 2017). However, forced change is often a ragged transition. In an introduction to a special issue on blended and online learning in technical writing and communication, Slattery (2021) expressed "mixed feelings about the sudden pivot online" (p. 4). On the positive side, educators were exposed to instructional technologies they might not have otherwise tried. That is the good thing about forced change -- it forces people to try new things. On the negative side, given that most faculty had a week or less to pivot online, there was little opportunity to examine and adopt best practices in eLearning. As Slattery (2021) pointed out, it can take years for experienced faculty to develop effective online programs and progress is often in "small, incremental revisions" (p. 4). Progress in best practices in eLearning has occurred over time. Arbaugh et al. (2010) did a thorough review of online and blended learning from 1994 to 2009. They found that the field "has seen dramatic conceptual, methodological, and analytical advances" (p. 39). However, within management disciplines, the progress has been uneven, with courses in organizational behavior and strategic management making the most progress, followed by human resource management, operations management, and international management. Entrepreneurship courses have seen little progress in adapting to eLearning, according to this review.

The current research focuses on the experiences of faculty at a college of business in making the pivot to eLearning under exigent circumstances. Given a high level of diversity in their prior experience with blended and online modalities and the variety of disciplines and instructional schemes being used, each faculty member's experience was unique. As Todd et al. (2017) observed in their meta-analysis, face-to-face, online, and hybrid approaches produce different outcomes for different course content. For example, process content worked better in face-to-face delivery whereas more structured content like compliance-based ethics instruction transitioned to eLearning more readily. For some disciplines, blended or hybrid methods produced the best instructional results. Emergency eLearning provided a social laboratory to observe and understand eLearning approaches as faculty were forced into change and to adopt unfamiliar methods and adapt well-developed approaches. This research will feature multiple cases describing the experience of faculty who had to adapt quickly to the realities of pandemic instruction. These lessons will provide the impetus for more ordered and deliberate progress in eLearning once the securitized restrictions have passed.

2. METHODS, PROCEDURES, AND RESULTS

2.1 Participants

The participants for this research were 10 faculty members at an AACSB-accredited college of business who were required to transition abruptly to various eLearning modalities in response to COVID-19 safety mandates. The participants represented several business disciplines including operations management, accounting, business law, business ethics, finance, marketing, and management. Some were broadly experienced in eLearning platforms and methodologies; others had little experience in eLearning. Some were new to higher education, filling in on short notice as COVID-19 disabled the faculty ranks because of health concerns while others were senior faculty with decades of experience in higher education. Additionally, each faculty member adapted using various eLearning modalities. Some transitioned their class to full online instruction. Others adopted a blended format of mediated synchronous instruction and asynchronous methods. A few continued face-to-face teaching with mandated rotating classroom attendance coupled with synchronous mediated instruction. Many possible permutations were represented in the case studies with a variety of outcomes.

2.2 Methods and Procedures

The primary intervention variable was the mandated transition from face-to-face instruction to eLearning. Faculty had one week to change over from face to face. Fortunately, the transition was over spring break when no instruction was scheduled so faculty could focus exclusively on the transition during that one-week period. The instructional options available were rotating face to face with supplementary synchronous delivery, full online delivery, and blended or hybrid instruction which involved mediated synchronous delivery using Zoom or Microsoft Teams coupled with asynchronous content. Faculty were free to choose their modality for the final several weeks of the semester. The three formats continued to be used during the summer session as well as fall and spring semesters the following year. Before the pandemic, the college made extensive use of Moodle as the primary learning management system (LMS); this factor, therefore, was a constant for this investigation.

Data were collected using email-mediated reports congruent with the methods employed in grounded theory research (see Strauss and Corbin, 1994). Faculty were requested to share their experience with the transition to eLearning mandated by the security protocols. The request asked faculty to included observations on the positives and negatives they encountered as they transitioned away from face-to-face instruction. This is similar to the methodology used by Müller et al. (2021) and provided a rich set of written protocols of the faculty's experience. Faculty were classified as having high, moderate, or low experience in higher education and high, moderate, or low experience in eLearning.

2.3 Results

Case 1 is a senior member of the faculty with 35 years of teaching experience at the university in operations management. This participant's pre-COVID experience includes extensive use of eLearning including full televised classes, the use of several LMSs, experience in multiple synchronous mediated learning platforms including Adobe Connect, Zoom, and Microsoft Teams and fully online instruction using an LMS, narrated Power Point slides, and video conference technology. This participant is classified as high in higher education experience and high in eLearning experience.

The forced transition for this participant was relatively smooth and easy. This participant had video recordings of each class lecture already on hand, having planned to move the class online in the near future. All the elements in the class were installed in the LMS and the class made extensive use of Pearson MyLab where students did homework and took quizzes. The only transition required was regular synchronous meetings with the class using Zoom. The only difficult transition was using Zoom without an instructional technologist since all of this participant's experience with Zoom had been with the assistance of these trained professionals (Campbell, 2008 and Sugar, 2005).

This participant's transition to eLearning is characterized as positive and opportunistic. The participant viewed the opportunity to manage their instruction using Zoom as a personal development opportunity. The flexibility of asynchronous instruction was also viewed as an opportunity. In addition to their regular university classes, this faculty member also teaches professional pre-licensing classes in real estate that are offered for credit through the university's Center for Extended and Lifelong Learning. These classes also had to abruptly move to remote eLearning, and this provided an opportunity to expand the reach of the class and the flexibility of the teaching format.

The participant observed that the exigencies of the pandemic accelerated the trend toward online and mediated learning modalities and provided an opportunity for other faculty to venture into this arena. Most students adapted to the eLearning modality adroitly. However, students who struggled with engagement did not fare as well. The lower level of accountability in eLearning allowed students who are less disciplined to disengage, fall behind, and perform poorly. The big question is now that we have demonstrated that significant instruction can take place using various forms of eLearning, will that be the administrative mandate in a post-COVID world?

Case 2 is a new faculty member recruited early in the pandemic to fill in for a faculty member who was adversely affected by the pandemic. This participant had limited experience in higher education and had no experience in eLearning. This participant would be classified as low in higher education experience and low in eLearning experience. The participant teaches business ethics and social responsibility.

A prime area of concern for this participant's classes during the pandemic was the use of class time. They teach three sections of Business Ethics, two of which are taught in a Hybrid format with one pre-recorded lecture and one live Zoom session per week and an additional online-only section with all material presented asynchronously. In this format, all sections of the class are receiving the same pre-recorded lectures on philosophical and business-oriented topics in ethics. Most of the content delivery on specific theories was reserved for the prerecorded lectures, which were done through annotated PowerPoints with voiceovers. This lecturing tool was used for the delivery of an 80-minute lecture on Nicomachean Ethics or Kantianism, lasting the entire class duration covering that specific material. For the Zoom sessions with the Hybrid classes, the live meetings of class were used to delve into thought experiments and more nuanced examinations of the theories. This combination of theory and practice may not have been possible in a pre-pandemic classroom environment given structured scheduling constraints. In order to discuss Kant's shortcomings by answering the "two rock" problem or Utilitarianism's tendency to aggregate the suffering of marginalized groups, students must first understand categorical imperatives or the greatest happiness principle. The prerecorded lectures allowed students to learn the theory at their own pace while watching the recordings and the synchronous sessions could be used for application.

On the negative side, since there has been no in-person interaction with students, there is the problem of not knowing what a vast majority of the students look like. With over 300 students having attended classes predominantly online, the familiarity the faculty have with the students is compromised. Synchronous Zoom sessions help but it is difficult to enforce having cameras on when the classes are at 8:00 am. Student participation was low during these class times even during face-to-face instruction so, on some mornings during the pandemic, it was like teaching to a computer screen.

The dynamic will change when the university returns to in-person teaching. But this unfamiliarity with the students compromises our department's emphasis on undergraduate education and to this faculty member's sense of belonging in the school community. As a faculty member who took on this teaching position full-time during the pandemic, it will take at least a full school year after in-person classes resume before the participant feels the same level of comfort in the department community as otherwise would have been the case.

Case 3 is a senior faculty member with high experience in higher education. The participant teaches accounting primarily face to face so the participant would be considered low in eLearning experience.

When face to face, their upper division accounting class was primarily working through problems on the analogue white board. Unassigned problems were also worked to introduce topics and homework problems were routinely reviewed. Both the faculty member and students were accustomed to this mode of teaching, so the transition involved an attempt to replicate this in an eLearning environment. A dedicated Zoom room with smart white boards, multiple cameras and displays, and multiple ceiling-hung microphones was used. The smart whiteboard was described as "clunky" and the Zoom signal gave students problems, especially the gallery display being on top of the shared whiteboard. With experience, both faculty and students learned how to move the gallery display or change it to speaker view, but everyone was in a learning curve.

Then the campus was closed, and this faculty member had to teach from home. The setup at home was better since they had a graphics computer with a writable screen, which worked better than the smart whiteboard. Zoom was used and problems were worked while writing on the screen in MS Word. When the actual problem was copied into Word, the process worked much better.

It took longer to write on a computer screen than an actual dry erase board in the classroom. About 15 minutes per 80-minute class was lost due to the slower medium and Zoom navigation time. The lost time required explanations to be recorded for quizzes and problems not covered in class. These were posted in Moodle.

When in the classroom, the experience reading the faces was important to the class pace and answering spontaneous questions. However, on Zoom, the "read the room" ability was completely lost. Students were asked to turn their cameras on, and that helped. Calling on students worked better but the asynchronous students fell behand as the class progressed. The University's "barrier-free" mandate in the transition required the faculty to allow asynchronous participation, but synchronous attendance would have served these students better.

Administration of quizzes required a significant adaptation. Quizzes were typically done at the start of class and time was called by watching to see when students were done or spinning their wheels. For eLearning, McGraw-Hill's Connect was used for quizzes. Time allocation was difficult to judge and some students said they did not have enough time. The online interface took longer and added complexities compared to paper quizzes.

Exams were also moved to McGraw-Hill Connect. However, exams took much longer, even for the "A" students who were not looking up many answers. Accommodating extended time was difficult and difficult to judge. Office hours were moved online via Zoom, but only a few students took the initiative to show up and participate.

Case 4 is an experienced management faculty member with significant experience in eLearning. The participant is classified as high in higher education experience and high in eLearning experience.

Prior to the pandemic the participant was teaching a section online, so the face-to-face section was easily moved online using the videos and other materials that were already created. In the participant's other classes, the students were focused on their team projects, so only regular office hours were required.

Several guest speakers were already scheduled, and they were still able to speak via Zoom and offered great insights into what their organizations were experiencing because of COVID.

In the fall, a previously scheduled online class was taught along with two sections of an MBA organizational behavior class which switched to remote. This transition was a little difficult, but the MBA students responded well to moving discussions into Zoom. These students were quite engaged throughout.

Students were required to keep their cameras on if they had the internet bandwidth to do so. This requirement made it a lot easier to have engaging discussions since everyone's faces were visible. The MBA students made the transition readily since most were accustomed to the hybrid program delivery in this program.

Case 5 is a relatively new member of the faculty who teaches specialty classes in an international business center. This participant is now teaching exclusively online. The participant is classified as low in higher education experience and moderate in eLearning experience.

The participant observes that teaching classes online expands the potential student base dramatically. But it becomes even more important to plan outstanding programming that can compete with many other options for online instruction. Another factor is the increasing desire by everyone to avoid adding one more Zoom session to the calendar. The participant observes that it is exhausting, and that everyone is becoming jaded.

Online instruction makes it far easier for people to make a dramatic shift in their educational plan and can change their loyalties among institutions and classes and can avoid moving to college. The power of individual personalities is muted and will not shine through enough in a virtual setting to drive student loyalty and retention.

Some suggested strategies to make eLearning more impactful include bringing in professional colleagues with granular information on specific topics and business leaders who are experiencing some of the issues being discussed in class. Another strategy is to call on individual students directly to address a question at the beginning and building this into the student expectations. A final suggested strategy is emphasizing the relevance of the material being covered to their existing and future business acumen and using private sector contacts to underscore this point.

Case 5 is a senior faculty member in management with high experience in higher education and moderate experience in eLearning.

On the negative side, this participant observes that the qualities of various remote teaching platforms have compromised interpersonal interaction because of the loss of nonverbal communication cues and the reduced ability of teachers and students to read interpersonal signals.

On the positive side, most students were described as "digital natives" (Prensky, 2001) and find the integration of technology into class both relevant and normal. Zoom, with its ability to chat while discussing material, allows multimodal learning in breakout rooms and enables students to create products like marketing plans or simple profit and loss statements for projects and then share their screen with the entire class for discussion.

Another positive is the ability for speakers to "join" classes through eLearning platforms from anywhere in the world; more professionals have been engaged without incurring pandemic risks and endangering students, guest lecturers, or instructors. Additionally, student projects, assigned at the direction of guest instructors, has resulted in content which is then immediately accessible for review and discussion. In some instances, that content has been used, with student permission, in the guest instructors' businesses.

Case 6 is a senior faculty member in marketing with high experience in higher education and high experience in eLearning through extensive teaching in the blended learning MBA program.

The biggest challenge reported by this participant was to get enough students to show up in the Zoom sessions and participate with good questions, answers, and comments to create a lively and engaging class. It is difficult to teach to the screen, but active and engaged students make it feel like a real classroom. Student participation can be tracked using Zoom recordings and saved chat dialogues. Students self-select active participation or chat discussion which satisfies everyone's interests and preferences.

The greatest positive is that office hours and meetings with students can be done on Zoom with individual students or the entire team for team projects. This mode is more convenient, productive, and easier to share screens and check student work. Plus, the ability to record project help sessions avoids debates on what was said and by whom. Zoom sessions can also make scheduling meetings at inconvenient hours more workable.

Case 7 is a mid-level faculty member in business analytics with moderate experience in higher education and moderate experience in eLearning.

This participant described the most significant insight during the transition to eLearning was coming to understand how much students had been collaborating on work. The transition to online learning created many impediments to this collaborative work which had been done primarily in person before the pandemic. Students had to go through a learning curve in using various eLearning platforms for these collaborations.

Case 8 is a mid-level member of the management faculty with moderate experience in higher education and high experience in eLearning. This participant had taught several MBA classes in online and blended formats prior to the pandemic and had a baseline understanding of the technology and its capability.

The most significant negative as the semester progressed was student fatigue and drop off in engagement. By fall, the big challenge was creating an engaging Zoom experience for a class with 150 students. The participant reported feeling like equal parts group therapist and radio talk show host. On a couple occasions, a graduate assistant was used to monitor the chat like a producer would in a radio broadcast. An adapted flipped classroom model worked best. Students were required to come to each class prepared to ask questions about topics related to the scheduled focus for the day. Current events, like the Facebook and Google anti-trust cases, provided a great foundation for illustrating various business concepts. For the spring 2021 semester, GameStop made an equally useful example.

The class format changed regularly so students could stay engaged. Some sessions were for the full group, others used small or large breakout groups. Some discussion prompts were very structured while others were open-ended. Constant experimentation and seeking student feedback on what worked and what did not was useful. This agile approach allowed the focus to be on what is important in a way that resonated with the students.

Case 9 is a senior member of the faculty in business law who has high experience in higher education. However, this participant is low in eLearning experience since all of this participant's experience with online and blended format was with the assistance of an education technologist (Campbell, 2008 and Sugar, 2005).

A major challenge is how to limit cheating on exams. The size of the classes and the variable time needed to complete the exams can allow some students to help others. Managing test integrity is a major issue. Another challenge has been how to engage with the students. In face-to-face classes, names could be associated with faces facilitated by name tents. Solid rapport could be developed, and this personal interaction contributed to an enriched learning environment. It was felt that Zoom compromises this interaction. It is difficult to get students to leave cameras and microphones turned on. Consequently, the interactivity of the class defaults to a small subset of the students. The students who engage regularly have a much richer classroom experience.

Another challenge has been individual interactions with students. Although individual Zoom sessions are regularly offered, few students take advantage of them. Only students who want to review exams want to make the effort to meet on Zoom and they were mostly MBA students.

One opportunity is how accommodating the online modality is for students' schedules. They can review the taped lectures and read the assigned materials at their convenience. Based on how quickly the classes filled during the spring 2021 registration, the two online sections filled up much earlier than the Zoom section did.

Another opportunity is the reduced "wear and tear" on faculty both physically and mentally. Multiple sections of the same class can be recorded once and recorded. Synchronous sessions can be scheduled once a week with recorded material filling in for the other class meetings. If students miss a class session, they can easily make it up by viewing the posted recordings.

Case 10 is a senior member of the faculty in finance who has extensive experience in eLearning prior to the pandemic. This participant is classified as having high experience in higher education and high experience in eLearning.

Prior to the forced transition, the participant had been teaching a finance class online, so the changeover was seamless. By fall, the participant was teaching both fully online sections and blended sections which incorporated some synchronous content. This participant noted no differences between the performance and engagement of the students in these two modalities. They used McGraw-Hill Connect with a Smart Book and this made the mediated instruction highly effective.

The primary challenge or negative aspect is that not all students have adequate equipment to fully engage in a remote environment which requires more bandwidth than fully online. Additionally, the pace of the class is slower than in the face-to-face mode, perhaps because it is more difficult to determine how they are learning the material.

On the positive side, the participant contends that quality does not have to suffer in an online environment. However, with online and remote learning, requiring assignments and other work on a specific schedule is essential to keep the students engaged.

3. CONCLUSION

Several themes emerged from these reflections that were similar to those noted by Müller (2021). The first and most obvious point is that those who were experienced in eLearning made the transition more readily than those who lacked the experience. But, as obvious as this observation is, there is an important implication: now that all the faculty have been forced through the learning curve for eLearning, the trend in that direction will speed up. Everybody gained valuable experience in eLearning because of the forced transition.

Student engagement in an eLearning environment is possible but the techniques and methods are different than in face-to-face modalities. More extroverted faculty, who relied on the force of their outgoing personalities to engage students, found that method of engagement significantly compromised in an eLearning environment. More structure and deliberate mechanisms to keep students on track are needed in online and blended environments. Some examples are structured discussion questions, requiring students to keep their cameras on, calling on students, requiring students to pose questions, and problem sets.

The faculty who used mediated learning platforms like, McGraw-Hill Connect and Pearson MyLab, found that these tools were indispensable in moving to online and blended modes of eLearning. Learning management systems like Moodle, Blackboard, and Canvas are basic infrastructure for eLearning as are conferencing software like Zoom and Microsoft Teams. But the content-specific platforms from the major publisher augment the eLearning process in a more structured and automated manner.

Exam security was a major issue, particularly for the more technical disciplines like accounting and finance. Proctoring systems like Proctorio and Respondus are used widely in the US and Canada (see Kimmons and Veletsianos, 2021), and their adoption by universities and colleges are necessary for a more secure move to eLearning modalities like online and blended instruction.

Additionally, students need the requisite technology to fully engage in an eLearning environment. Students who lack the bandwidth and computing power to take advantage of the multimodal eLearning environment are placed in a disadvantaged position (Chuang et al, 2003). This issue could differentially impact some minority and ethnic populations whose access to technology is already limited.

Finally, our entire set of respondents noted the positive flexibility for both students and faculty that the eLearning environment afforded. There is no disagreement that online and blended education will continue to increase in higher education. However, many students used this new flexibility to work or pursue other endeavors that competed for their attention with university classes. The COVID-19 pandemic will undoubtably accelerate the trend toward more eLearning in higher education. Hopefully, the resources necessary to take advantage of the positive aspects of eLearning and mitigate the potential negatives will be allocated to make this transition an improvement rather than merely a change.

This accelerated move to eLearning will make the online educational environment much more crowded and colleges and universities will have to develop specific strategies and branding to compete in the new arena. Lower on-campus student populations will present other challenges associated with bonding obligations, facilities maintenance, and participation in intercollegiate athletics.

These research findings are important and significant. The most important takeaway is that faculty were able to adapt and deliver a high-quality educational experience. Prior to the forced transition, many faculty voiced misgivings concerning the quality of courses delivered online. The data presented here support the conclusion that online does not necessarily mean lower quality. Online instruction can produce educational outcomes of equal quality as face-to-face instruction as (see Clouse and Evans, 2003). A second conclusion is that for most of the difficulties encountered during the transition, faculty were able to adapt, find or invent new methods, and generally make it work. Thus, the educational process is robust and can withstand external shocks! Perhaps the most significant and long-lasting conclusion from this research is that virtually all university faculty have now acquired the skillset necessary for online instruction. The silver lining in the COVID-19 pandemic for higher education is that, in a very short period, all the faculty members who participated in our research acquired the skills necessary to teach effective online courses. This will be a legacy and will inevitably expand the quality and scope of eLearning.

REFERENCES

Arbaugh, J. B., Desai, A., Rau, B., & Sridhar, B. S. (2010). A review of research on online and blended learning in the management disciplines: 1994–2009. *Organization Management Journal*, *7*(1), 39-55.

Campbell, T. (2008). The capacity of instructional technologists to provide systemic support for science education reform. *Teacher Development*, 12(1), 67-83.

Chuang, H. H., Thompson, A., & Schmidt, D. (2003). Faculty technology mentoring programs: Major trends in the literature. *Journal of Computing in Teacher education*, 19(4), 101-106.

Clouse, S. F., & Evans, G. E. (2003). Graduate business students' performance with synchronous and asynchronous interaction e-learning methods. *Decision Sciences Journal of Innovative Education*, 1(2), 181-202.

Kimmons, R and Veletsianos, G. (2021). Proctoring software in higher ed: Prevalence and patterns. Educause Cybersecurity & Privacy. https://er.educause.edu/articles/2021/2/proctoring-software-in-higher-ed-prevalence-and-patterns.

Müller, A. M., Goh, C., Lim, L. Z., & Gao, X. (2021). COVID-19 Emergency eLearning and beyond: Experiences and perspectives of university educators. *Education Sciences*, 11(1), 19. https://doi.org/10.3390/educsci11010019

Murphy, M. P. (2020). COVID-19 and emergency eLearning: Consequences of the securitization of higher education for post-pandemic pedagogy. *Contemporary Security Policy*, 41(3), 492-505.

Prensky, M., (2001). Digital natives, digital immigrants part 2: Do they really think differently? *On the Horizon*, 9(6), 1-6. https://doi.org/10.1108/10748120110424843

Shimoni, B. (2017). What is resistance to change? A habitus-oriented approach. *Academy of Management Perspectives*, 31(4), 257-270.

Slattery, D. M. (2021). Guest editor's introduction: Facilitating interaction, collaboration, community, and problem-solving capabilities in blended and fully online technical communication programs: An introduction to the special issue. *Journal of Technical Writing and Communication*, 51(1), 3-10.

Strauss, A. & Corbin, J. (1994). Grounded theory methodology. In N.K. Denzin & Y.S. Lincoln (Eds.) *Handbook of qualitative research* (pp. 217-285). Thousand Oaks: Sage Publications.

Sugar, W. (2005). Instructional technologist as a coach: Impact of a situated professional development program on teachers' technology use. *Journal of Technology and Teacher Education*, 13(4), 547-571.

Todd, E. M., Watts, L. L., Mulhearn, T. J., Torrence, B. S., Turner, M. R., Connelly, S., & Mumford, M. D. (2017). A meta-analytic comparison of face-to-face and online delivery in ethics instruction: the case for a hybrid approach. *Science and Engineering Ethics*, 23(6), 1719-1754.

FACTORS INFLUENCING STUDENTS' ACCEPTANCE OF E-LEARNING PLATFORMS IN PRIMARY AND SECONDARY SCHOOLS IN SAUDI ARABIA

Amani Bakarman and Nora Almezeini
Department of Management Information Systems, King Saud University
Riyadh, Saudi Arabia

ABSTRACT

Due to COVID-19 pandemic, the Saudi Ministry of Education decided to transform the educational process for both primary and secondary schools into electronic education for the first time. In this regard, it has established a new platform called Madrasti to ensure the effective transformation of learning. The study aims to highlight the features of the Madrasti platform and adopted the unified theory of acceptance and use of technology (UTAUT) to determine the factors that influence students' acceptance of e-learning platforms in primary and secondary education in Saudi Arabia. A total of 802 students from different levels responded to the survey on UTAUT constructs. Empirical data revealed that performance expectancy and social influence determine students' behavioral intention. Moreover, facilitating conditions and behavioral intentions determine students' use of e-learning platforms.

KEYWORDS

e-Learning Platform, Unified Theory of Acceptance and Use of Technology Model, Primary Education, Secondary Education, Saudi Arabia

1. INTRODUCTION

Electronic learning (e-learning) pertains to the use of information and communication technology in education (Elkaseh et al., 2015). e-Learning can be conducted through a virtual learning environment, which provides learning platforms consisting of databases, online tools, and resources (Gao et al., 2018). e-learning reduced the time and cost required for training and facilitated access to e-learning materials anytime and anywhere. Furthermore, e-Learning features several aspects, such as interactivity, flexibility, scalability, reduced costs, self-organization, rich content, self-directed learning, and immediacy, which play significant roles in the development of the educational sector in general. Moreover, e-learning promotes innovation among students, improves many skills, such as technical, management, critical thinking, analytical, and problem-solving skills (Farooq et al., 2020; Gowda & Suma, 2017).

The Ministry of Education (MOE) in Saudi Arabia provides an asynchronous e-learning system for students from different levels through educational channels via TV such as the Ein-National Education Portal, which includes 20 satellite channels for each level of education. The system presents lessons and reviews for all curricula aligned with the approved study plan of MOE. In addition, it supports the use of sign language to achieve optimal advantage for students under special education and enhances the use of new technologies in the educational process through augmented reality, Ein 3D, and play and learn (Ministry of Education, 2020).

However, the education in Saudi Arabia faced the formidable challenge of transforming into synchronous e-learning using learning management system (LMS) platforms due to the COVID-19 pandemic. For the first time, the country experienced a nationwide dilemma as the transformation includes students from all levels: primary, middle, and secondary schools.

Therefore, the MOE (2020) created a new platform called Madrasti for public and private schools to conduct distance learning for primary, middle, and secondary school students. Moreover, Madrasti was developed to ensure that educational outcomes are met by simulating traditional school classes while keeping learners safe. Madrasti (2020) is an LMS, which includes many electronic educational tools and features that support teaching and learning processes and contribute to the achievement of the educational goals of the curricula and decisions. Furthermore, it supports the achievement of skills, values, and knowledge to enable students to become up-to-date with present and future digital requirements.

Private schools in Saudi Arabia have the option to use other popular platforms for online learning, such as, Zoom, Microsoft Teams, and Classera. Zoom and Microsoft Teams provide synchronous e-learning with several features, such as online meetings, screen sharing, chatting, file sharing, and hand raising.

The majority of previous studies were conducted in higher education levels, such that relatively less is known about whether these factors apply to lower education levels. To address this research gap, the current study aimed to explore the factors that influence students' acceptance of e-learning in Saudi Arabia by conducting an empirical study with students under primary and secondary education as subjects.

The purpose of this study is to highlight the features of the Madrasti platform and investigate the effectiveness of its transformation by measuring students' acceptance of e-learning across platforms, such as Madrasti, Zoom, Classera, and Microsoft Teams, which were used by lower education levels. Previous scholars widely suggested the use of the unified theory of acceptance and use of technology (UTAUT) model to determine intentions to use an information system and resultant behaviors of such use (Ali et al., 2018). Thus, the current study employed the model to investigate the factors that influence students' acceptance of e-learning in general education in Saudi Arabia.

The remainder of the paper is structured as follows. Section 2 presents the features of the Madrasti platform. Related work is presented in Section 3. Furthermore, Section 4 introduces the research model and hypotheses followed by Section 5 with the research methodology. Section 6 analyzes contains data using several statistical techniques. The results are presented in Section 7. Finally, Section 8 concludes, provides several recommendations, and proposes further studies on e-learning in general education.

2. FEATURES OF THE MADRASTI PLATFORM

The main users of the Madrasti platform are students, teachers, parents, and school leaders. Accordingly, the platform enables users to take advantage of features and services depending on their roles and needs.

Madrasti provides a virtual classroom as a tool for delivering a safe environment for lessons over the Internet through Microsoft Teams, which enables a teacher to interact and discuss with students effectively, respond to inquiries, assign tasks and assignments, and motivate. Moreover, Madrasti provides more than 45,000 learning sources that consider differences between students. It provides visual and cartoon videos, educational games, augmented reality, 3D objects, interactive and fun experiments, and learning stories and books.

The platform features are improving student evaluation through electronic tests and assignments. Moreover, it facilitates exam preparation using a database of more than 100,000 approved questions for the majority of courses. Moreover, Madrasti provides spaces for discussion that enable interaction between teachers and students, between students and contents, and among students to enhance psychological and social communications skills. The Madrasti platform enhances the diversity of educational resources that make the education process more accessible through schoolbooks, Ein satellite channels, and discussion forums.

Besides, MOE provides many other tools to evaluate the new approach of e-learning, overcome obstacles as soon as possible, and ensure the quality of the education process electronically. It provides a technical team to assist the users of the platform and answers inquiries through technical support, automatic response, or contact to a unified number. Moreover, it creates electronic questionnaires to measure the quality of the Madrasti platform from the diverse perspectives of students, teachers, parents, and school leaders.

Madrasti provides several features that differ from one user to another to meet different needs. For students, the Madrasti platform provides a school schedule and educational enrichment foundation. A school schedule is a superior tool that ensures the arrangement of courses and enables each student to know and enter a specific course on time. For enrichment, it provides additional resources to expand and enrich student learning. Figure 1 demonstrates the student tools presented for each course separately.

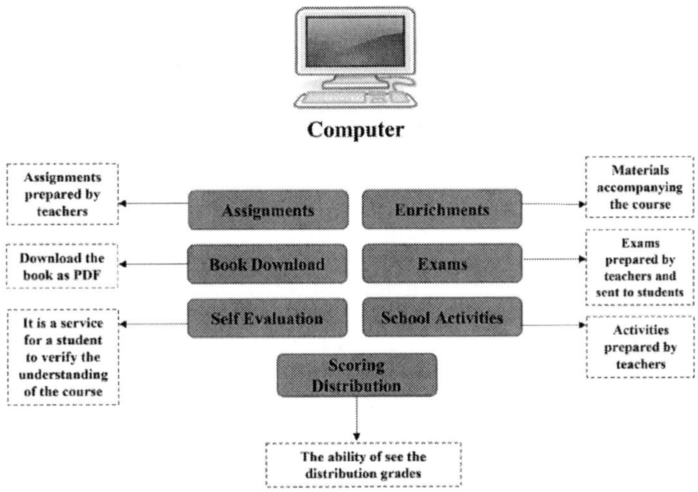

Figure 1. Students' Tools in Madrasti platform

Teachers use specialized tools in the Madrasti platform, such as electronic educational tools that develop students' skills, such as critical thinking, problem-solving, and innovation, which can help to overcome the educational gap and support students simultaneously. Moreover, teachers can conduct and attend virtual meetings with school employees and parents to serve the educational process. The evaluation process of teachers is dependent on the level of students' interaction and utilization of the platform. Therefore, teachers conduct a follow-up to improve students' performance and encourage them to increase their accomplishment. Teachers can also post students' grades and marks to be available on students' pages. Also, the teacher can monitor student absence or late attendance.

Moreover, Madrasti enables parents to supervise and follow up on the achievement of the children in the educational process through effective communication between parents, teachers, and school employees. Moreover, parents can view their children's data, such as attendance, assignments, and reports. The role of parents in supporting the educational process is to enter the system, selected the name of the child that requires a follow-up, and verify achievement and progress.

School leaders play an essential role in the traditional as well as the electronic educational process. For this reason, the platform provides beneficial tools for leaders to promote effective and efficient performance. Each school leader is responsible for essential tasks, such as adjusting the school schedule and ensuring that student information matches the appropriate level of education and teachers are assigned to appropriate courses. Lastly, school leaders are tasked with building and managing the school schedule for each classroom. The school leader can follow up the progress of the educational process in the virtual classroom by viewing the teacher's schedule, accessing any virtual classroom, and monitoring the progress of the educational process. (Ministry of Education, 2020).

3. RELATED WORK

In general, the acceptance of a new system is determined by the levels of users' adoption and usage. The significance of e-learning in the educational sector led researchers around the world to measure students' acceptance of e-leaning. For instance, Violaine (2019) used the UTAUT model to evaluate the factors that influence student's decision-making on the adoption of e-learning. Data were derived from higher education students in Rwanda. The study found that performance expectancy (PE), effort expectancy (EE), and facilitating condition (FC) are factors that significantly influence students' satisfaction with adopting e-learning, whereas social influence (SI) exerted no impact on students' adoption of e-learning.

In addition, Ameen et al. (2019) investigated the adoption of e-learning in Iraq. The authors surveyed a sample of 300 university students and used the TAM, UTAUT, and three factors to determine the factors that explain the adoption and effective use of e-learning system. The findings suggested that perceived usefulness (PU), perceived ease of use (PEOU), subjective norms (SN), information quality, system quality, technical support (TS), and self-efficacy (SE) are factors that have a significant impact on behavioral intention (BI). Thus, BI and TS have significant direct impact on the actual use of e-learning systems.

Utama et al. (2020) conducted a study in Indonesia and explored the perspectives of medical students toward e-learning during the COVID-19 pandemic. The researchers employed the UTAUT model to determine the factors that influence the medical students' acceptance of e-learning. The study found that PE was a significant factor that reflects the positive perception of medical students, which supports BI to use e-learning. In contrast, EE, SI, FC, and experience were considered as negative factors that limit the usage of e-learning.

Furthermore, Raza et al. (2020) used the extended UTAUT model to examine the factors that influence students' acceptance of e-learning during the difficult time of social isolation due to the COVID-19 pandemic. The results pointed to the strong relationships of PE, EE, SI, and social isolation to BI of e-learning. In addition, the results indicated a strong relationship between BI and students' usage behavior of e-learning.

In addition, Tiwari (2020) explored the core factors that influence university students to adopt and accept e-learning during COVID-19. The study was based on the UTAUT model, which identified perceived cost (PC) as an additional factor for explaining the relationship between students' attitudes and acceptance of e-learning. The findings revealed that PE, EE, and FC exerted a significant impact; SI displayed a weak impact; and PC had no impact on BI toward e-learning acceptance.

Al-Azawei and Alowayr (2020) conducted a comparative study between two Middle Eastern countries (i.e., Saudi Arabia and Iraq) using the modified UTAUT model to determine the factors that facilitate students' acceptance of ML. Although many constructs were significant for one country, they were not for other countries, and vice versa. The results revealed that the variances for BI and hedonic motivation were 56.1% and 40.7%, respectively, for Saudi Arabia and 51.1% and 41.9%, respectively, for Iraq. Such findings reflect the acceptance level of students toward ML for both countries.

In the same manner, many scholars measured acceptance of e-learning among teachers. For instance, Sarbaini et al. (2019) surveyed 200 lecturers in Indonesia to investigate the factors that influence their adoption of e-learning technologies. The researchers used the UTAUT model to examine the constructs that teachers considered the most relevant, such as PE, EE, SI, and FC. Moreover, the study further considered individualism–collectivism as an additional construct that influences the intention to use e-learning technologies among teachers. The findings indicate that high levels of relative advantage, individualism–collectivism, EE, and PE are significantly associated with increased intention to adopt e-learning technologies.

In addition, Buabeng-Andoh and Baah (2020) surveyed 361 teachers to explore the factors that influence teachers' intention to use LMSs as a form of e-learning system. The research model used was based on the UTAUT and TAM. The findings indicated that SI, EE, and PE influence teachers' attitude and BI to use technology in education, whereas FC exerted no effect.

4. RESEARCH MODEL AND HYPOTHESES

Several methods are utilized for analyzing technology acceptance. The Technology Acceptance Model (TAM) is the most popular and frequently used. In 2003, Venkatesh et al. (2003) theorized that the UTAUT model can present a comprehensive view of the acceptance process of new technologies compared with previous models. UTAUT was derived from the comparison and combination of eight theoretical models of intention and usage, namely, Motivational Model, Theory of Reasoned Action, TAM, Theory of Planned Behavior (TPB), combined TAM and TPB (C-TAM–TPB), Model of PC Utilization, Social Cognitive Theory, and Innovation Diffusion Theory (Mutambara & Bayaga, 2021). Each model uses different constructs to measure user acceptance of new technologies. The constructs of the eight models were compared and combined to formulate new constructs for the UTAUT model. Currently, the UTAUT model contains five constructs applicable to a wide range of fields and considered a decisive factor for user acceptance and behavioral usage.

The study employed the UTAUT as the research model. Under the UTAUT model (Lescevica et al., 2013), the acceptance of e-learning technology is determined using five constructs, namely, Performance Expectancy (PE), Effort Expectancy (EE), Social Influence (SI), Facilitating Conditions (FC), and Behavioral Intension (BI).

- PE pertains to the degree to which a student believes that the usage of a system will be useful and improve learning performance.
- EE denotes the degree of ease associated with using the system.
- SI stands for the degree to which a student considers the importance of the notion that other students should use the new system.
- FC represents the degree to which a student believes that an organizational and technical infrastructure exists to support system use.
- BI refers to the subjective probability of the student to perform the behavior in question.

The study presents the following hypotheses as shown Figure 2:

H1: Performance expectancy positively influences students' behavioral intention to use e-learning platforms.

H2: Effort expectancy positively influences students' behavioral intention to use e-learning platforms.

H3: Social influence positively influences students' behavioral intention to use e-learning platforms.

H4: Facilitating condition positively influences students' use e-learning platforms.

H5: Behavioral intention positively influences students' use of e-learning platforms.

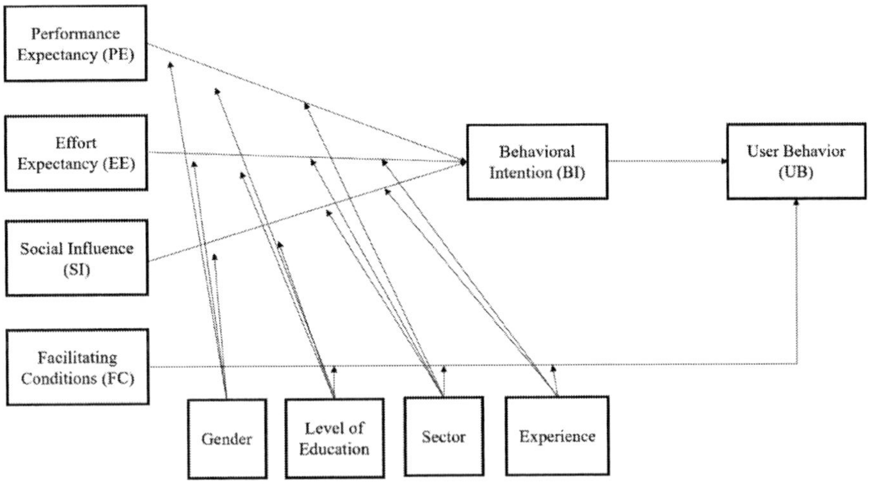

Figure 2. Research Model

5. RESEARCH METHODOLOGY

The study conducted a quantitative research in the form of a questionnaire, which was randomly distributed online to students at the primary, middle, and secondary school levels across public, private, and international schools. The questionnaire strictly followed the ethical guidelines of the institution. In the form of the questionnaire, the research purpose, the voluntary nature of participation, and the predicted time for completing the questions were noticed. The questionnaire aims to investigate the usage and acceptance levels of e-learning platforms among general education students. The questionnaire was developed based on the determining factors used in the UTAUT model. Items were rated using a five-point Likert-type scale ranging from 1 = strongly disagree to 5 = strongly agree.

As Arabic is the official language in Saudi Arabia, the original questionnaire was translated to Arabic by a professional translator. The authors reviewed the Arabic version and translated it back to English to ensure the same integrity of meaning.

Moreover, to ensure the reliability and validity of the results, a sample should represent a sufficient number of respondents that is representative of the general population. According to Hair et al. (2013), the sample size should be determined based on corresponding population sizes as shown in Table 1 .

Table 1. Determination of sample size based on population size

Population Size	Sample
10000	370
15000	375
20000	377
30000	379
40000	380
50000	381
100000	383
>100000	384

Note. Source: Hair et al. (2013)

According to the latest records published by MOE, the population of general education students is 6,187,776 as of 2020. Therefore, the study obtained 802 completed questionnaires, which reflects the optimal sample size required to produce reliable estimates. In this manner, the study can provide accurate answers and accurately reflect the results as representation of the population.

6. DATA ANALYSIS

6.1 Respondents' Profile

Table 2 presents the distribution of students according to gender, level of education, school type, e-learning platform used, and students' experience of using e-learning platform.

Table 2. Distribution of students

Distribution of students by:		Frequency	Percentage
Gender	Male	76	9.5
	Female	726	90.5
Education level	Elementary	230	28.7
	Middle	125	15.6
	High	447	55.7
School type	Public	725	90
	Private	51	7
	International	26	3
e-Learning platform	Madrasti+Microsoft Teams	706	88
	Zoom	28	3.5
	Classera+Microsoft Teams	44	5.5
	Microsoft Teams	24	3
Experience of using e-learning platform	Students with experience	227	28.3
	Students without experience	575	71.7

Table 3 and Figure 3 represent the most popular platform for each school type.

Table 3. Platforms used according to school type

School types	Platforms								Total	
	Madrasti+Microsoft Teams		Zoom		Classera+Microsoft Teams		Microsoft Teams			
	N	%	N	%	N	%	N	%	N	%
Public	707	99	9	32	3	6	6	37	725	90
Private	6	1	12	43	30	67	3	19	51	7
International	0	0	7	25	12	27	7	44	26	3
Total	713	100	28	100	45	100	16	100	802	100

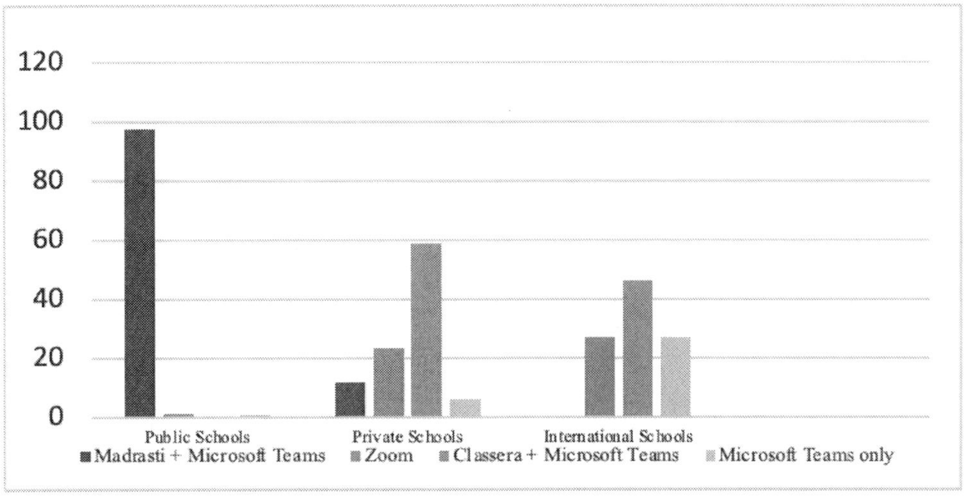

Figure 3. Relationship between platforms and school type

6.2 Reliability

The study employed Cronbach's alpha to test reliability. Table 4 indicates that Cronbach's alpha for the questionnaire is 0.944, which is a high value for stability (reliability). The table also presents that the validity and reliability of the items in the questionnaire are high and positive according "Pearson's correlation coefficient" with the highest and values at 0.916 and 0.758, respectively.

Table 4. Reliability statistics

	Cronbach's alpha	Items
	0.944	N = 16
	Performance Expectancy (PE)	Pearson's correlation
1	I found this platform useful in my learning process.	0.872**
2	Using this e-learning platform will help me accomplish tasks quickly.	0.877**
3	This platform will facilitate the effectiveness of learning.	0.900**
4	Using this platform will improve the quality of my learning.	0.881**
	Effort Expectancy (EE)	
1	My interaction with this e-learning platform is clear and understandable.	0.837**
2	I found this platform easy to use.	0.910**
3	Learning to operate this platform was easy for me.	0.916**
4	It was easy for me to become skillful at using this platform.	0.906**
	Social Influence (SI)	
1	People who influence my behavior (relatives) think that using this platform is easy for me.	0.807**
2	People who are important to me (non-relatives) believe that I should use this system.	0.758**
3	The Ministry of Education and my school encouraged me to use this platform.	0.825**
4	In general, I received sufficient supported in using this platform.	0.830**
	Facilitating Condition (FC)	
1	I have the resources necessary to use this platform.	0.866**
2	I have basic knowledge of using this platform.	0.874**
3	I have a support person/group (technical support team) who helps me with difficulties in using e-learning.	0.801**

Note. $^{**}p < 0.01$

6.3 Inferential Analysis

The study used two methods for inferential analysis, namely, correlation and regression, to describe the relationships between PE, EE, and SI (independent variables) and BI (dependent variable) and between FC and BI (independent variables) and use of e-learning (dependent variable).

Table 5 provides the results of correlation analysis to verify the proposed relationship among variables. First, a positive relationship was observed between experience and educational level. Students' experience of using e-learning is positively correlated with education level. Thus, high school students have more experience than elementary and middle school students. Second, a significant relationship was noted between experience and school type that differs from one school to another. For UTAUT factors, a significant relationship was found between PE and SI, between EE and BU, and between FC and BU. In contrast, no significant relationship was noted between other factors.

Table 5. Correlations between factors

	Gender	Education level	School type	Experience	BI	PE	EE	SI	FC	BU
Gender	1.000									
Education level	−.210**	1.000								
	.000									
School type	.284**	−.132**	1.000							
	.000	.000								
Experience	−.005	.160**	.197**	1.000						
	.891	.000	.000							
BI	−.005	−.006	−.001	.086**	1.000					
	.876	.837	.987	.007						
PE	−.035	.000	−.029	.081**	.512**	1.000				
	.246	.986	.320	.007	.000					
EE	−.024	−.038	−.009	.101**	.423**	.567**	1.000			
	.422	.187	.772	.001	.000	.000				
SI	−.014	−.033	−.019	.060*	.388**	.496**	.560**	1.000		
	.644	.252	.517	.046	.000	.000	.000			
FC	.003	−.032	.008	.093	.404	.578**	.687**	.679**	1.000	.779**
	.924	.372	.819	.009	.000	.000	.000	.000	.000	.924
BU	−.021	−.023	−.011	.091**	.637**	.706**	.699**	.650**		1.000
	.474	.411	.693	.002	.000	.000	.000	.000	.000	.000

In the proposed model, the study used path coefficients to reveal relationships between UTAUT factors and test the research hypotheses. Table 6 shows a statistically significant effect of BI, PE, and SI on e-learning ($p < 0.05$), whereas EE did not exert a statistically significant effect on intention to use e-learning ($p > 0.05$). Such findings support H1 and H3 ($p < 0.05$) but reject H2 ($p > 0.05$).

Table 6. Structural research model for behavior intention

Hypothesis	**Path**	**Unstandardized coefficients**		**Standardized coefficients**	**t-Value**	**Sig.**	**Remarks**
		B	Standard error	β			
H1	PE → BI	0.644	0.053	0.490	12.153	0.000	Supported
H2	EE → BI	0.114	0.062	0.084	1.844	0.066	Rejected
H3	SI → BI	0.168	0.063	0.110	2.659	0.008	Supported

Note. Dependent variable: behavior intention

Table 7 indicates the statistically significant effect of FC and BI, which are related to use of e-learning, on e-learning acceptance ($p < 0.05$). This result supports H4 and H5 ($p < 0.05$). Figure 4 shows the path coefficients of the hypotheses.

Table 7. Structural research model for use of e-learning

Hypothesis	Path	Unstandardized coefficients		Standardized coefficients	t-Value	Sig.	Remarks
		B	Standard error	β-value			
H4	FC → UB	0.342	0.009	0.537	39.409	0.000	Supported
H5	BI → UB	0.514	0.012	0.580	42.531	0.000	Supported

Note. Dependent variable: use of e-learning (User Behavior)

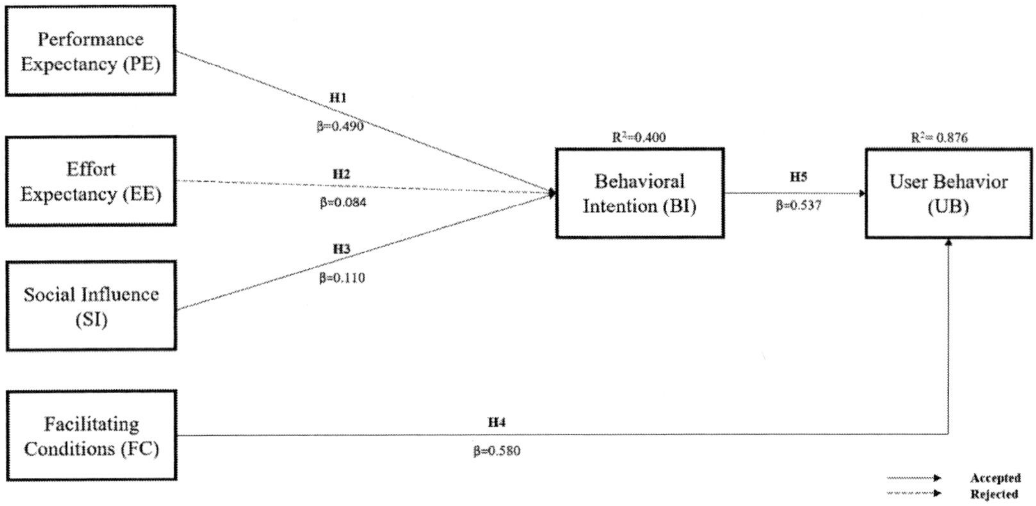

Figure 4. Path coefficients of the hypotheses

7. RESULTS AND DISCUSSIONS

The study investigated the main factors influencing students' use and acceptance of e-learning platforms as utilized by primary and secondary schools in Saudi Arabia in response to the COVID-19 pandemic. Analyses indicate that Madrasti is the most popular platform used for e-learning (88% of the total responses) and mostly used in public schools. Madrasti was selected by 88% of the respondents for its features and meeting the requirements of students in e-learning. Thus, Madrasti can be used across student levels and types of schools, which renders it a promising platform for potential use in other countries.

Moreover, the results revealed that the level of education of the students influence experience of using e-learning. As expected, high school students displayed more experience in using e-learning platforms compared with elementary and middle school students, whereas elementary students exhibited the least experience in using e-learning platforms. Moreover, 58% of international school students reported previous experience with using e-learning platforms followed by private (55%) and public (25%) school students.

The assessment of the core UTAUT variables in Figure 4 indicated that PE has a significant effect (0.490) (β-value) on BI to use e-learning platforms (H1) followed by SI (0.111) (β-value) (H2). The two constructs explain 40% (R2 value) of variance of BI. Moreover, FC has a significant effect (0.580) (β-value) on UB (H4) followed by BI (0.537) (β-value) (H5), which explains 87.6% of variance of UB.

Students reported efficient learning with the use of e-learning platforms, which are important tools for the rapid completion of tasks. Thus, PE is the most significant factor influencing BI to use e-learning platforms (49%). In addition, the efforts of the MOE are attributed for FC (58%), which enabled students to use e-learning platforms. Furthermore, students mentioned that the necessary resources, basic knowledge, and technical support were made available, which encouraged their acceptance and use of e-learning platforms.

In general, the results indicate high levels of acceptance of e-learning among students in the low level education scheme in Saudi Arabia. e-Learning in Saudi Arabia is undergoing constant development because it is predicted to be an approved approach to education in the future (Melibari, 2020).

8. CONCLUSION

The study used the UTAUT model to identify the factors that influence students' acceptance of e-learning platforms in general education in Saudi Arabia. The findings revealed that PE, SI, and FC were significant factors, whereas EE was not a significant factor for the acceptance of using e-learning platforms. Thus, EE can be considered an indicator of difficulties in using these platforms and lack of students' skills.

The research provided useful insights into students' acceptance and use of e-learning platforms. The model used laid the foundation for further research on the acceptance of e-learning platforms in general education. Therefore, future studies may use other methods used by international and private schools to gauge students' experience in using e-learning platforms. Moreover, researchers may explore possible techniques that can facilitate the use of e-learning platforms among students.

To encourage students to accept and use e-learning platforms, decision-makers in the MOE can use the results of the study to inform the design of such platforms with consideration of several aspects, such as ease of use, clarity, and understandability. Furthermore, enhancing the awareness and experience of general education students, especially elementary students, is important to promote acceptance of e-learning according to level of education. In addition, workshops and training courses may be conducted to aid students in the effective use of e-learning platforms. In this manner, the MOE can ensure that the largest possible number of students can make effective use of e-learning platforms.

ACKNOWLEDGEMENT

The authors thank the Deanship of Scientific Research and RSSU at King Saud University for their technical support.

REFERENCES

Al-Azawei, A., & Alowayr, A. (2020). Predicting the intention to use and hedonic motivation for mobile learning: A comparative study in two Middle Eastern countries. *Technology in Society*, *62*(March), 101325. https://doi.org/10.1016/j.techsoc.2020.101325

Ali, M., Raza, S. A., Qazi, W., & Puah, C. H. (2018). Assessing e-learning system in higher education institutes: Evidence from structural equation modelling. *Interactive Technology and Smart Education*, *15*(1), 59–78. https://doi.org/10.1108/ITSE-02-2017-0012

Ameen, N., Willis, R., Abdullah, M. N., & Shah, M. (2019). Towards the successful integration of e-learning systems in higher education in Iraq: A student perspective. *British Journal of Educational Technology*, *50*(3), 1434–1446. https://doi.org/10.1111/bjet.12651

Buabeng-Andoh, C., & Baah, C. (2020). Pre-service teachers' intention to use learning management system: an integration of UTAUT and TAM. *Interactive Technology and Smart Education*, *17*(4), 455–474. https://doi.org/10.1108/ITSE-02-2020-0028

Elkaseh, A., Wong, K. W., & Fung, C. C. (2015). A review of the critical success factors of implementing E-learning in higher education. *International Journal of Technologies in Learning*, *22*(2), 1–13. https://doi.org/10.18848/2327-0144/cgp/v22i02/49160

Farooq, A., Ahmad, F., Khadam, N., Lorenz, B., & Isoaho, J. (2020). The impact of perceived security on intention to use e-learning among students. *Proceedings - IEEE 20th International Conference on Advanced Learning Technologies, ICALT 2020*, 360–364. https://doi.org/10.1109/ICALT49669.2020.00115

Gao, H., Wu, H., & Wu, X. (2018). Chances and Challenges: What E-Learning Brings to Traditional Teaching. *Proceedings - 9th International Conference on Information Technology in Medicine and Education, ITME 2018*, 420–422. https://doi.org/10.1109/ITME.2018.00100

Gowda, Ramya S., & V. Suma. (2017). A Compartive Analysis of Traditional Education System vs. e-Learning. *IEEE International Conference on Innovative Mechanisms for Industry Applications, ICIMIA 2017 - Proceedings, Icimia*, 567–571. https://doi.org/10.1109/ICIMIA.2017.7975524

Hair, J. F., Ringle, C. M., & Sarstedt, M. (2013). Partial Least Squares Structural Equation Modeling: Rigorous Applications, Better Results and Higher Acceptance. *Long Range Planning*, *46*(1–2), 1–12. https://doi.org/10.1016/j.lrp.2013.01.001

Lescevica, M., Ginters, E., & Mazza, R. (2013). Unified theory of acceptance and use of technology (UTAUT) for market analysis of FP7 CHOReOS products. *Procedia Computer Science*, *26*(December), 51–68. https://doi.org/10.1016/j.procs.2013.12.007

Ministry of Education. (2020). *Madrasti Platform*. https://backtoschool.sa/

Melibari, G. T. (2020). *The challenges and opportunities facing the Saudi education system in coronavirus period*. Saudi Gazette. https://saudigazette.com.sa/article/591931

Mutambara, D., & Bayaga, A. (2021). Determinants of mobile learning acceptance for STEM education in rural areas. *Computers and Education*, *160*(August 2020), 104010. https://doi.org/10.1016/j.compedu.2020.104010

Rajab, K. D. (2018). The Effectiveness and Potential of E-Learning in War Zones: An Empirical Comparison of Face-To-Face and Online Education in Saudi Arabia. *IEEE Access*, *6*, 6783–6794. https://doi.org/10.1109/ACCESS.2018.2800164

Raza, S. A., Qazi, W., Khan, K. A., & Salam, J. (2020). Social Isolation and Acceptance of the Learning Management System (LMS) in the time of COVID-19 Pandemic: An Expansion of the UTAUT Model. *Journal of Educational Computing Research*. https://doi.org/10.1177/0735633120960421

Sarbaini, Jumadi, Abbas, E. W., & Rajiani, I. (2019). Managing e-learning in public universities by investigating the role of culture. *Polish Journal of Management Studies*, *20*(1), 394–404. https://doi.org/10.17512/pjms.2019.20.1.34

Tiwari, P. (2020). Measuring the Impact of Students " Attitude towards Adoption of Online Classes during COVID 19 : Integrating UTAUT Model with Perceived Cost. *Test Engineering & Management*, *83*(May), 8374–8382.

Utama, M. R., Levani, Y., & Paramita, A. L. (2020). Medical students' perspectives about distance learning during early COVID 19 pandemic: a qualitative study. *Qanun Medika - Medical Journal Faculty of Medicine Muhammadiyah Surabaya*, *4*(2), 255. https://doi.org/10.30651/jqm.v4i2.5000

Venkatesh, V., Morris, M. G., Davis, G. B., & Davis, F. D. (2003). User acceptance of information technology: Toward a unified view. *MIS Quarterly: Management Information Systems*, *27*(3), 425–478. https://doi.org/10.2307/30036540

Violaine, A. (2019). Key Factors Affecting Students' Satisfaction and Intention to Use e-Learning in Rwanda's Higher Education. *Journal of Digital Convergence*, *17*(5), 99–108. https://doi.org/10.14400/JDC.2019.17.5.099

THE DIGITAL LEAP OF E-LEARNING IN HIGHER EDUCATION

Kaikai Liu[1], Marja Liisa Tenhunen[2,*], Jun Chen[1], Hui Chen[3] and Jingjing Liang[1]
[1]*SHU-UTS SILC Business School, Shanghai University, Shanghai, China*
[2]*Shanghai University, Shanghai, China*
[3]*Henkel Co. Ltd., China*
[*]*Corresponding Author*

ABSTRACT

COVID-19 pandemic has led to the confrontation of higher education system with enormous challenges. This necessitated the urgent transition from face-to-face teaching to online teaching. A comparative study of digital education in seven different countries was conducted. This study established grey comprehensive evaluation model based on entropy weight method, which was successfully validated by reliability test. In general, developed countries tend to have high comprehensive evaluation value while Finland, South-Korea and Latvia have relatively low grey correlation coefficient in several certain indicators, leading to a sharp drop in the overall score. Romania ranked last while China ranked second as a developing country as well. This is followed by model optimization though input-output analysis method based on the upgrading of higher education system due to the pandemic's influence. The study launched a conclusion that research and development personnel, infrastructure funds and university financial investment in digital education have relatively more obvious effects on improving the quality of higher education system.

KEYWORDS

E-learning, Higher Education, Grey Comprehensive Evaluation Model, Sensitivity Analysis

1. INTRODUCTION

Online-teaching opens up as a smart solution for future education. In the field of education, a digital leap has been made in a short notice which has encouraged universities in the development of creative solutions. Concerns about educational inequality have risen in the process especially in the countries with short prior experience in online education. Despite the limitations in technological conditions, all possible efforts should be made when pursuing equality in online-education.

The global emergency of the COVID-19 pandemic confronts all people with unpredictable, disruptive situations which has changed our daily lives, economies, political decisions and universities. Important changes have been made in terms of online-teaching, admission and exam schedules, which have stirred discussions about future prospective in university landscape after the pandemic is over. Amid all the uncertainty and shock, universities are obliged to stick to their basic values and ethical responsibilities, which give academics a sense of direction and credibility. In any case, remote online teaching and learning cannot fully replace a face-to-face teaching and learning environment where teachers and students discuss with each other. Generally, online-teaching has been used to supplement the classroom teaching, which is called "blended learning". As the saying goes, "When there is a risk, there should be an opportunity". The late Austrian-American economist Joseph Schumpeter introduced the "creative destruction theory". The COVID-19 pandemic has been destructive, but it also, in a sense, has created some creative destruction. In the best scenario, teachers and students have got some benefits from online-teaching, which will equip them for the future learning and communication. For instance, teachers should consider the issues such as how to motivate students and encourage them to be proactively participate in real-time video class discussions, how to implement innovative teaching concepts more effectively, how to maintain care and guidance for individual students, and how to share and integrate online-teaching experiences with other colleagues. Teachers' creativity with online teaching can be a vital factor for stimulating students' autonomous learning, turning the epidemic "crisis" into an "opportunity" whilst reforming teaching and learning concepts. The university management should provide support in this process.

Throughout history, education has rarely been reformed or benefited from technological advances. Nowadays, with digital teaching allowing real-time interaction, many innovative teaching and learning methods can be attempted and implemented. The most powerful part of this new generation of real-time interactive teaching and learning is that it can simultaneously accommodate in scaling and personalized learning, which traditional classroom teaching cannot do. In traditional large classes, it is difficult for teachers to know how many of the students understand or master the contents of a class. However, if the teaching and learning activities are carried out online in real time, teachers' understanding of students' progress can change. For example, teachers can review the distribution of answers to certain multiple choice questions. They can recognize the number of students who answered incorrectly and where they went wrong through the interactive polling function. Based on a real-time data, teachers can better understand students' immediate responses and provide suitable assistance as quickly as possible in order to improve learning efficacy. The system can also guide students to review more challenging content. With the benefit of this experience, teachers can use similar functions in their traditional classroom teaching in the future to better understand students' personal progress and needs. The "flipped classroom" teaching method that has emerged in recent years is particularly applicable in a real-time video teaching environment. Students can watch the relevant teaching materials and videos in advance before the live online class so that the teacher can make better use of live class hours and focus on interactive discussion. This reduces the portion of unidirectional lecturing. During online teaching and learning, it is possible to reduce some of the limitations of traditional classrooms, which gives room to rethink how teachers can turn "classes" into better learning experiences and enhance teachers' mentoring and coaching roles.

2. AIM OF THE STUDY

COVID-19 created a digital leap in all around the world, including higher education. The starting point has varied from country to country and therefore, the changes that took place in the spring of 2020 vary. In some countries, a system for providing e-learning has been acquired on a fast schedule. Teachers have been introduced to new types of teaching, and only then has provision been introduced. Other countries have expanded only their previous offerings of courses. It will be interesting to compare the seven selected countries, China, Latvia, Mexico, Romania, Finland, South Korea and the United States at different levels of online education and to gather experiences of change for operational development. There is no return to yesterday, so institutions need to start from first principles, creating a vision for life after the pandemic, making hard choices based on data, creating new models, realigning priorities and entering a post-covid-19 world not in isolation but collaboration. The aim of this study is to compare the implementation, quality and quantity of online-education by a questionnaire method in seven different countries. The countries selected are China, Latvia, Mexico, Romania, Finland, South Korea and the United States. The countries have been selected on the basis of the researchers' teaching experience. The first electronic survey will be conducted for the management of every university and the second electronic survey will also be conducted for the academics including program directors. The third electronic survey in the study will be conducted simultaneously for groups of students of the same size in business administration.

3. THEORETICAL FRAMEWORK AND RESEARCH PROBLEM

There is no single or core theory which support online education. Research is linked to educational theories, mainly constructivism or exploratory learning. Constructivism is an international concept, so it is used is this research. Exploratory learning is actually a manifestation of constructivism. E-learning is implemented in as an opportunity to individualize teaching and it provides the preconditions for the realization of a constructivist view of learning better than mass-based teaching. The main research problem is as follows: The realization of a constructivist view of e-learning at universities in seven different countries. In the constructivism, knowledge and learning are related to action. Knowledge does not pass from the outside into the human mind, but each student constructs his or her own knowledge. Understanding cannot be transferred it is always the output of the student's own thinking. It is the student's own active knowledge construction process, in which the student selects and interprets information based on what he or she has previously learned and expectations. Learning includes, for example, self-perceived questions, self-experimentation, problem-solving, and understanding. According to the constructivism, the key to learning is the understanding and thinking. Learning is thus the active interpretation of an individual's observations and experiences and the construction of new meanings associated with them. Learning is situational and based on interaction. The student must be able to direct his or her own selective attention to what is relevant to what he or she is learning, and the student must also feel that the questions that arise are important and meaningful to him or her. Only then does learning happen. The results of the work of the different students form the basis for the teacher's own analysis of the matter.

The most important skill of a teacher is to create functional, appropriate learning environments that raise questions in the student's mind and help him or her construct answers by understanding what is being sought. In the learning environment created by the teacher, appropriate questions arise, the answers to which are sought under the guidance of the teacher on the basis of the student's own experimentation, understanding and thinking. The teacher trains students' thinking and comprehension skills by giving them the widest possible opportunities to receive feedback on their own operational processes. The learning environment includes situations of uncertainty (confrontations) initiated by the teacher. Through these, the student gets the opportunity to develop their own abilities to learn to learn. The appropriateness of the learning environment should be a conscious goal for all involved in the process.

Skills are developed through long-term and goal-oriented training at a variable, gradually decelerating pace. There are occasionally different levels of skill learning, during which a certain aspect of a skill is automating, but overall performance suffers. The development of skills at the highest level means the persistent continuation of practice even after the pace of skill development has slowed down. Peak performance can be achieved by avoiding the formation of rigid routines. The student has to face challenges that break with familiar patterns and force the student to stretch his/her own skills. Simply maintaining the level of performance achieved is not enough. The most difficult of these skills are often thinking skills. In order to develop, the student must constantly and consciously refine both his/her own actions and his/her own thinking. Action and thinking develop intertwined. A well-developed and unified way of acting and thinking is typical of an expert. Self-assessment skills (metacognitive skills) are needed to develop expert thinking. The student cannot get them naturally, because the assessment and development of student's own internal models and skills requires acceptance that the student does not yet know everything.

New creative and evolving expertise is needed when the operating environment changes and old and proven models do not work. An innovative expert constantly strives to invest in learning new things and is also willing to question his or her own previous beliefs. It is impossible to teach different core skills such as problem solving and interaction skills in isolation. Also, the ability to collaborate, creativity, knowledge of different learning styles, assessment of one's own learning and the use of knowledge never arise in a vacuum, but are best learned in a relevant context. E-learning is implemented in as an opportunity to individualize teaching and it provides the preconditions for the realization of a constructivist view of learning better than mass-based teaching. If e-learning is used only to share material and tasks used in face-to-face teaching without pedagogical vision and reflection, e-learning does not take advantage of the new opportunities to apply constructivism that e-learning offers to interactive learning. It could also be stated that not only a new kind of pedagogical approach, e-learning also requires more work from the teacher than lecture-based contact teaching. A priori reflection on the preconditions of constructivism in e-learning provides subjects to the theoretical part and the surveys.

4. METHODS

4.1 Data Collection

Data collection of this study was conducted as digital surveys. Target survey-takers were divided into 3 groups: (1) University management: What role does e-learning play in the current strategy of the university? How do they see the change in the future? Also management was asked about their views on learning and whether they relate to some general theories or whether they exist at all. (2) Academics including program leaders: What kind of experience have they had with e-learning technical solutions, software, content, and guidance? What is the key feedback from academics and program teachers? What are the key successes, what about failures? How do program managers and academics see the connection of e-learning to students working life after graduating? How have been the reactions of the partner companies to e-learning? (3) Students: What kind of experience have they had with e-learning technical solutions, software, content and guidance? How has their studies progressed? What are the key successes and failures? How do students see the connection of e-learning to working life after graduation? The collection of questionnaire data plays a significant role on the application of our model. The extensiveness and reliability of the data could ensure the model feasible with practical significance. This study selected managers, students and academics engaged in higher education as investigation objects. The survey was conducted from August 2020 to March 2021, finally collecting data from the selected countries including China, Finland, Latvia, Mexico, Romania, South-Korea and the United States of America. A total of 160 questionnaires were issued in this survey. After eliminating 4 invalid questionnaires, 156 valid ones were obtained with an effective recovery rate of 97.50%.

4.2 Variable Description

This study selected 17 indicators from *Scale of e-learning in higher education*, *Input of digital education during the COVID-19 crisis* and *Impacts of e-learning on higher education during the COVID-19 crisis* to accurately evaluate the implementation, quality and quantity of digital education in each country. First, *Scale of e-learning in higher education* reflects the basic development of digital education. Enrollment number of graduate students and number of doctor students could represent this index. Second, *Input of digital education during the COVID-19 crisis* is the core reflecting the driving force of digital education development under the influence of the pandemic. Among them, number of R & D personnel has attracted our special attention in terms of manpower investment in scientific research. Last, *Impacts of e-learning on higher education during the COVID-19 crisis* could reflect the ability of digital education to serve the current community. Wen's article (2013), one of the most cited articles in this field, mentions that intensity of students' performance evaluation, grade for academics' online teaching skills and grade for managers' digital working efficiency are important indices to measure the significance of digital technologies in higher education. Table 1 provides the list of variables.

Table 1. Parameter list

Primary variable	Secondary variable	Symbol
Scale of e-learning in higher education	Enrollment	X_1
	Number of graduate students	X_2
	Number of doctoral students	X_3
Input of digital education during the COVID-19 crisis	Proportion of e-leaning in higher education	X_4
	Number of teachers implementing online-teaching	X_5
	Number of R & D personnel in digital education	X_6
	Infrastructure funds	X_7
	Financial investment provided by universities	X_8
	Online education expenditure per capita	X_9
	Research funds on digital technologies	X_{10}
	Inherent assets	X_{11}
Impacts of e-learning on higher education during the COVID-19 crisis	Total use frequency of digital technology	X_{12}
	Intensity of students' performance evaluation	X_{13}
	Grade for academics' online teaching skills	X_{14}
	Grade for managers' digital working efficiency	X_{15}
	Number of temporary forms of academic employment	X_{16}
	Opportunities for equity, diversity and inclusion	X_{17}

4.3 Factor Analysis

Due to the considerable number of indicator selection, there might be high internal correlation between different indicators and unstandardized structure of observation data resulting in inconsistent analysis results. In order to facilitate the subsequent data analysis, we hope to reduce the number of variables and improve the model accuracy through factor analysis. The basic principle is to find out the representative factors that can reflect the overall characteristics in multi-dimensional variables, and classify the same essential variables into one factor. These unobservable synthetic indicators are public factors. The model is as followed:

$$X_i = \mu_i + a_{i1}F_1 + \cdots + a_{iq}F_q + \varepsilon_i \quad (1)$$

Note: $X = (X_1, X_2, X_3, \ldots, X_p)'$ *is a p-dimensional random vector with a mean value of* μ *.* $F = (f_1, f_2, \ldots, f_q)'$ *is a q-dimensional random vector.* ε_i *is a special factor.* $E(F) = 0$, $E(\varepsilon) = 0$; $Cov(F, \varepsilon) = 0$; $D(F) = 1$.

4.4 Grey Comprehensive Evaluation Model Based on Entropy Weight

After the dimensionality reduction by factor analysis, grey comprehensive evaluation method was conducted to test. This method assesses the pros and cons of each comparison sequence by calculating the similarity between the comparison sequence and the reference sequence. However, the traditional grey comprehensive evaluation method simply samples the average value of the correlation coefficient of each index when solving the sample correlation degree, which obliterates the heterogeneity between the indexes. While in accordance to the background of this topic, different elements of the data have different significance to digital education system. Therefore, it is of great priority to distinctly set the reasonable and scientific weights for these indicators so as to represent different elements' value. To improve the traditional one, this study integrated the entropy weight method and the grey comprehensive evaluation method to analysis the quality of digital education in various countries.

4.4.1 Dimensionless Processing of Data

The standardization of data to solve the error caused by the disunity of measurement units was conducted. We use semi-ascending trapezoidal fuzzy membership function for non-dimensionalization where r_{ij} is the actual value of the jth index in the ith province, x_{ij} is its fuzzy membership value, r_{min} and r_{max} are the minimum and maximum values of the jth index respectively.

$$x_{ij} = \begin{cases} 0, & r_{ij} \le r_{min} \\ \frac{r_{ij} - r_{min}}{r_{max} - r_{min}}, & r_{min} \le r_{ij} \le r_{max} \\ 1, & r_{ij} \ge r_{max} \end{cases} \quad (2)$$

4.4.2 Entropy Method

Entropy method and Analytical Hierarchy Process (AHP) are regarded as the most commonly used methods in the field of scientific empowerment. Since AHP method has the subjective and optional drawbacks, we choose entropy method which overcomes the subjectivity in determining the weight and is more appropriate in this case. Entropy weight method is usually used in comprehensive evaluation problems to carry on the weight analysis to the importance of the assessment index.

Firstly, we calculate the information entropy of each index, and its formula is as follows:

$$E_j = -\ln(n)^{-1} \sum_{i=1}^{n} p_{ij} \ln p_{ij} \quad (3)$$

$$p_{ij} = \frac{Y_{ij}}{\sum_{i=1}^{n} Y_{ij}} \quad (4)$$

Then we determine the weight of each index. According to the calculation formula, the information entropy of each index is E_1, E_2, E_3......E_k. The weight of each index is calculated by information entropy, and the formula is as follows:

$$W_i = \frac{1 - E_i}{k - \sum E_i} (i = 1,2,3 \ldots \ldots k) \quad (5)$$

4.4.3 Grey Comprehensive Evaluation Method

In this method, we firstly select the optimal sequence. Since the indexes described above are positive indicators, the maximum value of the same index for each evaluation object is taken as the optimal value of the index. The sequence composed of the optimal values of each indicator is called the optimal sequence, and is denoted as $X_0 = (x_{01}, x_{02}, \ldots x_{0n})$. Secondly, to figure out the grey correlation coefficient, we set the comparison sequence and the reference sequence respectively. Continue to the previous step, the optimal sequence is taken as the reference sequence. And the sequence composed of the index values of each evaluation object as the comparison sequence, denoted as $X_i = (x_{i1}, x_{i2}, \dots x_{in})$, i=1, 2, ...m. The grey correlation coefficient between the ith evaluation object and the jth index in the reference sequence is denoted as γ_{ij}, which is expressed as:

$$\gamma_{ij} = \frac{\min_i \min_j |x_{ij} - x_{0j}| + \rho \max_i \max_j |x_{ij} - x_{0j}|}{|x_{ij} - x_{0j}| + \rho \max_i \max_j |x_{ij} - x_{0j}|} \qquad (6)$$

In formula (6), ρ is the resolution coefficient, $\rho \in [0,1]$. Here, we take ρ as 0.5.

Last step is to calculate the grey correlation degree which reflects the closeness of the comparison sequence to the reference sequence. The greater the degree of association, the closer the comparison sequence is to the optimal value. Therefore, the pros and cons of each evaluation object can be evaluated according to the degree of grey correlation of each comparison sequence. Taking into account the heterogeneity between different indicators, different weights are assigned to the indicators according to the relative importance of each indicator. The grey correlation degree of the ith evaluation object is defined as:

$$\gamma_{i0} = \sum_{j=1}^{n} \omega_j \cdot \gamma_{ij} \qquad (7)$$

Among them, ω_j is the weight of the jth index. The index weight is determined by the above-mentioned entropy weighting method. Then we calculate the grey correlation degree of each country based on this.

5. RESULT ANALYSIS

5.1 Evaluation Results

Before factor analysis, it is necessary to judge whether the variables selected are suitable for factor analysis. According to the data, a group of observations with 5 related variables and 12 sample size are obtained for analysis. In order to prevent the occurrence of multicollinearity, we need to estimate the correlation between the selected variables before factor analysis. In this study, we use SPSS 25.0 statistical software to test the collected data. The test results are shown in Table 2. Although the significance level of Bartlett sphericity test is less than 0.01, the KOM value is 0.495, less than 0.6, which does not pass the KMO test indicating that the selected variables are not suitable for factor analysis.

Table 2. Results of KMO and Bartlett's test

Kaiser-Meyer-Olkin Measure of Sampling Adequacy		.495
Bartlett's Test of Sphericity	Approx. Chi-Square	58.196
	Df.	10
	Sig.	.000

When the index data does not meet the KMO test, the factor analysis method is not applicable. Fortunately, the grey correlation analysis does not require the distribution of sample data, nor does it require sample data to meet statistical tests, which can make up for the defects of the above methods. Therefore, we directly evaluate all these seventeen indicators adopting grey comprehensive evaluation model based on the entropy weight. Using the collected data of 7 countries in the questionnaire, the entropy weighting of each evaluation index is carried out according to the steps of solving the entropy weight. The weight of each indicator is shown in Table 3.

Table 3. Results of weight calculation

Index	Weights	Index	Weights
X_1	4.160%	X_{10}	4.123%
X_2	4.357%	X_{11}	6.732%
X_3	4.048%	X_{12}	3.040%
X_4	4.301%	X_{13}	11.589%

X_5	11.296%	X_{14}	5.055%
X_6	9.562%	X_{15}	4.615%
X_7	1.924%	X_{16}	4.804%
X_8	4.822%	X_{17}	3.549%
X_9	12.024%		

According to formula (6), first obtain the grey correlation coefficient matrix of each country, as shown in Table 4. According to formula (7), the grey correlation degree of each country is calculated, that is, the comprehensive evaluation value of the development level of digital education. Table 5 demonstrates the value and rank.

Table 4. Grey correlation coefficient matrix

Index	U.S.	South-Korea	Romania	Mexico	Latvia	Finland	China
X_1	1.00	0.33	0.33	0.35	0.39	0.35	0.45
X_2	0.35	0.33	0.33	0.34	0.47	0.37	1.00
X_3	1.00	0.33	0.33	0.33	0.49	0.37	0.47
X_4	0.59	0.49	0.33	1.00	0.58	0.36	0.75
X_5	0.59	0.33	0.34	0.34	0.36	0.35	1.00
X_6	1.00	0.37	0.36	0.33	0.45	0.98	0.34
X_7	0.66	0.38	0.47	0.41	0.47	1.00	0.71
X_8	1.00	0.33	0.34	0.41	0.40	0.34	0.34
X_9	1.00	0.56	0.38	0.39	0.55	0.37	0.36
X_{10}	0.40	0.66	0.37	0.34	1.00	0.35	0.33
X_{11}	1.00	0.68	0.36	0.35	0.40	0.40	0.35
X_{12}	1.00	0.33	0.34	0.38	0.34	0.45	0.43
X_{13}	1.00	0.33	0.34	0.43	0.34	0.48	0.57
X_{14}	1.00	0.33	0.34	0.33	0.34	0.36	0.35
X_{15}	0.43	0.33	0.34	0.35	0.34	0.53	1.00
X_{16}	0.35	0.34	0.35	0.33	0.33	0.89	1.00
X_{17}	0.35	0.35	0.33	0.33	0.34	0.95	1.00

Table 5. Comprehensive evaluation value

Country	Comprehensive evaluation value	Rank
U.S.	0.7709	1
China	0.5387	2
Finland	0.4988	3
Latvia	0.4751	4
South-Korea	0.4192	5
Mexico	0.3786	6
Romania	0.3495	7

5.2 Analysis of Results

It is widely accepted that developed countries tend to have high comprehensive evaluation value, including the United States, Finland, South-Korea and Latvia. However, Finland, South-Korea and Latvia have relatively low grey correlation coefficient in several certain indicators such as "Research funds on digital technologies" with heavy entropy weight, leading to a sharp drop in the overall score. Notably, Romania ranks last. This is because Romania's digital education penetration is still relatively low. It can be found from the Table 4 that the number of enrolled students (number of undergraduates, graduate students and doctoral students) is particularly low.

In general, as a developing country, all digital education evaluation index values in Mexico seem to be tremendously low. The number of academic staff implementing online-teaching continues to decrease and their quality could not be guaranteed significantly. On the other hand, what is puzzling is that China ranks second as a developing country as well while the various evaluation index values have a relatively large gap, showing that China has an unbalanced level of resource development when the digital education system has obvious room for improvement.

In terms of that, Liu and Ru (2018) demonstrate that for the large number of students in China, the phenomena of uneven distribution in higher education resources are increasingly obvious. For example, the resources of scientific research personnel attracted by various schools and the financial resources invested by the state are uneven. Jiang (2020) discovers that only a few universities are considered to be highly efficient in digital R&D. Since schools without national key construction projects lack national financial support, the research efficiency is relatively low. According to the analysis of China's grey correlation coefficient, it can be found that the statuses of scientific research, university construction investment as well as university financial investment are far below the optimal sequence. Furthermore, the entropy weights of R&D personnel, university financial investment and digital research funding are relatively large. Therefore, we select China whose digital education system has room for amelioration as the object for further optimization and evaluation with focus on the mentioned five aspects.

6. MODEL OPTIMIZATION

COVID-19 pandemic has led to the confrontation of higher education system with enormous challenges. This necessitated the urgent transition from traditional teaching mode to e-learning. Therefore, redesigning a more appropriate model to evaluate the improvement of digital education is deemed necessary for the provision of quality online-education without compromising the established standards amidst rampant outbreaks. Specifically, the model is mainly optimized from five dimensions which were extensively improved during the pandemic, namely number of R&D personnel in digital education, research funds on digital technologies, infrastructure funds, inherent asset investment and financial investment provided by universities. For different aspects, we have selected adjusted indicators as the basis for optimization. The descriptions and explanations of each index are shown in Table 6.

Table 6. Descriptions and explanations of optimization basis index

Optimization	Index	Symbol	Explanation
Number of R&D personnel in digital education	X_6/X_2	A1	It represents the selection probability of talents cultivated by higher education for scientific research. The larger the proportion, the more attractive the digita technology research work.
Research funds on digital technologies	$\frac{X_{10}}{(X_{16}+X_{17})}$	A2	The ratio of scientific research funding input to output of achievement. It indicates the effectiveness of scientific research funding. The smaller the input-outpu ratio, the more efficient the use of research funding on digital technologies.
Infrastructure funds	X_7/X_1	A3	Per capita infrastructure funding, inherit asset investment and university financial investment indicate the campus resources available to each student, whethe it is electronic facilities or online help. The more digita resources available to each student, the better.
Inherent asset	X_{11}/X_1	A4	
Financial investment provided by universities	X_8/X_1	A5	

The original data is used to calculate the values of these five indicators in seven countries, and the results are shown in Table 7. According to published peer-reviewed literature, under the principle of realizability, we conduct following analysis and optimization.

A1: Developed countries pay more attention to technology and craftsmanship and have a sound intellectual property system. Funds are guaranteed in the transformation of scientific and technological achievements (Cheng et al. 2020). The lack of these resources in China has led to fewer people willing to continue to do research on digital education, especially under the the pressure of economic contraction during the pandemic. Therefore, we use the index value of the United States as a major technological power considering its value is not too high for China to reach the level.

A2: R&D expenditure has an important position in the digital world, and especially research funds of universities have a positive impact on employment (Baş & Canöz 2020). The original data demonstrates that

China's R&D expenditure is relatively high. In addition, it is found that China has the highest digital research funding input-output ratio, according to further optimization basis index calculations. Therefore, we maintain the value of China's research funding or keep with a little fluctuation.

A3&A4: In order to build a research university that is in line with international education and research standards, the Romanian government focuses on upgrading existing higher education institutions to adopt online-teaching. In the context of the Belt and Road Initiative, China-Romania multilateral education cooperation has become closer (Liu & Yan 2020). Therefore, it has realizable reference significance in terms of university's infrastructure construction and the proportion of available inherent asset resources.

A5: In many developed countries, government expenditure on higher education accounts for a particularly important part of government expenditure, which makes it one of the elements of national competitiveness. Therefore, we choose the number of indicators in the Finland as the optimized value. This is not only the standard of major developed countries, but it can also be achieved under China's economic conditions.

Based on the current situation of higher education system adapting to the pandemic, while the values of other indicators remain unchanged, we adjust the number of R&D personnel in digital education to grow threefold (0.18/0.06) when infrastructure funding, inherent asset investment and university financial investment respectively increase by 24%, 4.5 times and 3.2 times. In addition, it would be the relatively ideal state that the research funding could keep remind when we suggest that the quality of digital technological research output should be improved. The optimization of selected indicators is listed in Table 7 as well.

Table 7. Calculation results and optimization results

Country	A1	A2	A3	A4	A5
U.S.	0.18	38634.40	609.40	16.93	8036.84
South-Korea	3.76	277321.98	42284.57	2439.35	6475.04
Romania	1.19	26087.95	74772.35	370.44	32116.82
Mexico	0.09	50964.19	3857.52	19.43	28104.57
Latvia	3.04	946737.27	1923.56	20.63	9718.12
Finland	0.39	720.99	13971.89	74.74	2470.46
China	0.06	240.46	1613.44	4.33	756.62
Optimization	**0.18**	**240.96**	**3857.52**	**19.43**	**2470.46**

According to the optimization index value calculated in the previous section, we change the value of X_6, X_7, X_8 and X_{11} in turn. The obtained indicators are substituted into the entropy weight and grey comprehensive evaluation model to recalculate the score in turn, and the new score is compared with the original data to calculate the change rate. The results are shown in the Table 8.

Table 8. The score and rate of exchange of the optimized objective

The optimized variable	Score	Rate of change
Initial value	0.5388	-
X_6	0.5565	3.29%
X_7	0.5462	1.37%
X_8	0.5691	5.62%
X_{11}	0.5706	5.90%

It can be found that the original data in X_6, X_7, X_8 and X_{11} are all improved. And the change of inherent assets has the greatest impact on the score of digital education system with a 5.90% increase in the evaluation score. The inherent assets of colleges and universities are the hardware guarantee and basic conditions for the running of digital education, which may determine the essential material basis of the development of digital education. Therefore, when facing teaching restrictions resulted from the COVID-19 pandemic, increasing the investment of inherent assets can continuously promote the ability of online-teaching and scientific research activities, thus increasing the output of digital education and optimizing the whole higher education system. Secondly, the score increasing rate of digital education system caused by the increase of university financial investment is 5.62%. Generally speaking, the sufficient balance of investment funds can provide more opportunities for recovering and developing digital education system during the pandemic. Meanwhile, it could also improve the income of online-teaching staff. As a consequence, the quality and quantity of academics would be positively affected to a certain extent, therefrom improving the education output and the overall level of higher education (Trostel, 2009).

7. SENSITIVITY ANALYSIS

To improve the accuracy of the data and avoid being affected by extreme values, this section takes the mean value of each variable to process. The comprehensive score is calculated by using grey comprehensive evaluation model. According to the basic principle of sensitivity analysis, this section mainly studies the sensitivity of a systems' state to the change of system parameters, which is equivalent to the method of controlling variables. The parameters needed for analysis are increased or decreased by a range, such as 5%, 10%, etc. When the control parameter value X^k remains unchanged, the sensitivity response of overall function $F_j(X)$ to the variable X^i can be calculated by the formula:

$$S_{ji} = \frac{\partial F_j(X)}{\partial X_i} \quad X = X^i \quad (j=1, 2, \ldots, m;\ i=1, 2, \ldots, n) \qquad (8)$$

$|S_{ji}|$ is the sensitivity level of function $F_j(X)$ to X_i. The higher the value of $|S_{ji}|$, the more sensitive of the effect of X^i on the function.

This section uses the monofactor change method of sensitivity analysis to test the response of higher education level to X_6, X_7, X_8, X_{10} and X_{11}. Set the initial value of each variable as shown in Table 9.

Table 9. The initial value

Variable	Value	Variable	Value
X_1	7263217	X_{10}	17730716.35
X_2	1982246	X_{11}	23108306.06
X_3	320913	X_{12}	548959
X_4	17.5083	X_{13}	537064
X_5	2286878	X_{14}	53994
X_6	31899	X_{15}	408624
X_7	11588547175	X_{16}	863610.8333
X_8	5789665133	X_{17}	110129.8333
X_9	3104.3226		

Firstly, X_6 is selected for sensitivity analysis, while keeping other variables unchanged. This index is set to be increased and decreased by 5%, 10% and 20% respectively. Each time the parameters are changed, the model is run and the corresponding digital higher education level score is output as the basis of sensitivity analysis. The calculation process of other variables is similar to the sensitivity calculation process of X_6, according to which the sensitivity coefficients of each factor can be calculated respectively. The results are shown in the Table 10.

Table 10. The Sensitivity coefficients of selected variables

	Sensitivity coefficients					
Parameters	**-20%**	**-10%**	**-5%**	**5%**	**10%**	**20%**
X_6	-0.184	-0.146	-0.0739	0.0760	0.154	0.137
X_8	-0.060	-0.045	-0.015	0.015	0.031	0.061
X_7	-0.045	-0.018	-0.009	0.007	0.014	0.025

The sensitivity coefficients of digital technology research funds and inherent assets are close to 0, which indicates that these two variables have little influence on the digital higher education system. The changes of X_6, X_7 and X_8 are in direct proportion to the changes of the level of higher education system, which shows that with the increase of input in these aspects during the COVID-19 pandemic, the higher education system has a certain improvement. Among all the selected variables, X_6 has the greatest impact. The higher education system has a greater change in X_6, and the sensitivity order is $|S_{X_6}|>|S_{X_8}|>|S_{X_7}|$, while the effects of X_{10} and X_{11} are not obvious. Controlling other variables unchanged, we make the value of X_6 and X_8

fluctuate by 20% and calculate the corresponding score of higher education level after fluctuation. Then we draw the diagram between X_6/X_8 and higher education level by using MATLAB software. As shown in figure 1 and figure 2, the more intuitive performance of the improvement of higher education level is more sensitive to these two variables. Therefore, during the outbreak of the pandemic, the increasing input on the number of R&D personnel in digital education, university financial investment and infrastructure investment may have a positive influence on higher education, while that of promoting the digital technology research funds and inherent assets is relatively ineffective.

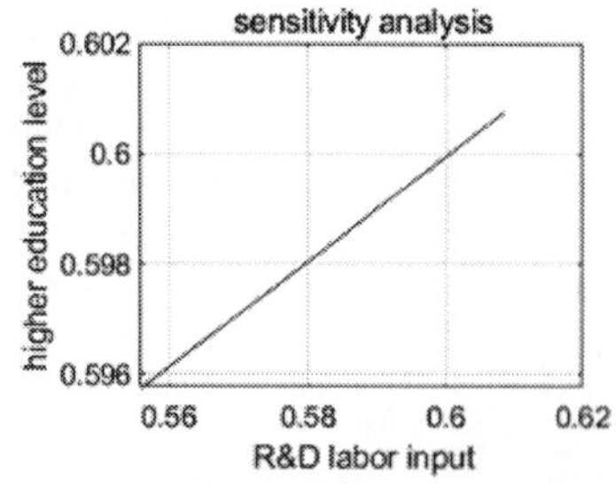

Figure 1. Sensitivity of X_6

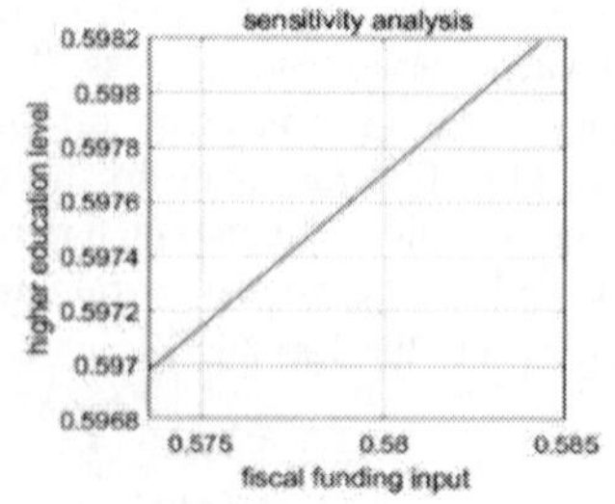

Figure 2. Sensitivity of X_8

8. VALIDATING THE MODEL

Reliability refers to the consistency of the evaluation results, that is, how many people can trust the evaluation score. This section mainly selects the reliability test method $\mathrm{L.J.Cronbach} - \alpha$, which tests the reliability based on the consistency of all internal items. The mathematical model is:

$$\alpha = \frac{k}{k-1}\left(1 - \frac{\Sigma S_i^{2}}{S_k^{2}}\right) \tag{9}$$

K is the number of indicators. S_i^2 is the variance of the score of an evaluation index. S_k^2 is the variance of the total score. When α is between 0.95 and 0.99, the reliability of the index system is high, but it is not common. It is usually a good result when α is between 0.8 and 0.94. It can be used when α is between 0.7 and 0.79. However, if α is below 0.7, it indicates that the error is large, and the index system cannot be used.

We use SPSS25.0 statistical software to obtain the reliability analysis results according to the score coefficient matrix, as shown in Table 11 and Table 12.

Table 11. Reliability coefficient table

Reliability Statistics		
Cronbach's Alpha	Cronbach's Alpha Based on Standardized Items	N of Items
.817	.837	17

Table 12. Results of variance analysis

ANOVA						
		Sum of Squares	df	Mean Square	F	Sig
Between People		5.655	11	.514		
Within People	Between Items	5.273	16	.330	3.499	.000
	Residual	16.577	176	.094		
	Total	21.849	192	.114		
Total		27.504	203	.135		
Grand Mean = .367569756356655						

It can be seen from Table 11 that the reliability coefficient α of the evaluation system is 0.817, and the standardized α is 0.837, which indicates that the evaluation system has high homogeneity reliability and the evaluation results have high reliability. In addition, in the results of ANOVA in Table 12, F is 3.499, P is less than 0.001, which is quite significant. It indicates that the re-use effect of the digital education evaluation system is good.

9. CONCLUSION

Economic and cultural globalization has ushered in a new era in higher education. Because of its immersion in knowledge, higher education plays a particularly important role in global knowledge economies. However, the current Covid-19 pandemic is making it trapped in a development burden. To cope with the challenges posed by this crisis, transformation from traditional face-to-face teaching to online-teaching should be timely implemented in higher education system. This research offered insightful analysis and established grey comprehensive evaluation model based on entropy method, which followed by model optimization according to the improvement of higher education system due to the pandemic's influence. Although COVID-19 has restricted mobility, the research result promotes the development work and internationalization of higher education institutions, which could serve as a credible reference for the higher education reform. In the future, more cross-border e-learning will be offered and implemented. The expansion of e-learning across national borders implements internationalization in an economic and efficient way. In particular, the study is likely to stimulate discussion with business representatives on issues related to employability as well as on the achievement of lifelong learning objectives.

ACKNOWLEDGEMENT

This research is funded by the National Social Science Fund of China (Project No. 16BJY057). The authors acknowledge valuable support from MD, PhD(Med.)-student of Annika Eurola in University of Helsinki who has prepared the survey document and students in SILC Business School of Shanghai University who have handled the data collection.

REFERENCES

Ba, H., & Canz, S. (2020). The Role of R&D Investments on Labor Force: The Case of Selected Developed Countries. Strategic Priorities in Competitive Environments.

Cheng Long, Cao Xianyu & Zhang Zhigang. (2020). An Empirical Study on the impact of labor relations on the innovation and entrepreneurship willingness of University researchers -- the interactive effects of welfare, fairness and promotion. *Journal of University of Electronic Science and Technology (SOCIAL SCIENCE EDITION) (04)*, 105-112.

Electronical version: Acta Electronica Universitatis Tamperensis; 365, Tampereen yliopisto 2004. ISBN 951-44-6024-3, ISSN 1456-954X. http://acta.uta.fi.

Hakkarainen, K. & Lonka, K. & Lipponen, L. (2004): Exploratory learning, Reason, emotions and culture as igniters of learning.

Hasan, N., & Bao, Y. (2020). Impact of "e-Learning crack-up" perception on psychological distress among college students during COVID-19 pandemic: A mediating role of "fear of academic year loss". *Children and Youth Services Review*, 118, 105355.

Jiang M.J. (2020). Assessing the research efficiency of Chinese higher education institutions by data envelopment analysis. *Asia Pacific Education Review*, 21.

Kärnä, Maija (2011): Virtual data building mode to support problem-based learning. University of Lapland. Acta electronica Universitatis Lapponiensis. http://urn.fi/URN:NBN:fi:ula-201108221152.

Kilpinen Kari (2004): Reflective teacher using the computer-network in teaching; how the psycho-epistemological learning styles help to better design learning environments.

Liu J. & Yan X. M. (2018) One belt one road: the higher education status and development trend of the countries along the line (tenth) -- taking Latvia as an example. *World Education Information* (15), 30-33. doi:CNKI: SUN:JYXI.0.2018-15-009.

Liu, W. H., & Ru, M. A. (2018). Regional inequality of higher education resources in China. *Frontiers of Education in China*, 13(001), 119-151.

Rizwana Shahid, & Arsalan Manzoor Mughal. (2020). E-learning: A way out in COVID-19 Crisis. *Journal of Rawalpindi Medical College*, 24(3), 180.

Trostel, P. A. (2005). The effect of public support on college attainment. *Higher Education Studies*, 2(4).

Wen, F. (2013). Retracted: a mathematical model for higher education input–output efficiency analysis.

GENERAL (APTITUDE) MATH EXAMS AND SUCCESS IN MATHEMATICAL CLASSES AT UNIVERSITY: A CROSS-COUNTRY COMPARISON

Genady Grabarnik[1], Luiza Kim-Tyan[2] and Serge Yaskolko[3]
[1]*Dr., Department of Math & CS, St. John's University, Queens, NY, USA*
[2]*Dr., Department of Mathematics, NUST MISIS, Moscow, Russia*
[3]*Dr., AD&D, College Board, Pittsburgh, PA, USA*

ABSTRACT

The goal of the paper is to understand to what degree the student success depends on teaching practices and materials, and to what degree it is due to differences in background, including prior knowledge, skills, preparation, abilities, etc. We analyzed the existing research on outcomes of the SAT and ACT in the United States and the Unified Country Exam (UCE/ЕГЭ) in the Russian Federation, since those exams usually considered as a good indicator of skills, preparation, and abilities. In the US, exams concentrate on identifying success in college studies. In the RF, exams concentrate on identifying gifted students. According to our analysis, the tests are based on different goals which they respectively satisfy.

KEYWORDS

College Readiness, Assessment, Aptitude Tests, Predicting Success in College STEM Courses

1. INTRODUCTION

In our daily work, we aim to help STEM majors succeed in their college-level math and statistics studies. The metric for success in math classes is typically a grade of "B" or higher. We want to understand to what degree the results and outcomes of our work depend on our teaching practices and materials, and to what degree student success is due to differences in background, including prior knowledge, skills, preparation, abilities, etc. To this end, we set out to research commonly accepted college entry exams. Because we have access to educational systems in two counties — the United States (US) and the Russian Federation (RF) — we have compared cross-country approaches to identifying the educational readiness of university STEM majors studying math.

We analyzed the existing research on test results such as the SAT and ACT in the United States and the Unified Country Exam (UCE/ЕГЭ) in the Russian Federation. To our surprise, the goals of each country exams differ significantly. The SAT, for example, is used to measure literacy, numeracy and writing skills needed for academic success in college. Likewise, the ACT is used to measure high school students' general educational development as well as ability to complete college-level work. The UCE, by contrast, assesses knowledge acquired in school, but considers as its main goal providing students with equal opportunity and exam transparency. It is also intended to minimize the possibility of college entry-related corruption.

Several research studies show a good correlation between SAT/ACT grades and success in college studies (Willingham, 1990, Young, 2001, Hezlett et al, 2001, Radunzel, Noble, 2012, Allen 2005).

The predictive power of UCE results for success at college studies is statistically and significantly less (SAT~70+% vs UCE~38%). To make sense of the difference in results, we investigated the exam problems and exam structure in question. The SAT and ACT usually contain a larger number of simpler problems, while the UCE contains a smaller number of problems divided into two parts: A basic section devoted to very simple problems, and an advanced section devoted to some very challenging problems. The latter section is intended for students seeking to enter a STEM program. To some extent, it is similar to SAT subject tests. It differs, however, in the complexity of problems contained therein.

The UCE is meant to create equal opportunity for gifted students of varying educational backgrounds across RF regions. Being gifted does not guarantee success in college math studies. We conclude that college entry exams in different countries (US and RF) are aligned with their respective goals.

In the US, exams concentrate on identifying success in college studies. In the RF, exams concentrate on identifying gifted students.

The SAT/ACT and UCE exams, while similar in form, are based on quite different concepts and, hence, provide quite different outcomes. We conclude that in order to estimate the quality of STEM education we need to take into account the predictive power of college entrance exams.

The paper proceeds as follows. In the introduction section we outline the problem and provide a brief overview of results and a conclusion. Section 2 provides necessary background with a brief historical overview of the SAT, ACT, and UCE exams; gives necessary references to the papers analyzing the tests' college success predictive power (CSPP) and summarizes CSPP per exam. Section 3 describes the structure of the exams and provides typical questions of varying relative complexity per exam and focuses on problem complexity and quantity and time allocated per exam. Section 4 cites statistical analysis of the CSPP, analyses problem complexity and quantity as reasons for possible outcome and offers a hypothesis as to why such a difference in the predictive power exists. Section 5 summarizes our paper results and conclusions.

2. CURRENT COLLEGE ENTRY EXAMS IN USA AND RUSSIAN FEDERATION

We study three main entrance exams available to us from two countries, USA and Russian Federation (RF) as well as their prediction capabilities of future college success.

2.1 USA Entrance Exams: SAT, ACT

In the USA there are two main college entrance exams - the SAT and ACT. We briefly describe them here.

2.1.1 SAT

As defined in (Kobrin, Michel, 2006), "The College Board is a not-for-profit membership association whose mission is to connect students to college success and opportunity. As defined in (Kobrin, Michel, 2006, Goldman, 1976), "The College Board is a not-for-profit membership association whose mission is to connect students to college success and opportunity. Founded in 1900, the association is composed of more than 5,000 schools, colleges, universities, and other educational organizations. The SAT Reasoning Test™ (SAT®) is the most widely used standardized test for college admissions.". The first Scholastic Aptitude Test (SAT) was administered on June 23, 1926 to 8,040 students. The SAT was designed primarily to assess aptitude for learning rather than mastery of subjects already learned. In 2019 over 2 million senior students took the SAT.

The SAT also provides separate subject tests including: foreign languages (Spanish, French, Chinese, Italian, German, Modern Hebrew, Latin, Japanese, Korean), English, physics, chemistry, biology, mathematics (I and II) and history (US and World).

2.1.2 ACT

Another popular college entrance exam in the US, introduced in 1959, is the American College Test (ACT). According to the Princeton Review (*What is ACT?,* 2020, Goldman, 1976) "the purpose of the ACT test is to measure a high school student's readiness for college and provide colleges with one common data point that can be used to compare all applicants." Additionally, the new test should be used not just for admissions but placement as well. It should primarily be useful as an indicator of academic preparation, i.e., it should be an *achievement* test (Sawyer, 2010). Over 75,000 senior students took the ACT in 1959. In 2019 almost 1.8 million seniors took the ACT.

In short, the ACT is more an entrance exam than a "college readiness" predictor. Like the high school GPA (HSGPA), it is more a measure of student's current knowledge base.

2.2 RF Entrance Exam: Unified Country Exam

Introduced in 2009, the Unified Country Exam (UCE/ЕГЭ) in RF is both part of the final certification for educational programs in secondary general education and an entry exam to the higher education institutions. The exam has two mandatory parts: Language (Russian) and Mathematics as well as voluntary parts, which might be needed for entering various Universities (История ЕГЭ, 2020). It still causes a lot of controversy and debate among scientists, university professors, teachers, parents etc. (Неретин, 2016). It has been adopted, nevertheless, by the state and currently the results of the exam are one of the main criteria for enrolling students in universities.

Two of the UCE's mandatory sections - Language (Russian) and Mathematics - are now needed to get one's high school diploma and to apply to a university. Most universities also require some voluntary parts, which include foreign languages (English, German, French, Spanish, Chinese), physics, chemistry, biology, geography, literature, history, basics of social sciences and computer science. The closest US analogy to these voluntary parts are the SAT Subject Tests.

3. STRUCTURE AND CONTEXT COMPARISON OF THE COLLEGE ENTRY EXAMS

In this section we compare structural organization and complexity of the test problems. We will concentrate more closely on the Math part of the exams (Sánchez, 2020).

3.1 SAT

The SAT (excluding SAT Subjects) has three required sections and one optional, with each required section grade in interval 200-800 points:

- Reading, 52 questions, 65 mins.
- Writing, 44 questions, 35 mins.
- Math (includes Science and History/Social Sciences sub-scores), 58 questions, 80 mins.
- Essay (optional), 1 question, 50 mins.

The required SAT test math section contains 58 questions of approximately three levels of complexity. The SAT's typical simplest problems (Stiggins, 1989):

1. If (x-1)/3=k and k=3, what is the value of x?
2. If y=kx, where k is a constant, and y=24 when x=6, what is the value of y when x=5?

The SAT's typical mid-range problems:

1. 3x+4y=−23
   2y−x=−19

What is the solution (x,y) to the system of equations above?

A food truck sells salads for $6.50 each and drinks for $2.00 each. The food truck's revenue from selling a total of 209 salads and drinks in one day was $836.50. How many salads were sold that day?

The SAT's typical difficult problems:

1. If (ax+2)(bx+7)=15x2+cx+14 for all values of x, and a+b=8, what are the two possible values for c?
2. For a polynomial p(x), the value of p(3) is −2. Which of the following must be true about px()?

A. x−5 is a factor of p(x).
B. x−2 is a factor of p(x).
C. x+2 is a factor of p(x).
D. The remainder of p(x) divided by x−3 is −2.

3.2 ACT

The ACT has four required sections and one optional of the following structure and time allocation (Saupe 2000):

- Language (English), 75 questions, 45 min.
- Math, 60 questions, 60 mins.
- Reading, 40 questions, 35 mins.
- Science, 40 questions, 35 mins.
- Writing (optional)

All the math questions are five-choice, multiple-choice questions. Total ACT score runs up from 1 to 36.

3.3 UCE

The UCE has two required sections and many optional sections (much like the SAT Subject Tests). They are administered one subject per day:

- Language (Russian), 39 questions, 210 mins.
- Math; basic level: 20 questions, simplest problems, 180 mins; profile level: 19 questions, 8 multiple choice, simplest problems, 4 short answer average problems, 7 difficult problems extended answer, total 235 mins.

The UCE typical simplest problems:

1. Calculate: 2.4(6.7-3.2)
2. Ivan earned 20,000 rubles last month. He paid 13% of federal tax. How much money does he have left after paying the tax?

The UCE typical mid-range problems:

1. If $S=v_0t+at/2$ what is the value of S when $v_0=6$, $t=2$, $a= -2$?
2. Find the negative solution of $x^2-x-6=0$

The UCE typical difficult problems:

1. In a cylindrical glass, water reaches a height of 80 cm. The water is poured into another cylindrical glass, whose radius is four times more than the first one. What height, in centimeters, will the water reach in the new glass?
2. The rectangle is divided into four smaller ones by two straight linear cuts. The perimeters of three of the smaller rectangles, starting with the upper left and counting clockwise are equal to 24, 28 and 16 respectively. Find the perimeter of the fourth rectangle.

Typical UCE problems appear to be harder than problems from the SAT and ACT. More time is allocated to their solution. The SAT and ACT tests basically cover the same knowledge/skills base. However, the SAT has much finer granularity with scores ranging 400-1600 points, while the ACT scores range 1-36.

The UCE test covers a knowledge/skills base in mathematics similar to the SAT and ACT (*Демоверсии ЕГЭ 2020 по математике*, 2020).

3.4 Tests Widespread

Both SAT and ACT tests are almost equally popular with about 2 million US students who took the SAT during high school in 2018 compared with about 1.9 million who took the ACT during high school in 2018.

The UCE test was administered to about 0.75 million RF students in 2018 (see also Clinedinst, 2011).

4. COMPARISON OF THE UNIVERSITY SUCCESS PREDICTIVE POWER OF SAT VS UCE

In this section we discuss CSPP across all tests.

4.1 Methodology

We match the test result with the first-year college GPA (FGPA) as the criterion of the test's predictive power. When comparing the predictive power of the tests, we observed that different tests tend to provide different measures for describing CSPP. A little work is done on comparison of the CSPP across different exams (Noble, 2007).

Typically, the R2 coefficient from linear regression both for single and multiple variables (for that methodology see (Koretz, et al, 2016, Miles, Shevlin, 2001, Noble, 2002) is used. In (Cohen, 1988) a rule of thumb was suggested for evaluation of correlation. If absolute value of correlation exceeds .50 it is large, if absolute value is between .30 and .50 it is medium, and if absolute values less than .30 it is small. In addition to general issues using R2 as a measure of prediction power (Miles, Shevlin, 2001), referred here papers used different units and scales. Thus, just normalization of results does not make the outcomes comparable (Green, 2012).

We use the match of the test result and FGPA approach, and re-evaluated data provided in the cited papers to compute the match measure of CSPP (Tinto, 2002), and, hence, compare similar results (Lotkowski 2012, Moore, 2009).

4.2 SAT

Since 1950s, multiple research studies have been conducted that looked at the SAT score as a predictor of student college performance. The earlier studies are summarized in (Fishman, Pasanella, 1960, Willingham, 1990). One recent study was performed by (Young, 2001). Another work worth mentioning is (Hezlett et al, 2001), which presented a comprehensive meta-analysis of about 3,000 validity studies covering more than one million students. The Hazlett study concludes that the SAT is a reasonable predictor of FGPA ranging from .66 to .85. It is summarized in the following table (Kobrin, Michel, 2006):

Table 1. Accuracy Rates for Logistic Regression Models for Total Sample

Success Criterion Level FGPA	Model	Accuracy Rate Overall
2.0	HSGPA Only	87.0
	SAT Only	87.1
	SAT&HSGPA	87.0
2.5	HSGPA Only	72.4
	SAT Only	71.4
	SAT&HSGPA	73.7
3.0	HSGPA Only	67.5
	SAT Only	66.2
	SAT&HSGPA	69.7
3.25	HSGPA Only	73.8

	SAT Only	73.8
	SAT&HSGPA	75.7
3.5	HSGPA Only	83.3
	SAT Only	83.6
	SAT&HSGPA	84.0
3.75	HSGPA Only	99.3
	SAT Only	99.3
	SAT&HSGPA	99.3

The SAT is mostly a better predictor of college success than an average HSGPA. More detailed results stratified by various socio-economical, racial and gender groups can be found in (Kobrin, Michel, 2006).

4.3 ACT

A good source for data on ACT as a college success predictor is (Radunzel, Noble, 2012, Allen 2005). In particular, it gives the following data for ACT/HSGPA predictive power, comparable to the above data for SAT. The ACT is a reasonable predictor of FGPA ranging from .58 to .68 (see also Schmitt, 2009).

Table 2. ACT Predicting Levels at Four-Year Institutions

Success Criterion Level FGPA	Model	Accuracy Rate Overall
3.0	HSGPA Only	70
	ACT Only	68
	ACT&HSGPA	71
3.25	HSGPA Only	63
	ACT Only	64
	ACT&HSGPA	67
3.5	HSGPA Only	56
	ACT Only	61
	ACT&HSGPA	63
3.75	HSGPA Only	50
	ACT Only	58
	ACT&HSGPA	59

4.4 UCE

According to (*Психолого-педагогический анализ успеваемости студентов по высшей математике*, 2018, Хавенсон, Соловьева, 2014, Польдин, 2011), the UCE is not as good a predictor of FGPA as the SAT or ACT. The sample sizes used in (Польдин, 2011) are not large enough though to make reasonably definite conclusions compared with the above data for the SAT and ACT. The UCE is a predictor of FGPA with predictive power ranging from .33 to .48 (see also Sackett, 2009).

Table 3. UCE Predicting Levels at Four-Year Institutions

Success Criterion Level FGPA	Model	Accuracy Rate Overall
3.0	UCE Only	35
2.0	UCE Only	33
1.0	UCE Only	48

5. CONCLUSION

In order to understand to what degree the results and outcomes of our work depend on our teaching practices and materials, and to what degree student success is due to differences in background, including prior knowledge, skills, preparation, abilities, etc., we considered the commonly accepted college entry exams.

We have compared cross-country approaches to identifying the educational readiness of university STEM majors studying math available to us via US and RF college entry exams. We analyzed test structure and content. For the US, tests contain more questions, with time per question under 1 minutes 30 seconds, and with questions being relatively simple. For the RF, tests contain fewer questions with over 10 minutes allocated per question, with questions being relatively more difficult.

In the US the main college entry exams, the SAT and ACT, are used to measure literacy, mathematical and writing skills necessary for academic success in college. In the RF the UCE is used to provide equal opportunity for students as well as to fight corruption.

In the US, exams concentrate on identifying success in college studies. In the RF, exams concentrate on identifying gifted students. According to our analysis, the tests are based on different goals which they respectively satisfy.

REFERENCES

ACT, 2012. *ACT scores and postsecondary degree attainment: What's the connection?* ACT Information Brief No. 2012-11). Iowa City, IA.

Allen, J., & Sconing, J., 2005. *Using ACT Assessment scores to set benchmarks for college readiness.* (ACT Research Report No. 2005-3). Iowa City, IA: ACT, Inc.

Clinedinst, M.E., Hurley, S.F., et al, 2011. *2011 State of College Admission.* Alexandria, VA: National Association for College Admissions Counseling.

Cohen, J., 1988, "*Statistical Power Analysis for the Behavioral Sciences (2nd ed.)*", Hillsdale, NJ., Erlbaum

Fishman, J.A., & Pasanella, A.K., 1960, "*College admission selection studies*", Review of Educational Research, 30(4), 298–310

Goldman, R.D., & Widawski, M.H., 1976. *A within-subjects technique for comparing college grading standards: Implications in the evaluation of college achievement.* Educational and Psychological Measurement, 36, 381–90.

Green, C., & Radwin, D., 2012. *Characteristics of associate's degree attainers and time to associate's degree.* (Web Tables NCES 2012-271). Washington, DC: U.S. Department of Education.

Hezlett, S.A., et al, 2001, "*The effectiveness of the SAT in predicting success early and late in college: A comprehensive meta-analysis.*",The annual meeting of the National Council on Measurement in Education, Seattle, WA

Kobrin, L.L., Michel, R.S., 2006, "*The SAT® As a Predictor of Different Levels of College Performance*", https://files.eric.ed.gov/fulltext/ED563073.pdf

Koretz, D., Yu, et al, 2016, "*Predicting Freshman Grade Point Average from College Admissions Test Scores and State High School Test Scores.*", AERA Open

Lotkowski, V.A., Robbins, et al, 2004. *The role of academic and non-academic factors in improving college retention.* Iowa City, IA: ACT, Inc.

Miles, J., Shevlin, M., 2001, "*Applying regression and correlation: A guide for researchers.*", London, SAGE.

Moore, C., Shulock, N., et al, (2009. *Steps to success: analyzing milestone achievement to improve community college student outcomes.* Sacramento, CA: Institute for Higher Education Leadership & Policy. National Governors Association Center for Best Practices & Council of Chief State School

Noble, J., & Radunzel, J., 2007. *College readiness = college success beyond the first year.* Paper presented at the Annual Forum of the Association for Institutional Research, June 2–6, Kansas City, Missouri. 51

Noble, J., & Sawyer, R., 2002. *Predicting different levels of academic success in college using high school GPA and ACT composite score.* ACT Research Report Series, Iowa City, IA: ACT, Inc.

Radunzel, J. Noble, J., 2012, "*Predicting Long-Term College Success through Degree Completion Using ACT® Composite Score, ACT Benchmarks, and High School Grade Point Average*", http://www.act.org/content/dam/act/unsecured/documents/ACT_RR2012-5.pdf

Robbins, S., Allen, J., et al, 2006. *Unraveling the differential effects of motivational and skills, social, and self-management measures traditional predictors of college outcomes.* Journal of Educational Psychology, 98, 598-616.

Sackett, P.R., Kuncel, N.R., et al 2009. *Does socioeconomic status explain the relationship between admission tests and postsecondary academic performance?* Psychological Bulletin, 135(1), 1-22.

Sánchez H., Comeaux E., et al, 2020. *Report of the UC Academic Council Standardized Testing Task Force*, https://senate.universityofcalifornia.edu/_files/underreview/sttf-report.pdf

Saupe, J.L., & Curs, B.R., 2008. *Deriving enrollment management scores from ACT data.* (IR Applications No. 16). Tallahassee, FL: The Association for Institutional Research.

Sawyer, R., 2010. *Usefulness of high school average and ACT scores in making college admission decisions.* (ACT Research Report No. 2010-2). Iowa City, IA: ACT, Inc.

Schmitt, N., Keeney, J, et al, 2009. *Prediction of 4-year college student performance using cognitive and noncognitive predictors and the impact on demographic status of admitted students.* Journal of Applied Psychology, 94(6), 1479-1497.

Stiggins, R.J., Frisbie, D.A., et al, 1989. *Inside high school grading practices: Building a research agenda.* Educational Measurement: Issues and Practice, 8(2), 5–14.

Tinto, V., 2002. *Enhancing student persistence: Connecting the dots.* Paper presented at the Optimizing the Nation's Investment: Persistence and Success in Postsecondary Education conference sponsored by the Wisconsin Center for the Advancement of Postsecondary Education.

What is ACT?, 2020, https://www.princetonreview.com/college/act

Willingham, W., Lewis, C., et al, 1990. *Predicting college grades: An analysis of institutional trends over two decades.* Princeton, NJ: Educational Testing Service.

Young, J.W., 2001, "*Differential validity, differential prediction, and college admission testing: A comprehensive review and analysis.*", College Board Research Report N 6. New York: The College Board

Демоверсии ЕГЭ 2020 по математике, 2020, https://4ege.ru/matematika/58234-demoversii-ege-2020-po-matematike.html

История ЕГЭ, 2020, http://edu.glavsprav.ru/spb/ege/history/

Неретин Ю.А., 2016, "*ЕГЭ и агония математики в школе*", Математическое образование. № 4 (80). С. 2-14, http://mi.mathnet.ru/mo583

Польдин, О.В., 2011, "*Прогнозирование успеваемости в ВУЗе по результатам ЕГЭ*", Прикладная Эконометрика, #1(21), http://www.appliedeconometrics.ru/general/upload/articles/pe2111-56-renamed.pdf

Психолого-педагогический анализ успеваемости студентов по высшей математике, 2018, http://adlog.narod.ru/st/statia13.htm

Хавенсон, Т.Е., Соловьева А.А., 2014, "*Связь результатов Единого государственного экзамена и успеваемости в вузе*", Вопросы образования, https://vo.hse.ru/2014--1/117875470.html

BASIC MATHEMATICAL MODELLING COMPETENCIES FOR NON-STEM HIGHER EDUCATION

Marina Marchisio, Fabio Roman and Matteo Sacchet
Department of Molecular Biotechnology and Health Sciences, University of Turin
Via Nizza 52, 10126 Torino, Italy

ABSTRACT

The role of mathematical modelling pertains several disciplines, both STEM and non-STEM, and various fields: education, academy, work, everyday and social life. Despite its importance, it is not uncommon to see university students facing difficulties with the use of Mathematics to create models, even when mathematical entities that play a role in facing a problem belong to the study programs of secondary schools, and should thus be familiar also to students without a specific background in Mathematics. Difficulties can arise in various phases of modelling: in the comprehension of the problem, in the translation into mathematical formulas, in the resolution process or even in the interpretation of the results. In this paper, we give an analysis of an online test taken by 75 non-STEM students. The 10 questions of the test focused on specific items in mathematical modelling. During the test, students had to write down the reason why they chose a specific answer. The test allowed us to find and categorize the common errors students make and the phase in which it happens, suggesting actions in order to prevent them. Results show percentages of errors and discuss students' arguments.

KEYWORDS

Higher Education, Mathematical Modelling, Mathematics Education, Modelling Mistakes, Modelling Process, STEM Education

1. INTRODUCTION

Mathematical modelling plays a prominent role in various disciplines: it is important to many categories of students. Solving a problem contextualized in the reality is a task that occurs well beyond Mathematics: for this reason, every student of a scientific course could take advantage of mathematical modelling. These non-mathematical students need modelling the most since they are usually less fond of Mathematics. Furthermore, problems occur and need to be solved even outside STEM disciplines, thus making modelling an important component also in courses not belonging to a scientific area. Since mathematical modelling is a wide concept, it is generally not easy to state for it a precise and unique definition. Mathematical modelling is a cognitive activity in which the situation, the system, the phenomenon or the problem is understood, described in mathematical terms (objects, formulas, language, entities...) and this representation helps to mathematically solve problems, discuss solutions, interpret their results, predict future behaviors and build new models. The depth-complexity of the model depends on the theoretical background owned by the person that creates the model. In this study, we will focus our interest on the *basic* level, affordable by a large majority of secondary or university students since it largely relies on concepts acquired during the mandatory school years. Mathematical modelling consists of several phases. First, the "modeler" must understand the phenomenon and the related textual resources, and this is not always trivial since Mathematics requires a rigor that does not pertain the regular, simpler language. Secondly, a translation from common to mathematical language is necessary: words and sentences have to become formulas and equations, again by taking into account the need to be rigorous. Thirdly, the problem itself has to be solved, by using the proper mathematical tools and instruments close to the knowledge of the solver. The final step is the interpretation of the results. A correct interpretation may lack even at the end of the process, thus resulting in having "the right numbers" but the wrong meaning. Mathematical modelling is not only useful while studying, i.e. at school or at university: its importance also emerges during the working life. Furthermore, in the social and collective life of the present world, citizens need to be conscious in order to contribute to the development of a better society: in this sense, mathematical modelling is also useful to form a conscious citizen. A study on mathematical modelling could be food for thought for teachers, since it invites them to understand where the students encounter difficulties during the modelling process. In this paper we analyze results from a test targeted at finding evidence of difficulties during one or more of the mathematical modelling phases, in order to propose a proper action to overcome them. 75 students who will become non-STEM graduates took the online test remotely from home. Ten questions, which require a specific mathematical modelling skill, alternate with an open answer in which students had to write down their reasoning. The aim of this research is finding the most relevant mistakes that students face while modelling. Students were aware of the research purposes and were invited not to cheat. The paper is organized as follows: Section 2 presents the state of the art and some related works on the topic, while Section 3 is devoted to the research question and methodology. Section 4 contains the results of our research, and finally some concluding remarks are contained in Section 5.

2. STATE OF THE ART AND RELATED WORKS

Problem solving and mathematical modelling concern various disciplines. As a general competence, problem solving includes mathematical modelling as a mean to solve problems (Noble, 1982). Nonetheless, the latter one can also imply other activities; it could be simply the description of a system or of a phenomenon, even without a proper solving. Within the problem solving and the mathematical modelling setting, students activate certain cognitive processes: it is therefore natural to ask which mistakes are made more frequently when activating such processes. Several studies have addressed the topic: (Clement et al., 1981) considered how, during the translation into an algebraic notation, a common error of college science students was to reverse the variables in an equation, by writing for example $2A = 3B$ instead of $3A = 2B$. The authors called this error the Reversal. The percentage of Reversal error was 37% over 150 calculus-level students, while 57% over 47 non-science students attending college algebra. Another source of error could even be students' previous knowledge and preconceptions, even when attending a hard STEM like Physics for engineers (Clement, 1981). In (Haines et al., 2001), the authors dealt with distractors in a multiple-choice, real-world setting. Moreover, the authors listed two more steps in the modelling process, namely evaluating the model and refining the model. Apart from the tests, a worker could also need to make a mathematically supported decision among a limited set of choices, with the risk of making a wrong one if the situation is not analyzed with care. (Houston and Neill, 2003) gave suggestions about how to assess modelling skills, basing them on a real experience at the University of Ulster, where students faced real-world problems, both in a third year industrial placement and in a return to university for their final year. This research emphasizes the connection of modelling with the real jobs. The mathematician Felix Klein already started a reform process at the beginning of the 20th century. The main focus was on functional thinking. In the context of the reform of Merano, a utilitarian principle was propagated: enhance our capability of dealing with real life with a mathematical way of thinking (Greefrath and Vorhölter, 2016). In (Schukajlow et al., 2018) a survey of various empirical studies in the field is presented. They state that researchers in modelling have paid more attention to the theoretical foundation of research questions and to using appropriate research methods in their studies. However, the authors suggest enhancing and promoting this kind of research. In (Marchisio et al., 2020) an application to a scientific track belonging to a *soft* STEM discipline is depicted by means of a blended mathematical course for biotechnologists, in which mathematical modelling is enhanced by proper digital resources. On the other hand, (Fissore et al., 2020) involves also students belonging to a course in Strategic Sciences, for which (apart for the name) science does not cover the majority of their program. In this context, the enhancement of mathematical modelling skills passes through students' submission of a worksheet, in which they state, analyze, solve and interpret a problem based on real-life context. In such case, students had to work with the Advanced Computing Environment (ACE) *Maple*. The ACE allows to propose different kinds of interactive resources, useful for learning and modelling (Barana et al., 2020). Moreover, in these courses, the Automatic Assessment System (AAS) *Mobius Assessment* was adopted to evaluate how much a student is prepared by using automatic, randomly generated questions with mathematical content, since the ACE behind the AAS is able to evaluate various types of mathematical expressions, stating in particular whether they are correct or not (Galluzzi et al., 2021). Furthermore, the AAS comes with several tools devoted to the analysis of what the students submitted: close and open-ended answers, even when automatically assessed (Barana et al., 2018), can be revised, and the teacher can change their evaluation manually (Barana et al., 2019). This is important especially when students are given the possibility to try an answer more than once: it is thus possible to see every attempt, gaining precious information about their reasoning. For teachers, analyzing errors allows to remodel the didactics on students' needs, since it can give a strong help in tracking difficulties. This is true for university teachers, but certainly also for secondary school teachers, since it is important for them to train their students according to what the university will require, in a vertical curriculum framework.

3. RESEARCH QUESTION AND METHODOLOGY

In several hard science study courses, students have to deal with Mathematics in order to learn about tools that they are asked to use in relation with the central topics of their courses. Mathematics and mathematical modelling characterize large parts of these courses. It is important to keep in mind that they have been studying the subject since long before entering university, for 12 or 13 years of school (from elementary to high school, in a K-12 like setting). Thus, it is licit to assume that they have already acquired a certain amount of knowledge, competencies and some modelling skills. With regard to Mathematics, the university study program of soft sciences often consists of a simple first-year basic mathematical course. In this research, we want to verify what the students' skills are in solving problems through mathematical modelling, and, in case of poor modelling, why did they not perform better. The research question is: *how is it possible to find and understand the difficulties in basic mathematical modelling, encountered by non-mathematical students?* Our sample consists of 75 students, which are attending the third year of a program devoted to the training of military officers, in a collaboration between the University of Turin and the Italian Army. These students already attended several basic mathematical courses, from school to former university years, even with different backgrounds since they come from all over the country and there are even some foreign students. They just attended, almost completely online, a short modelling-oriented course with a duration of 21 hours (1 ECTS), for which they are going to take the exam, too. We constructed an online test consisting of ten questions, in which the prerequisites and competences required were lower than those needed for these students, since the skills acquired in secondary school were sufficient for the task. They read as:

- Q1: *By law, for every 15 square meters of living space, there have to be 3 square meters of windows, in order to enlighten the environment. Write a relation between S (for the living space) and F (for the windows' surface) which represents the described situation.*
- Q2: *A runner is doing a 2-kilometers race on a 400 meters long track; at the end of every lap, the time elapsed is detected. After a distance of 400 meters, 2 minutes have elapsed; after 800 meters, 4 minutes; after 1200 meters, 6 minutes; after 1600 meters, 8 minutes; after 2000 meters, 10 minutes. Write a formula between T (for time) and D (for distance) allowing to predict distance as a function of time. [data were shown in a table]*
- Q3: *In a clothing store, every five clothes bought, two gadgets are given for free. Write a formula between V (for the number of clothes) and G (for the number of gadgets) which represents the described relation.*
- Q4: *We want to measure the height of a building, given that an observer, placed 25 meters far from its base, sees its top under an angle of 67 degrees. Which geometrical object is necessary in order to compute the height of the building? [answer: triangle]*
- Q5: *During the emergency due to the SARS-CoV-2 pandemic, with the level of restrictions orange, from the municipalities constituted by less than 5,000 inhabitants it is possible to move without valid reason up to 30 kilometers from home. Which geometrical object could approximate the area in which a citizen residing in a municipality constituted by 3,500 inhabitants can move without valid reason? [answer: circle]*
- Q6: *While performing a goal kick, the goalkeeper kicks the ball in order to resume playing. Which geometrical object can describe the trajectory of the ball? [answer: parabola]*

- Q7: *A university student obtained the following grades: 24 for an exam of 6 ECTS, 30 for an exam of 3 ECTS, 25 for an exam of 12 ECTS, 28 for an exam of 6 ECTS. Which grade must the student obtain for the last exam of 9 credits, in order to achieve a weighted average of 28? [data were shown in a table]*
- Q8: *Figure 1 depicts on the left the observations of the pollution agent PM10 (mg/m3) in some provinces of Piedmont during the last week of February and the first days of March 2021.*
  - Which province has the highest number of days below the 40 mg/m3 threshold?
  - In which day the sum of the PM10 values, in the various provinces, is minimum?
  - In which day the sum of the PM10 values, in the various provinces, is maximum?
  - Can we state that a province performed always worse than another one in terms of pollution? Select all the right choices between:
  (i) Alessandria w.r.t. Asti; (ii) Torino w.r.t. Alessandria; (iii) Asti w.r.t. Novara;
  (iv) Novara w.r.t. Biella; (v) Biella w.r.t. Novara; (vi) Torino w.r.t Biella;
  (vii) Alessandria w.r.t. Vercelli; (viii) Novara w.r.t. Torino; (ix) Alessandria w.r.t. Biella;
  (x) Asti w.r.t. Biella.
- Q9: *5 printers print 5 copies of a book in 5 minutes. How much it would take 100 printers to print 100 copies of the same book?*
- Q10: *Figure 1 contains on the right a data frame about people detained in jail relative to the Italian regions. Select all the right choices between:*
  (i) Toscana has the highest number of detained which are foreign citizens ("di cui stranieri");
  (ii) Lombardia has the highest number of detained people ("detenuti presenti – totale");
  (iii) It exists at least one region with more women detained ("donne") than foreign citizens;
  (iv) It exists at least a region with less detained people w.r.t. capacity ("capienza regolamentare");
  (v) Regions having more jails ("numero istituti") have also higher capacity;
  (vi) The percentage of women is about 4% of the total number of detained people;
  (vii) At least ten regions have overcrowded jails.

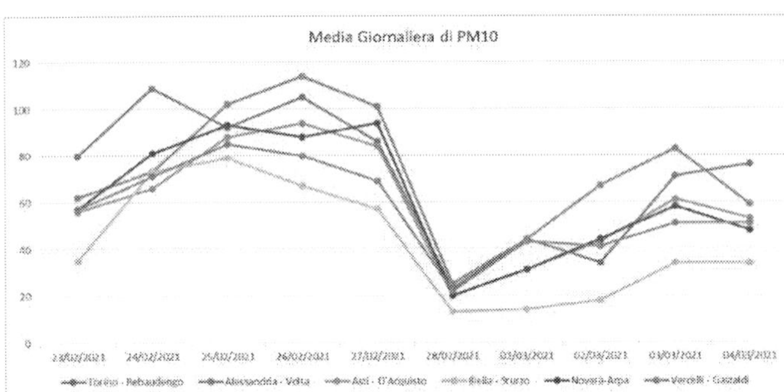

Detenuti presenti e capienza regolamentare degli istituti penitenziari per regione di detenzione
Situazione al 28 febbraio 2021

Regione di detenzione	Numero istituti	Capienza Regolamentare (*)	Detenuti Presenti		di cui Stranieri	Detenuti presenti in semilibertà (**)	
			Totale	Donne		Totale	Stranieri
ABRUZZO	8	1.658	1.622	48	281	12	3
BASILICATA	3	401	390	0	44	1	0
CALABRIA	12	2.704	2.520	60	448	27	0
CAMPANIA	15	6.054	6.519	317	867	149	0
EMILIA ROMAGNA	10	2.993	3.270	146	1.541	56	12
FRIULI VENEZIA GIULIA	5	467	637	20	264	10	4
LAZIO	14	5.230	5.692	375	2.131	45	3
LIGURIA	6	1.120	1.318	71	711	24	11
LOMBARDIA	18	6.143	7.766	370	3.499	80	13
MARCHE	6	846	857	20	319	20	5
MOLISE	3	271	344	0	100	6	1
PIEMONTE	13	3.918	4.144	138	1.613	67	18
PUGLIA	11	2.686	3.538	182	509	72	2
SARDEGNA	10	2.609	2.019	33	475	29	0
SICILIA	23	6.447	5.793	191	1.026	91	4
TOSCANA	16	3.098	3.124	87	1.532	85	25
TRENTINO ALTO ADIGE	2	498	379	18	235	3	2
UMBRIA	4	1.324	1.301	43	390	4	0
VALLE D'AOSTA	1	177	172	0	100	1	0
VENETO	9	1.907	2.292	133	1.221	24	7
Totale	189	50.551	53.697	2.252	17.306	806	110

Figure 1. Data relative to questions Q8 and Q10

This allowed us to consider all of them at the same level, regardless of how much Mathematics they did at university during the first two years, in which they were in another city with different teachers. The test was mandatory, but it did not grade students, in order to have them answer calmly, without distractions and avoiding cheating behaviors. Since the test has not been designed as summative, it possesses a formative significance, which extends its usefulness also beyond the scope of our research. We delivered the test electronically, by means of the AAS *Mobius Assessment*, which collected all the data we needed for our analyses. The response areas required answers in different forms: formulas, text, numbers, and check boxes, in order to allow the exploration of various kinds of reasoning; in particular, they were not limited to multiple choices (Wiggins, 1993; Barana et al., 2015). For every question, they had two attempts: on one side, this reduced the risk of accidental errors, but on the other side, this allowed to detect cases in which the reasoning leading to the first attempt was conceptually wrong, and where the second time the student answered correctly by changing the reasoning. This happened possibly thanks to the information given by the error made in the first instance, in a simple example of "learning through errors" (Scriven, 1967). Halfway between two questions, the students had to write in detail, in an open answer setting, why they gave a certain answer, and how they reasoned in order to choose it. The test referred to all knowledge, competencies and abilities in Mathematics according to the Italian educational system: Numbers (arithmetic), Space and Figures (geometry), Relations and Functions (logic, algebra and analysis), Data and Forecasts (probability and statistics). After the test, we analyzed all the results with descriptive statistics and discussed the reasoning process, especially where errors occurred.

4. RESULTS

As a first result, it is interesting to note how many students would have passed the test, if the test had been graded. Even with a generous evaluation, for example by giving full score to only partially corrected answers (some questions were multipart), and setting the passing score to 5 out of 10 (while usually more than the 50% is required), only 76% of students would have obtained a positive outcome. This means that a quarter of them was not capable of developing basic mathematical models, although they all graduate, and they are going to obtain a Bachelor's Degree at the end of the present year. Entering into the detail of the 10 questions, almost all the students answered correctly to the three geometric questions (Q4, Q5, Q6), in which they were asked to apply elementary shapes to reality. Although the number of correct answers is very high (98.6% for Q4, 93.0% for Q5, 97.2% for Q6), some remarks still need to be made. For example, almost half of the students was overabundant in the reasoning about Q4: most of them brought up extensive trigonometric computations, for instance, while the question simply asked them to determine the geometrical object, not to compute the height of the building. In real life, the completion of a task properly and as fast as possible is a key success factor, so it would have been better had unnecessary aspects been put aside. In Q6, almost half of the students answered reasoning by comparison (43%): they are military, so they know very well the parabola as the trajectory of a projectile, thus being able to compare it explicitly to the trajectory of a ball (with standard modelling assumptions, even if not elicited). If on one side this is undoubtedly positive, since it shows their capabilities in generalizing concepts learned for specific contexts, on the other side we could argue whether they would have been able to still answer correctly without this knowledge; this can be tested in the future with students belonging to other courses.

Speaking of weaknesses, the question with the lowest performance was the problem on impossibility inside a certain context, namely Q7. Although not specified in the text, it was implicit that the highest grade was 30, since the Italian university system gives grades in thirtieths. By doing computations, it results that the value 34 arithmetically solves the problem: without solving in detail, we can directly compute the total number of credits as 36, and:

$$24\cdot(6/36) + 30\cdot(3/36) + 25\cdot(12/36) + 28\cdot(6/36) + \mathbf{34}\cdot(9/36) = 28$$

However, a student cannot obtain 34 as a grade since the maximum is 30. Nonetheless, more than half of the students did not take that into account, and answered 34: by excluding those answering 34 at the first attempt and correctly at the second one, we still have 66% of students. The majority of them (36%) did not even refer in the reasoning to the actual impossibility of reaching 28 as the average; the overall percentage of students forgetting the context is even higher (51%). Only a minority of them (30%) mentioned (directly or indirectly, e.g. answering – again wrongly, but at least respecting the context – 30 the second time) how it was impossible to reach 28, possibly after noticing the wrongness of the answer 34. Along with other errors, this resulted in only 27.1% of students answering correctly, even if they had two attempts.

About the other questions, Q1-Q3 resulted in middling percentages (70.4% for Q1, 84.6% for Q2, 64.2% for Q3), but two main errors arose. Some of them wrongly input the answer in the AAS (which is flexible, but especially when it comes to formulas, it requires some precision in the syntax), or exchanged the role of the two variables, by writing a wrong relation of proportionality, like the error described in (Clement et al., 1981). Last but not least, the three final questions Q8-Q10, concerning interpretation, resulted in variable percentages (77.6% for Q8, 90.4% for Q9, 50.8% for Q10), although for example in Q8 we considered as correct some partial answers. It is noteworthy to remark how in Q10 60% of the students gave a reasoning that was very short, such as "data comparison" or "analysis of values", or a bit longer but essentially without giving real information on how they reasoned. Table 1 shows the global situation: this is not necessarily an exhaustive classification, but it takes into account the main peculiarities we found in students' answers; more than one of them can refer to the same question for the same student, so the sums in the columns can exceed 100%. Note that following a correct approach did not result necessarily in answering correctly, as the example of Q7 shows, where the quota interpreting correctly the question exceeded the quota writing a correct answer, due to other errors. Furthermore, some students did not attempt one or more questions, and this is why every question totalized a number of answers lower than 75.

Table 1. Percentages of correctness and peculiarities, relative to the ten questions administered

	Q1	Q2	Q3	Q4	Q5	Q6	Q7	Q8	Q9	Q10
Total answers	71	65	67	70	71	72	70	58	73	61
Correct answers	50	55	43	69	66	70	19	45	66	31
Wrong answers	21	10	24	1	5	2	51	13	7	30
Correct answers (%)	70.42	84.62	64.18	98.57	92.96	97.22	27.14	77.59	90.41	50.82
Errors (%)										
Forgotten datum	1.41		1.49		1.41		1.43			
Input error	28.17	23.08	13.43							
Forgotten context							51.43			
Extra variables	1.41	4.62								
Reading error			2.99						10.96	
Exchanged proportionality	19.72	1.54	31.34							
Inverted proportionality	1.41									
Inadequate formula		1.54								
Correct approaches (%)										
Numerical example	8.45	6.15	14.93							
Correct interpretation	50.70	66.15	38.81	34.29	77.46	47.22	45.71	17.24	84.93	14.75
Comparison						43.06				
Overabundant reasoning				45.71	5.63	1.39				
Change between attempts	11.27	4.62	13.43		7.04	1.39	27.14		10.96	
Other (%)										
Incomplete reasoning	7.04	4.62	8.96	14.29	7.04	6.94	1.43	10.34	2.74	37.70
Absent reasoning	2.82		1.49	1.43	1.41		1.43		1.37	
Inconsistent reasoning			2.99		4.23					
Answer not making sense	5.63	9.23	8.96	1.43	4.23	1.39	2.86			
Answer only partially correct								70.69		47.54
Computation error	2.82						2.86		2.74	

4.1 Categorization of Errors

We now want to categorize the errors in relation to the phases of mathematical modelling we presented in Section 1. First, it has to be noted how it is not always possible to precisely place an error within such a categorization: sometimes, for example due to steps that are not sufficiently explicated, it is hard to precisely determine where the mistake lies. Nonetheless, in certain cases, the form of the very answer (formula, number, etc.) is sufficient to give proper suggestions. A valid categorization can be given as:

- Category 0, technical difficulties: this includes errors due to wrong input in the AAS, which occurred not unfrequently in Q1-Q3.
- Category 1, misunderstanding of the text: the error lies in a not correct understanding of the problem, in a wrong identification or interpretation of significant data, or in relating them wrongly.
- Category 2, translation from common to mathematical language: the error lies in the wrong writing of formulas, equations, or other mathematical tools representing what the text states.
- Category 3, solving process: the error lies in the misuse of the mathematical concepts needed, in the wrong formulation of strategies, in the wrong consideration of formal tools, or in the wrong development of procedures and computations.

- Category 4, interpretation of results: the error lies in not correctly contextualizing the results in the environment the problem is defined in.

Table 2. Categorization of the errors depicted in Table 1

Error	Category	Error	Category
Forgotten datum	1	Inadequate formula	2
Input error	0	Incomplete reasoning	3
Forgotten context	4	Absent reasoning	
Extra variables	2	Inconsistent reasoning	3
Reading error	1	Answer not making sense	
Exchanged proportionality	2	Answer only partially correct	
Inverted proportionality	2	Computation error	3

The types of error depicted in Table 1, along with the items referred to as "Other" (which are often indicative of incorrectness too), can be categorized as in Table 2. Of course, it is not possible to categorize a reasoning that is completely absent, or an answer that does not make sense at all, while errors in only partially correct answers can depend on various categories. We see how the errors made by the students cover every category: if, as already stated, a Category 0 error occurred in Q1-Q3, a Category 1 error occurred in Q9, where the repetition of the number 5 three times could have triggered a similar repetition for the number 100, while in fact the answer was still 5. Category 2 errors were detected again in Q1-Q3, where students tend to get confused: for example, in Q1 the right relation was $S/15 = F/3$, or equivalently $3S = 15F$, but some of them wrote instead $15S = 3F$, possibly because 15 referred to the living space and 3 to the windows (Clement et al., 1981). Category 3 errors occurred in Q10, causing a large number of answers which were only partially correct, but also in Q4, involving even students answering correctly to the question (but not motivating their answer in a fully proper way). The latter occurrences are noteworthy, since they show how some errors can be made independently from the correctness of the answer: maybe the student is able to identify the right item, but not to give a precise motivation about their own choice. In all likelihood, this does not only mean that the student is unable to give a proper explanation, but it can also mean that he or she does not even know why that answer is the correct one. Possibly the student was helped by intuition, which is of course very useful in Mathematics, but should be accompanied by capabilities related to knowledge and rigor. Finally, a Category 4 error occurred often in Q7 where, as already stated, the arithmetical result was unfeasible due to a practical constraint: it is likely that the students simply proceeded mechanically, not thinking about the meaning of the quantities involved in the real context. A reflection going beyond this categorization, but interesting as well, concerns the capabilities of the students to argue. An argumentation should comment and justify with proper means the choice of the solving strategy, the fundamental steps of the executive process, and the consistency of the results with regard to the context of the problem. A case could occur when the students express themselves in a way that is not objectively very clear, but for which their teacher is able to understand them, because he or she followed their learning path. This is a double-edged sword: if on one hand this can be indicative of a good understatement between the two sides of the cathedra, on the other hand this makes their argumentation of scarce use outside the assessment of their teacher. The latter aspect collides with the aim of teaching them Mathematics and mathematical modelling in order to use it beyond educational contexts.

5. CONCLUSION

This study allowed us to answer to the research question of Section 3: we were able to find specific difficulties students have in basic mathematical modelling, and to quantify them, by also taking into account their status as non-mathematicians. The sample was quite homogeneous, due to the origin of students from all over the country and the presence of some foreign students. Furthermore, the difficulties were numerous and of various kinds, thus configuring a situation which generally saw students being not too confident about mathematical modelling. In order to overcome these difficulties, it would be proper, in secondary schools (within a vertical curriculum framework) but also at university, especially during the first years, to devise actions with the aim of developing problem solving competences through mathematical modelling. As future work, it could be devised to perform starting and final assessment for a comparison of pre- and post- course status to evaluate teaching approaches and propose new ways for teaching mathematical modeling. While working on this, an idea is to consider also metacognitive and affective measures, since emotions, beliefs or motivation are worthy to be investigated further (Schukajlow et al., 2018). In addition, it would be possible to focus on the development of mathematical modelling and pedagogical skills of pre-service and in-service teachers, through country-wide actions that involve distance education and math teachers' training (Barana et al., 2017).

REFERENCES

Barana, A. et al, 2015. Automated Assessment in Mathematics. *Proceedings of IEEE 39th COMPSAC Conference*. Taichung, Taiwan, pp. 670-671.

Barana, A. et al, 2017. Teacher training: a model for introducing innovative digital Methodologies for learning Mathematics. *Proceedings of 3rd International Conference on Higher Education Advances (HEAd'17)*. Valencia, Spain, pp. 608-616.

Barana A. et al, 2018. Model of automatic assessment and interactive feedback. *Proceedings of IEEE 42nd COMPSAC Conference*. Tokyo, Japan, pp. 1016-1025.

Barana, A. et al, 2019. Advantages of Using Automatic Formative Assessment for Learning Mathematics. *Proceedings of the 2018 International Technology Enhanced Assessment Conference (TEA2018)*. Amsterdam, The Netherlands, pp. 180-198.

Barana, A. et al, 2020. The creation of animated graphs to develop computational thinking and support STEM education. *In: Gerhard J., Kotsireas I. (Eds.), Maple Conference 2019: Maple in Mathematics Education and Research*, Cham, Springer, pp. 189-204.

Clement, J. et al, 1981. Translation Difficulties in Learning Mathematics. *American Mathematical Monthly*, Vol. 88, No. 4, pp. 286-290.

Clement, J. 1981. Students' preconceptions in introductory mechanics. *American Journal of physics*, Vol. 5, No. 1, pp. 66-71.

Fissore, C. et al, 2020. Development of Problem Solving Skills with Maple in Higher Education. *Proceedings of Maple Conference 2020*, Waterloo, Canada (virtual), accepted.

Galluzzi, F. et al, 2021. Mathematics in higher education: a transition from blended to online learning in pandemic times. *Proceedings of IEEE 45th COMPSAC Conference*. Madrid, Spain (virtual), accepted.

Greefrath, G. and Vorhölter, K., 2016. Teaching and Learning Mathematical Modelling: Approaches and Developments from German Speaking Countries. *In the homonym book, part of the ICME-13 Topical Surveys book series (ICME13TS)*, pp. 1-42.

Haines, C. et al, 2001. Understanding Students' Modelling Skills. *In: Matos, J. F. et al (Eds.), Modelling and Mathematics Education,* Woodhead Publishing, pp. 366-380.

Houston, K. and Neill, N., 2003. Assessing Modelling Skills. *In: Lamon, S. J. et al (Eds.), Mathematical Modelling*, Woodhead Publishing, pp. 155-164.

Marchisio, M. et al, 2020. Teaching Mathematic in Scientific Bachelor Degrees Using a Blended Approach. *Proceedings of IEEE 44th COMPSAC Conference*. Madrid, Spain (virtual), pp. 190-195.

Noble, R.D., 1982. Mathematical modeling in the context of problem solving. *Mathematical modelling,* Vol. 3, pp. 215-219.

Schukajlow, S. et al, 2018. Empirical research on teaching and learning of mathematical modeling: a survey on the current state-of-the-art. *ZDM Mathematics Education*, Vol. 50, pp. 5-18.

Scriven, M. 1967. The Methodology of Evaluation. *In: Gagné R. M., Tyler R. W., Scriven M. (Eds.), American Educational Research Association Monograph Series on Curriculum Evaluation, vol. 1: Perspectives of Curriculum Evaluation*. Rand McNally, Chicago, USA (Illinois).

Wiggins, G.P., 1993. *Assessing student performance. Exploring the purposes and limits of testing*. Jossey-Bass Publishers, San Francisco, USA (California).

USING LOGIC TO DETERMINE KEY ITEMS IN MATH EDUCATION

Manuel Ojeda-Hernández, Francisco Pérez-Gámez, Ángel Mora Bonilla and Domingo López-Rodríguez
Departamento de Matemática Aplicada - E.T.S.I.Informática – Universidad de Málaga, Spain

ABSTRACT

Due to the COVID-19 restrictions, high-schools in Spain are having both online and in-class lectures. As a result, the students can use not only the information provided by the teachers in class, but they can also use several other methods such as videos and online examples that allow the students to have materials from different places. In this paper, we analyse the Mathematics results of the first two terms in a secondary school from Andalusia. This analysis can help find the central units of the subject found, that is, giving enough background knowledge to keep up with the module. When these are found, the teachers can improve the learning and the results in the following years.

KEYWORDS

e-Learning Assessment Tools, Formal Concept Analysis, Knowledge Mining, Implications

1. INTRODUCTION

e-Learning is an exciting approach to learning that we can use to improve the teaching and learning process quality. It has advantages such as allowing self-paced learning for each of the students, availability of the content at any time, and community-based support, given in the form of forums where the students can ask and solve their questions and their partners'.

A mixture of e-Learning and classical learning is Blended Learning (Dziuban et al., 2018). This term refers to every teaching style that combines traditional face-to-face lectures with an online platform where some content is uploaded, namely, theoretical material, quizzes, tasks, and other stuff related to the module.

Usually, nowadays, we could say we approach our teaching using Blended Learning. That is, we provide on-site courses with live instruction but with solid support from online systems.

In the Spanish Education System framework, the use of Learning Management Systems such as Moodle is widely extended (Almansa-Martinez, 2019) (Cabero-Almenara, 2019). Moodle (Modular Object-Oriented Dynamic Learning Environment) is, at the moment, the most popular system for e-Learning purposes.

The wide use of e-Learning platforms has brought about a massive amount of data that, with proper processing, may bring out meaningful information beneficial for teaching purposes. Anyone with minimal technical knowledge can use classical techniques like Machine Learning or Data Mining to extract knowledge from data.

In recent years, there have been many different approaches in the literature showing the advantages of using methods of Machine Learning or Data Mining to e-Learning (Mohamad, 2013) (Romero, 2008), (Viloria, 2019). For example, it is possible to develop systems that adapt or recommend modifications of particular contents according to different students' aspects defined by their behaviour (Ashraf, 2020) (De Maio, 2012) (Asil Oztekin, 2013) (Hooshyar, 2020). Other applications of this kind of techniques to e-Learning are the development of tools to detect and prevent academic dropouts (Burgos, 2018), (Chung, 2019), (Chui, 2020), (Gray, 2019) (Blundo, 2021), the detection of problematic aspects in evaluation tasks (García 2011), the representation of feelings or preferences of students (Carmona, 2007), (Zengin, 2011) or the measurement of the student experience during an e-course (Shukor, 2015), (Hew, 2020) among others.

Since one of the main goals is to provide an understandable analysis of datasets, we chose to use Formal Concept Analysis (FCA) tools. FCA is a solid mathematical framework to manage information based on logic, lattice theory and Galois connections. It defines two explicit representations of the tacit knowledge present in a dataset (called formal context). One of these representations is in the form of concepts, which are closed sets under a closure operator, entities characterised by the non-formalized relationships among the attributes or features in a dataset.

The other representation of the information is in the form of implications, which are exact association rules. The use of implications extracted from a dataset allows us to employ logic to reason with them. The implications obtained by this method capture all the non-trivial knowledge included in the dataset.

FCA provides the methods to find those representations and extract the concepts and implications that can be deduced from the dataset, introducing logic tools to reason and infer new knowledge. In this sense, FCA allows discovering knowledge in datasets analogously to what other techniques (e.g. in Machine Learning) do. Still, this logic-based approach is more suitable to provide explainable answers when dealing with real-world datasets. Comparing our system with other techniques used in machine learning and data mining, such as association rules, FCA extracts more knowledge. It gives the implications (exact association rules) and the concepts organised in a hierarchical structure, called the concept lattice. Moreover, our team is exploring the use of logic, specifically the Simplification Logic (see Mora 2012), to manipulate implications and build automated methods to reason.

In this work, we use FCA to retrieve the implications from a dataset with the exam marks obtained in the different Maths subject lessons, inspect them, and acquire valuable knowledge for the teacher.

Mainly, our research deals with searching for hidden patterns and relationships between different courses or lectures in pre-university degrees. Specifically, in this paper, we present some preliminary results obtained using FCA techniques to the data collected from the Maths subject in High School, taught following the Blended Learning scheme, due to the COVID-19 restrictions. Data collected in this course include mainly exam marks. Other researchers (Buldu, 2010) (Yahya, 2019) have addressed this general problem of finding links between different lessons. Still, the difference concerning our approach is that we use Formal Concept Analysis (FCA) (Ganter, 1999) (Ganter, 2019) as the tool to extract the knowledge from the data. Although FCA has been applied in the context of e-Learning, e.g., in (De Maio, 2012), to the best of our knowledge, it has never been used for this specific goal, which is studying the weight of each unit within the subject, thus helping the teacher improve the marking scheme for the following year, rather than giving result statistics.

In this way, Section 2 describes the subject details and how we have approached FCA's use to extract knowledge. The results obtained are explored in Section 3, and some conclusions and future works appear in the last section.

2. MATERIALS AND METHODS

In this paper, we analyse the marks obtained in mathematics in a class of the third and fourth year of compulsory education in Spain. The data used has been taken from a secondary school in Andalusia (Spain). The third year class has forty-seven students and the fourth year class has fifty-five students. We cannot give more information about the dataset due to the data protection regulations in Spain.

This year, due to COVID restrictions, the students have both in-class and online teaching, i.e., one day they have in-class lectures, and the following one, they have online classes. This way, there are weeks when they have three math classes and others where they have only two. In the days with online lectures, the students must do some different exercises to check that everything they were taught in class was understood. Some other online activities include watching videos that explain some theory in order to solve some exercises later on.

Although we do not have many students in these groups, we have analysed the qualifications obtained from different exams and courseworks made in the first and second term (see Table 1) to check if any implications would lead us to pass the term.

Table 1. Table of the exams analyzed

Third course	Fourth course
First term:	
Integers and fractions	Real numbers
Decimal numbers and scientific notation	Polynomials and algebraic functions
Polynomials and numerical sequences	Equations, inequations and systems I
Mark of the first term	Coursework I (solving eq. systems)
	Mark of the first term
Second term:	
Equations and systems of equations	Equations, inequations and systems II
Functions and graphs	Elemental functions and characteristics
Coursework I (Geogebra)	Similarity, applications and trigonometry
Mark of the second term	Coursework II (Geogebra)
	Mark of the second term

This way, the teachers can focus on those exams or exercises in the following years to get better results and a more balanced marking scheme. The students also have different activities where they get the skills and knowledge necessary to get a high level in maths this year and further years due to mathematics being a pyramidal study. The students need a good background if they want to improve their knowledge and add new information about the subject.

Even though the subject's teacher thinks that the work made so far has been satisfactory enough to get that background needed for further courses, analysing the data could potentially provide new (hidden) information. For instance, the teacher could determine the most critical unit that gives the students the mindset needed to understand the latest concepts and pass the terms.

In summary, the goal of the paper is to extract interesting knowledge from this data. Some questions that we want to answer are the following:

- Is there any exam or set of exams important enough to imply passing the two terms?
- Is there any connection between the exams, i.e., is there any implication telling that if a student passes an exam, they will pass any of the following ones?

The method chosen to analyse this dataset and answer these questions is Formal Concept Analysis (FCA). Since it is based on Logic and Lattice Theory, this technique can provide more interpretable answers to the questions above.

FCA is useful to capture and infer knowledge stored in binary data sets, usually referred to as formal context. Usually, this formal context is described as tables where the rows are called objects and the columns are called attributes. Also, the formal context can be given as $\boldsymbol{K} = \preccurlyeq G, M, I \succ$ where for all $g \in X$ and $m \in M$ $\preccurlyeq g, m \succ \in I$ if and only if the object g has the attribute m .

To capture the information we use the following mappings:

$X^{\uparrow} = \{m \in M \mid \preccurlyeq g, m \succ \in I, for\ all\ g \in X\}$ i.e. given a subset $X \subseteq G$ the subset $X^{\uparrow}$ is the subset of all attributes shared by all the objects in X.

$Y^{\downarrow} = \{g \in G \mid \preccurlyeq g, m \succ \in I, for\ all\ m \in Y\}$ i.e. given a subset $Y \subseteq M$, $Y^{\downarrow}$ is the subset of all objects that have all the attributes in Y.

With these mappings, we can form the so-called formal concept: a pair of subsets (A,B) where A is the set of objects that share all the attributes in B whilst they do not share any other attribute.

We can define an order among formal concepts as $(A_1, B_1) \leq (A_2, B_2)$ if and only if $A_1 \subseteq A_2$ or (equivalently) if $B_2 \subseteq B_1$. This way, the set of all the formal concepts will have a structure (the concept lattice) to give important information about the formal context. This concept lattice has already been used previously to infer hidden knowledge in Maths education (Pérez-Gámez, 2020).

However, in this paper, we are going to use the implications, we call implication to any expression $A \to B$ where A and B are subsets of M. We say that an implication $A \to B$ is valid in a formal context if and only if $A^{\downarrow} \subseteq B^{\downarrow}$, that is if every object satisfying the attribute set A also satisfies the attribute set B..

Due to the length restrictions, we do not introduce an extensive summary of Formal Concept Analysis. See (Ganter, 1999) and (Ganter 2011) for more details about FCA.

We have used the R language to develop the analysis of the data using FCA and, specifically, the R package named **fcaR**[1]. This package allows extracting the knowledge inside a binary dataset using FCA.

Using **fcaR**, the user can easily extract the formal concepts, the whole concept lattice, relationships between attributes. In the following section, we show how we have used **fcaR** to extract the valid implications in the provided datasets.

3. RESULTS OF THE ANALYSIS

To answer the questions posed above, we have introduced in R the information provided by the High School. This data could be simply an excel file or a CSV file. Then, the data has been binarized; that is, all the passed items were put to 1, and the rest were put to 0. Therefore, we get a formal context having the students as objects, the exams as attributes, and a binary relation representing ``a student is related to an exam if and only if the student has passed the exam".

The package **fcaR** allows us to use the latter defined formal context as such and, hence, compute its basis of implications, also called Duquenne-Guigues basis (Duquenne-Guigues, 1986). All the implications were computed with **fcaR** using the **find_implications** command. The following are all the implications obtained from the third course database.

Implication set with 13 implications.

- Rule 1: {Functions, Geogebra} → {2nd term}
- Rule 2: {Equations} → {2nd term}
- Rule 3: {Polynomials, Equations, 2nd term} → {1st term}
- Rule 4: {Decimals, 2nd term} → {1st term}
- Rule 5: {Decimals, Geogebra} → {1st term}
- Rule 6: {Decimals, Functions} → {1st term}
- Rule 7: {Decimals, 1st term, Equations, 2nd term} →{Integers, Functions}
- Rule 8: {Decimals, Polynomials} → {1st term}
- Rule 9: {Decimals, Polynomials, 1st term, Geogebra} → {2nd term}
- Rule 10: {Integers, 2nd term} → {1st term}
- Rule 11: {Integers, 1st term, Equations, 2nd term} → {Functions}
- Rule 12: {Integers, Equations} → {1st term}
- Rule 13: {Integers, Decimals} → {1st term}

Even though the package gives the implications on its own, some may be a little confusing. Moreover, the rules extracted have a high degree of redundancy. Thus, these implications have been simplified using logical simplification rules, which give a simpler read but contain the same amount of information.

3.1 Analysis of the Third Year Class

Among the total number of implications, we will only consider the ones with the first or the second term mark as a consequent. This is due to these implications being the most important to both teachers and students.

[1](https://CRAN.R-project.org/package=fcaR). See https://github.com/Malaga-FCA-group/fcaR for some vignettes explaining the use of this package.

1st term: Implication set with 8 implications.

- Rule 1: {Polynomials, Equations, 2nd term} → {1st term}
- Rule 2: {Decimals, 2nd term} → {1st term}
- Rule 3: {Decimals, Coursework} → {1st term}
- Rule 4: {Decimals, Functions} → {1st term}
- Rule 5: {Decimals, Polynomials} → {1st term}
- Rule 6: {Integers, 2nd term} → {1st term}
- Rule 7: {Integers, Polynomials} → {1st term}
- Rule 8: {Integers, Decimals} → {1st term}

This set of implications shows a balanced weight of each unit during the first term. This is by rules 5, 7 and 8. These rules show that a student passing any two exams during the term will pass the module. This is desirable from a teaching point of view because students pass two out of three exams. In addition, if they fail one, it is with a high mark; that is, students fail the exam but are not completely unaware of the unit contents. This good balance does not appear in the second term results.

2nd term: Implication set with 3 implications.

- Rule 1: {Functions, Coursework} → {2nd term}
- Rule 2: {Equations} → {2nd term}
- Rule 3: {Decimals, Polynomials, 1st term, Coursework} → {2nd term}

On the one hand, notice that rule 2 gives a privileged weight to the Equations unit. Every student who passes the Equations exam gets to pass the second term. This makes sense from a theoretical point of view because the first Equations unit is a milestone to every math student and understanding it makes every other unit easier. Still, the term's weight should be more balanced since this unit is not the most important in the whole course. For instance, every student that chooses the Mathematics module in higher years must have Functions as background knowledge, which is not ensured with this marking scheme.

On the other hand, rule 1 ensures that every student who has passed the Functions exam and the Coursework passes the second term. This is interesting since the coursework's contents are function graph representations in Geogebra. Therefore, a good knowledge of Functions ensures a satisfactory result in the whole term. Again, Functions is one of the most important units in the whole course, but notice that it is not strong enough to be independent of the other exams, particularly the Geogebra coursework.

This set of implications suggests that the first term's marking scheme is well balanced, but the one of the second term should change to give less importance to the Equations unit and try to balance it with the Functions one.

3.2 Analysis of the Fourth Year Class

As in the previous section, we will consider the simplified set of implications. From this set, the implications taken into account are again only the ones such that the consequent is either the first or the second term mark.

1st term: Implication set with 6 implications.

- Rule 1: {Functions} → {1st term}
- Rule 2 : {Equations II, 2nd term} → {1st term}
- Rule 3: {Equations II, Geogebra} → {1st term}
- Rule 4: {Eq. Project, Equations II} → {1st term}
- Rule 5: {Equations I} → {1st term}
- Rule 6: {Polynomials} → {1st term}

From this set of implications, we observe the following conclusions. From rule 1, we infer that if a student does not have enough knowledge to pass the first term, then they are going to fail the Functions unit because it uses information learnt in the first term such as Equations and Polynomials. Also, in rules 2 and 3, we see the same idea: if a student has not passed the first term, they will not pass the second term as they do not have enough knowledge to pass the second term. In rules 5 and 6, we find that Equations I and Polynomials are important enough on their own to assure passing the first term. It could be because if a student passes one of these exams, they are probably going to pass another of the exams from the first term as they need a good knowledge of real numbers to work with polynomials and equations. Also, deep knowledge of polynomials is needed to understand equations.

2nd term: Implication set with 10 implications.

- Rule 1: {Trigonometry, Geogebra}→ {2nd term}
- Rule 2: {Functions} →{2nd term}
- Rule 3: {Equations II, Geogebra} →{2nd term}
- Rule 4: {1st term, Equations II} → {2nd term}
- Rule 5: {Eq. Project, Equations II} → {2nd term}
- Rule 6: {Equations I, 1st term, Geogebra} → {2nd term}
- Rule 7: {Reals, 1st term, Trigonometry} →{2nd term}
- Rule 8: {Reals, Eq. Project} → {2nd term}
- Rule 9: {Reals, Equations I, 1st term}→ {2nd term}
- Rule 10: {Reals, Polynomials, 1st term}→ {2nd term}

In rule 2, again, we find that Functions is the central unit of the course; if a student passes the Functions exam, this means that they have enough knowledge to pass the two terms. In rule 4, we have that if a student understands the first term and Equations II, then they are going to pass the second term. In rule 6, we have again that if a student passes the first term, Equations I and the Geogebra coursework, they will pass the second term. In rules 4, 7, 9 and 10, we have that passing the first term along with other exams implies passing the second term. This could happen because if a student has passed the first term, they should have enough knowledge to afford the second term. In rule 1, we have that if a student passes Trigonometry and Geogebra, they are going to pass the second term. Hence, Trigonometry and Geogebra are important information within the second term. Lastly, in rule 3 again we find Geogebra along with Equations II showing the importance these units have in order to pass the second term.

4. CONCLUSIONS

We have presented our results of the analysis of the evaluations in two courses in a High School in Andalusia. We have analysed some exams and projects made during the first and second term.

In this work, we have used FCA tools to extract logical implications between the exams, coursework and the marks obtained in the first and second terms, finding some of them very interesting from the teachers' point of view. For instance, some exams are relevant enough to make a student pass both terms. The teachers can use this information to improve their lecturing in the following years so that students can get a bigger background knowledge and be better prepared for higher levels. This is not an analysis to be used midterm but from one course to another.

One of the main restrictions during the development of this study is having the data of half a course and not a full course. Therefore, we look forward to extending this study to one taking into account all the exams of the course. Besides, we plan to do a longitudinal study where we consider not just one year but also the following courses, even university studies. Of course, all the teachers and professors will have all this information available from that study to improve their lectures and increase the math level in high schools and universities.

Another direction to improve our study is taking into account not only the fact of passing or failing the exams but also if they get a letter mark such as A, B, C, D, E, F, FF, G or H. This way, a deeper analysis could be made because it would give much more information than a binary set of pass/fail data.

ACKNOWLEDGMENT

This work has been partially supported by the FPU19/01467 internship granted by the Ministry of Science and Innovation, PRE2018-085199 and the research projects TIN2017-89023-P of the Science and Innovation Ministry of Spain, co-funded by the European Regional Development Fund (ERDF), UMA18-FEDERJA-001 and PIE15-130.

REFERENCES

Almansa-Martínez,et al. 2019. *Functionalities of moodle and edmodo in the middle and higher educations. In Revista de Comunicación de la SEECI, (Vol 50, 87-105).*

Asil Oztekin, et al, 2013. *.A machine learning-based usability evaluation method for e-Learning systems. In Decision Support Systems (Vol 56, pp 63-73)*

Ashraf, M. et al, 2020. An Intelligent Prediction System for Educational Data Mining Based on Ensemble and Filtering approaches. *In Procedia Computer Science (Vol. 167, pp. 1471–1483). Elsevier B.V.*

Blundo,C., et al, 2021. A time-driven FCA-based approach for identifying students' dropout in MOOCs, *International Journal of Intelligent systems,*

Buldu, A. and Üçgün, K, 2010. Data mining application on students' data. *In Procedia - Social and Behavioral Sciences (Vol. 2, pp. 5251–5259). Elsevier.*

Burgos, C. et al, 2018. Data mining for modeling students' performance: A tutoring action plan to prevent academic dropout. *Computers and Electrical Engineering, 66, 541–556.*

Cabero-Almenara, et al, 2019. *Technical and Didactic Knowledge of the Moodle LMS in Higher Education. Beyond Functional Use. Journal of New Approaches in Educational Research,* (Vol 8, 25-33)

Carmona, C., et al, 2007. *Discovering Student Preferences in e-Learning.*

Chui, K. T. et al, 2020. Predicting at-risk university students in a virtual learning environment via a machine learning algorithm. *Computers in Human Behavior, 107, 105584.*

Chung, J. Y. and Lee, S., 2019. Dropout early warning systems for high school students using machine learning. *Children and Youth Services Review, 96, 346–353.*

De Maio, C. et al, 2012. RSS-based e-Learning recommendations exploiting fuzzy FCA for Knowledge Modeling. *Applied Soft Computing Journal, 12(1), 113–124.*

Dziuban, C. et al, 2018. Blended learning: the new normal and emerging technologies. *International Journal of Technology in Higher Education. 15(3)..*

Ganter, B. and Wille, R. (1999). Formal Concept Analysis: Mathematical Foundations. Springer.

Ganter, B. and Obiedkov, S. (2016). Conceptual Exploration. Conceptual Exploration, 1–315.

Ganter, B. and Obiedkov, S. 2016 *Conceptual Exploration Springer.*

García, E. et al, 2011. A collaborative educational association rule mining tool. *Internet and Higher Education, 14(2), 77– 88.*

Gray, C. C. and Perkins, D., 2019. Utilizing early engagement and machine learning to predict student outcomes.

Computers and Education, 131, 22–32.

Hew, K. F. et al, 2020. What predicts student satisfaction with MOOCs: A gradient boosting trees supervised machine learning and sentiment analysis approach. *Computers and Education, 145, 103724.*

Hooshyar, D. et al. 2020. Open learner models in supporting self-regulated learning in higher education: A systematic literature review. *Computers and Education, 154, 103878.*

Mohamad, S. K. and Tasir, Z., 2013. Educational Data Mining: *A Review. Procedia - Social and Behavioral Sciences, 97, 320–324.*

Mora, A. et al, 2012. Closure via functional dependence simplification, *International. Journal of Computational Mathematics, 89,4, 510-526*

Pérez-Gámez, F et al, 2020. Using Formal Concept Analysis to Explore Hidden Knowledge in the Assessment of a Math Course. *International Conference e-Learning.*

Romero, C., et al, 2008. Data mining in course management systems: Moodle case study and tutorial. *Computers and Education, 51(1), 368–384.*

Shukor, N. A., et al., 2015. An Examination of Online Learning Effectiveness Using Data Mining. *Procedia - Social and Behavioral Sciences, 172, 555–562.*

Viloria, A. et al, 2019. Determinating student interactions in a virtual learning environment using data mining. *In Procedia Computer Science (Vol. 155, pp. 587–592). Elsevier B.V.*

Waheed, H. et al, 2020. Predicting academic performance of students from VLE big data using deep learning models. *Computers in Human Behavior, 104.*

Yahya, A. A. and Osman, A., 2019. Using Data Mining Techniques to Guide Academic Programs Design and Assessment. *In Procedia Computer Science (Vol. 163, pp. 472–481). Elsevier B.V.*

Zengin, K., Esgi et al, 2011. A sample study on applying data mining research techniques in educational science: Developing a more meaning of data. *In Procedia - Social and Behavioral Sciences (Vol. 15, pp. 4028–4032). Elsevier.*

PROPOSAL OF A LEARNING DESIGN MODEL DEVELOPED FOR THE CREATION OF TRAINING COURSES COBOL PROGRAMMING COURSE CASE STUDY

Rosa Reis and Bertil P. Marques
GILT, ISEP, IPP
Rua Dr. António Bernardino de Almeida, 431, 4249-015 Porto - Portugal

ABSTRACT

In this paper we present a model for designing professional courses in a blended learning context as a tool to help the interaction between students, teachers and learning resources.
This model aims to promote new concepts, new approaches and new strategies that have been changing the paradigm of teaching and learning. To develop a course based on these objectives, a systematic process, driven by a series of well-defined phases and activities, is required to help us to effectively develop high-quality applications. The research presented here focuses on an improved design model in a blended learning context and consists of four main phases: requirements definition, planning, design of learning activities, implementation, and evaluation. The whole process begins with an analysis of the students and the characteristics of the environment. Content analysis is conducted to explore the structure of the course. The identification of learning events, learning units, and instructional methods are included in the design of learning activities. As evaluation is a critical factor, this model incorporates a questionnaire, whose purpose is to ensure a well-designed blended learning course. This questionnaire tries to answer the key points that determine the structure of the course and to check the satisfaction of the learners with the context taught. One of the main contributions of this research is allowing the requalification of professionals who meet the needs of professional staff in Information and communications technology (ICT).

KEYWORDS

Blended Learning, Collaborative Tools, Distance Education, Online Learning

1. INTRODUCTION

SARS-CoV-2, known as the coronavirus, has drastically changed the routine of the world population. Organisations have had to adapt to the new context, especially educational institutions, reinventing themselves with technological tools and instruments that allow teachers and students to continue their teaching and learning processes.

At an early stage of this pandemic, the Ministry of Education did not foresee the cancellation of teaching activities and those educational institutions would comply with the recommendations of the General Health Directorate (DGS), such as the distance of individuals and the use of a mandatory mask. These rules obliged educational institutions to apply a hybrid teaching model that would allow students to have both face-to-face and online classes. This model implied that online classes were alternated with face-to-face classes, allowing the reduction of the number of students travelling to school across several classrooms, given the high number of students per class. Based on these premises, it was necessary to restructure the vocational training courses, namely their design. This restructuring aimed to reflect on the strategies to be created, on new practices and methodologies to be applied to analyse and define new forms of assessment.

2. TEACHING HYBRID

In the educational scenario, proposals have emerged that combine active methodologies in hybrid contexts, joining the classroom to online learning, thus emerging the so-called hybrid education.

Hybrid Learning is a teaching methodology that combines online and offline learning spaces, mixing moments in which the student performs activities in the virtual environment with others in which learning occurs in person, reinforcing peer interaction and between the student and the teacher (Moran, 2015).

This teaching methodology stands out for its flexibility, mixing and sharing spaces and activities, making hybrid education "a formal education programme in which a student learns at least in part through online learning, with some element of control over the time, place, mode and/or pace of study, and at least in part in a supervised physical location outside their home" (Christensen *et al*, 2013).

To apply this type of teaching methodology, it is necessary, considering the materials available and the students' profile, that learning focuses on collaboration between the actors in the environment. Hybrid teaching allows students to study at their own pace and devote more time to the subjects that interest them most; it allows them to interact with colleagues and teachers, and to take responsibility for their own learning. Therefore, personalisation and teaching, in hybrid form, is related, e.g., personalisation is enabled by Hybrid Learning (Fagundes *et* al., 2021).

2.1 Types of Hybrid Education

Teachers who apply hybrid teaching in their curricular units can opt for different modalities. The most well-known modalities are the following (Evolua, 2020):

Flipped classroom - this is a different concept, which has nothing to do with the position of the chairs in the classroom. What changes is the concept of a place of learning. Students learn at home through online classes. The time in the classroom is used for additional projects spent by the teacher or instructor.

Rotating lab - this type is very similar to the previous hybrid learning. The difference is that here the online learning period takes place in a specific laboratory provided by the school. Allowing the student to have contact with other education professionals.

Flex - the basis of this model is e-learning and personalised teaching. Here everything is flexible: the hours of face-to-face classes, the support of the teachers, the subjects to be taught. With that, everything must adapt to the student's profile.

Hybrid Collaborative Synchronous - Feature's classroom communication, with teacher support for face-to-face and remote students. Using tools integrated with a learning platform, students can establish synchronous or asynchronous communication.

2.2 Aspects to Consider When Designing Courses

Hybrid education, as we discussed in the previous section, consists of integrating technology, which is very present in students' lives, with education. It mixes traditional methodologies with interactive methodologies. However, it is not enough to place a few computers in classrooms and let students' study on their own. According to Evolua (Evolua,2020), the organisation of the classroom, the preparation of the teaching plan and the control of school time are issues that are questioned in any course proposal with these characteristics. When we decide to design a course, we should pay attention to the following aspects.

2.2.1 Application

For hybrid teaching to be applied effectively, the focus of discussions should be on personalising learning, both for students and for trainers and/or teachers. From there, one can think about infrastructures, training of trainers and/or teachers. Here we are talking about education associated with technology, so investment in technological equipment is paramount. It is investing in Internet packages and in the computers offered, these will be decisive for the development of the work.

2.2.2 Rotations

There are two types of rotations in hybrid education. To share, the student's experience of the learning journey and the student's interaction with technology are considered. Let us see:

Rotation of seasons - the school builds its students' learning journey based on the seasons. Students alternate the way they learn per term, one of which is entirely online.

Individual rotation - the student rotates the learning according to the seasons. However, the schedule control is carried out individually by a teacher or software. Thus, the maximisation of the personalisation of teaching is considered here. The management of the rotation is done according to the profile of each student.

In addition to the models described above, there are 2 more:

A la carte - This model is 100% online. The course is entirely online, and the student also contacts the teacher/trainer. Therefore, besides ensuring the personalisation of teaching, it is a great choice for schools that cannot offer specific professionals in cases of free courses.

Virtual enriched - The virtual enriched type of hybrid education is ideal for schools that are fully online. It follows the concept of the flipped classroom with the difference that face-to-face meetings, although mandatory, do not require daily attendance.

2.2.3 Advantages of Hybrid Learning

One of the advantages of hybrid education and the most significant is the greater involvement of students, it allows the student to be the protagonist of their own learning. With this, they learn more and better prepare themselves for the labour market.

For the students, it is a way of offering a quality and differentiated education that solves their needs.

Teachers, on the other hand, are empowered to teach through collaborative learning, demystifying their role as holders of knowledge.

Another positive point of hybrid education is the possibility of a school management system. Thus, we can reduce bureaucratic processes and automate them, in addition to saving time. The system will monitor the school's results.

Another aspect that we can consider, is hybrid business education, which besides being an alternative to traditional education, hybrid education is also present in the business world. Study has no age and keeping up to date is essential. This type of education being highly flexible is its main difference. It has a direct positive impact on productivity.

3. COURSE DESIGN MODEL

As mentioned in the introduction section, the pandemic led to teaching being adapted and the teaching-learning process being restructured. To minimise student contacts at school, the teaching-learning process in our educational institution started to operate by alternating face-to-face teaching with online teaching. This required mental and technical preparation of teachers and students, and it was necessary to implement the courses with several additional tools and activities to support the communication between these actors. The general framework and main elements comprising the courses taught during the pandemic period were developed as shown in Figure 1.

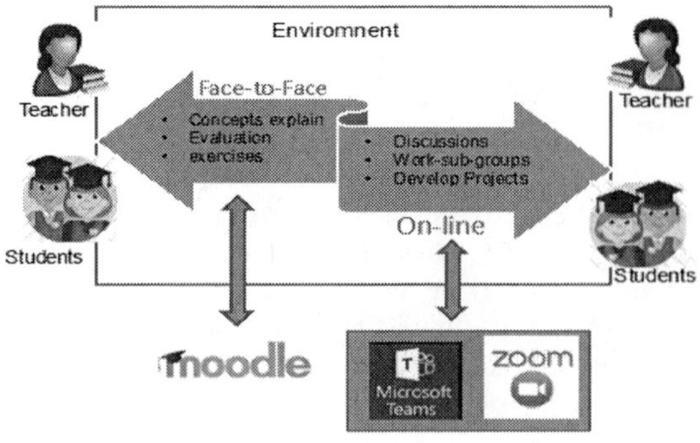

Figure 1. A general framework of learning approach for building courses with lectures, laboratory classes and other activities

The face-to-face learning component aims to allow course content and learning material to be taught in person to a group of students. The learning is essentially a teacher-centred teaching method and the interaction between student-student and student-teacher is more active, ensuring a better understanding and recall of the lesson content.

The online component aims to allow the teacher to have the mission of facilitating learning and motivating the student to perform their tasks autonomously. The teacher needs to remain flexible and ready to assume any necessary role (e.g., guide, coach and/or student) to maintain the focus on learning (Ramos, 2018).

The student becomes more autonomous, and has a more active attitude, and their responsibility in learning. However, to be able to implement the course, we need to do more demanding development work and acquire new and challenging skills (Addis, 2009).

One of the aspects to consider when implementing this type of course is the interaction between the two stakeholders, which according to our point of view should be provided by the course design. This interaction depends on the learner and the intended effectiveness of the course, so it is necessary to take into consideration some artefacts, which are:

1. clear learning objectives.
2. find the right blended learning model that works for the organisation and the learners.
3. learning must be ubiquitous.
4. microlearning (we should use easy to understand elements like bullet points, quizzes to increase students' involvement).
5. evaluation in e-learning.

3.1 Course Design Steps

The design of courses, whether they are intended for vocational education students, requires a development methodology that goes through several interconnected phases and leads the development team to consider several essential aspects such as collaborative work, assessment, active learning techniques. This allows learning activities that involve a systematic combination of face-to-face interaction and technology-mediated (online) interactions between students, teachers and learning resources to offer greater flexibility and deeper learning. In this sense, the course proposal presented here considered several phases, as shown in figure 2.

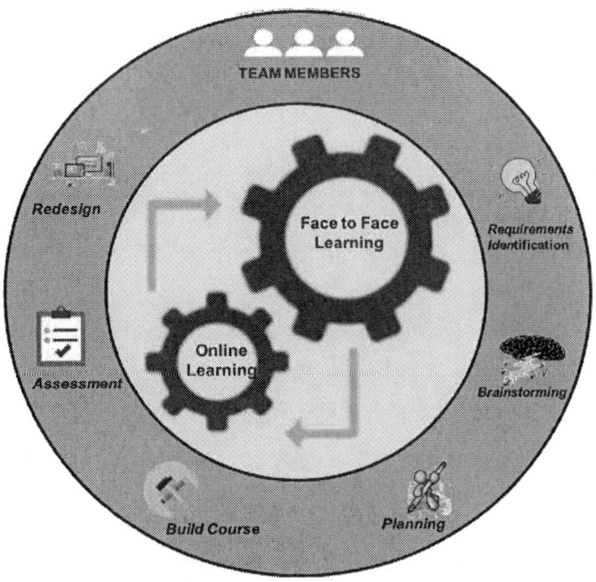

Figure 2. Design course phases

The first two phases, called requirements identification and brainstorming, allow us to achieve a balance between the two learning models (face-to-face and online), being necessary to define the instructional objectives, identify the characteristics of the students (target audience), define the online resources available, choose the platform that will host all the contents and activities related to the course, define the types of interaction and the method(s) of student assessment and, finally, define which collaborative platform to adopt in the online model. The second phase, called planning, follows on from the previous two, allowing teachers to define a training plan, which will be supported by the virtual learning environment chosen for the course, which will also include distance sessions. After identifying these points, we can start implementing the course and, during this phase, we should make an evaluation, to achieve the proposed requirements. This will help the course participants to improve the course design to include the following teaching strategies, as we believe they can contribute to improve the course design:

- Process-oriented - progressive activities that culminate in performance or evaluation (e.g., peer reviews, brainstorming sessions, etc.)
- Project-oriented activities that go step by step, with benchmarks that the students should perform in a certain order. The outcome is not the only important thing here, but the way students create the project is also important (e.g., case studies, online group collaboration, blogs, etc.)

When designing the course, we should keep in mind that students should have time to think about what they know and what they do not know about the subject in question. Thus, we can achieve an optimal environment for metacognitive development (McGee & Reis, 2012). Do not forget that this will only be possible if the technology we incorporate in the course is simple and free, so that students can engage it and can use it according to their needs.

Finding the right balance between face-to-face and online activities are the biggest challenges of designing such a course. The course structure should be carefully created with the learner at the centre of the redesign. Sessions should not be randomly held online or in class, but rather complement each other to take advantage of the online or in class environment. Figure 3 shows the different phases and the different artefacts to be built for our model to be proposed.

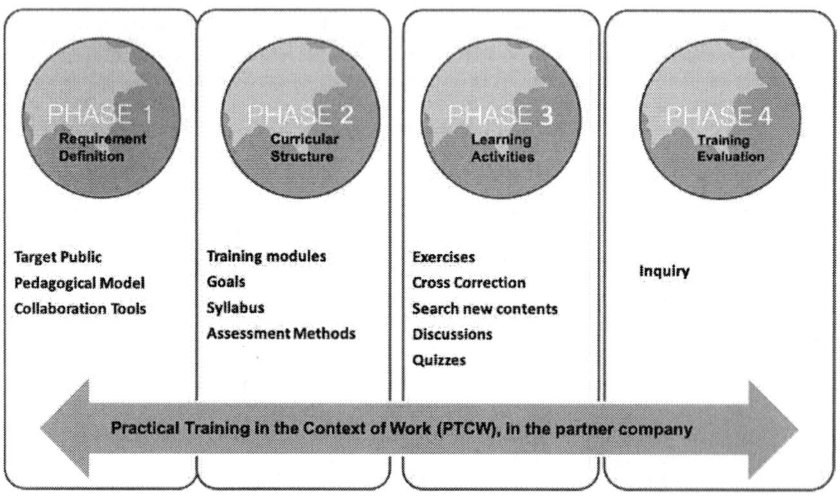

Figure 3. Stages of development of the proposed model

4. CASE STUDY

The study focused on the development of a programming course in Cobol, which took place within the Upskill programme. This training course with the duration of 700 theoretical and theoretical-practical hours is carried out on a work basis, in the facilities of PORTIC - Research, Technology and Innovation Centre of Porto, 7h/day and 5 days/week in schedules that can go from 8:00 am to 6:00 pm and up to 35 hours per week.

The objective of the course was to allow trainees to receive training based on training references, methodologies, and work processes, applied to their professional output in accordance with the conditions of health, hygiene and safety at work required by the legislation in force.

Based on these assumptions, we will demonstrate all the steps taken to achieve the proposed objective, where we intend to create an educational scenario that combines active methodologies in a hybrid context, combining the classroom with online classes, making use of Digital Information and Communication Technologies.

4.1 Definition of Requirements

4.1.1 Target Audience

The target audience, trainees, of the course are employed and unemployed people, preferably with training levels 3 to 6 of the National Qualifications Framework (NQF), which can also cover levels 7 and 8 of the NQF. The target audience should preferably be people who are unemployed and underemployed at the time of enrolment in the course (Proença & Marques, 2020). A situation of underemployment is one where the person holds a contract to perform functions or services for which the qualifications required are lower than those held by the contractor.

Trainees have certain obligations, which are:

1- Each trainee may not record more than 10% of absences which are measured according to the workload of the theoretical training course. If he exceeds 5% of justified absences, he loses the right to the training grant, maintaining the right to meal allowance. In the case of exceeding 10% of absences, justified and/or unjustified, it is the responsibility of the IHE training manager to approve the continuity of the trainee in action, provided that, according to the opinion of the training team, this does not prevent the trainee's certification and if there is evidence of recovery work done by the trainee. But absences that occur for reasons such as illness, family assistance, provision of assessment tests, or others foreseen in the Labour Code, are justified. Proof of the reason for the absence must be provided within a maximum period of 5 consecutive days from the day of the facts that gave rise to the absence.
2- Attend the training course with assiduity and punctuality to acquire the theoretical and practical knowledge given, in accordance with the Internal Regulations in force for theoretical and practical training.
3- Use carefully and ensure the proper preservation of equipment and other property entrusted to them for training purposes.

4.1.2 Pedagogical Model

Considering the specialised and intensive nature of the training that requires a very close follow-up of the work done by the trainees in a tutorial logic, the pedagogical model has the following format:

- classroom training, corresponding to 50% of the theoretical training hours.
- Non-contact training, in asynchronous mode, corresponding to 50% of the theoretical training hours, oriented towards the development of autonomous work by the trainees, in a logic of exercise / project / work accompanied by the trainer / tutor.
- the evaluation of the training in the different modules is supported by the development of exercises / works / projects by the trainees which allow the training of the acquired skills and their demonstration in results made available to the trainers / tutors.
- The training is organised by a team of trainers coordinated by a person in charge of organising the content of the training and supervising the team of trainers.
- the training has a Scientific-Pedagogical Manager.
- the scientific-pedagogical manager will liaise with the companies to ensure that the contents and projects carried out throughout the course are consistent with the type of competencies and activities that are expected to be accomplished in the FCT and in the context of professional integration.
- It is also foreseen that the scientific-pedagogical supervisor will monitor the activities developed by the trainees during the FCT, through mechanisms of regular contact with the trainees and the tutors in the companies.

The model may have to be conditioned by the contingencies resulting from the pandemic, and in defined circumstances it may be necessary to move from face-to-face to distance learning in synchronous mode if there are indications from health authorities for this to happen. The technical conditions for the transition to distance learning are fulfilled if this proves to be mandatory.

4.1.3 Collaboration Tools

Collaborative tools help to promote interaction between students and student teachers. In a distance environment, all interaction is mediated through a technological medium. Since the proposed model is based on blended learning and some training sections will be carried out at a distance, it was necessary to choose a collaborative tool. Thus, the platforms used during the training to support face-to-face and online classes were -Moodle and MSTeams. Both platforms were properly configured to support the designed course and the students who would attend the course were enrolled on them (Proença & Marques, 2020).

4.2 Curricular Structure

This course implemented, was intended for trainees with any area of origin. With this principle, its content was initially designed to provide and level the basic concepts, followed by the more practice-oriented component of programming in Cobol language (Proença & Marques, 2020).

The programming component in Cobol language is divided into two training units, one for the programming itself and the other for the laboratory where trainees are expected to apply the skills acquired or developed in the previous training units in the analysis, design, and programming of applications specially prepared for this purpose.

There are several variants of the Cobol programming language. With this observation in mind, the Programming training unit is designed to contain a generic and more specialised component - adaptable for each edition - in the desired Cobol variant.

The course also includes a training unit on emotional management with the aim of providing trainees with motivation, resilience, and strategic skills to manage emotional states, preparing them for job interviews and teamwork.

With this training action, the trainee acquires knowledge and skills to:

- Develop programs in Cobol language.
- Understand and evaluate the best way to store data.
- Analyse a problem in a structured way.
- Design a problem solving with recognised standards.

The modular list of the "Cobol" training course with a duration of 700 hours, regarding its theoretical component, is presented in the following table (Table 1), to which 480 hours of Training in the Work Context (TWC) are added.

Table 1. Theoretical component of Cobol

Modules / Training Units Theoretical Training Component	**Total (hours) 700h**
Emotional Management in Professional Reframing	60
Introduction to Programming	120
Information Representation	60
Programming	320
Laboratory	140

4.3 Curriculum Plan

In this section, information is presented on the curricular plan and on each of the training units that make up the modular list of the "Cobol" training action lasting 700 hours, on its theoretical component (see Table 2). The content can be adjusted according to factors considered relevant by the training team (Proença & Marques, 2020).

Table 2. Curricular Plan of the Training Unit: Introduction to Programming

Training Unit: Introduction to Programming		**Hours:** 120 hours, compulsory, 60 hours synchronous.
Objectives	**Content**	**Evaluation**
Understand and apply fundamental programming concepts. - Identify the requirements of a problem, analyse it, create an algorithm for its computational solution and design an appropriate test plan for its validation. - Understand and apply the software development process. - Understand the concept of programming language. - Identify the most widely used languages and their field of application. - Understand the concepts of source, object, and executable code.	Algorithmic - Algorithm testing - Good practices in application development - Application development life cycle - Programming languages - The programming process: source code, object, and executable code - Compilation errors and execution errors	Daily worksheets submitted on Moodle - Group work and presentation - Two assessment tests, the second being taken in the last session of the module - Classroom performance and posture evaluation

This course is intended for trainees with any background area. On this basis, its content is designed initially to provide and level basic concepts, followed by the more practice-oriented component of programming in the Cobol language.

The Programming training unit is designed to contain a generic and more specialised component - adaptable for each edition - to satisfy the Cobol language variants in the intended Cobol. Issues such as access to existing and/or to be created data in files of various formats are the subject of a structural viewpoint in the programming unit and applied in the laboratory unit.

At the end of the course, trainees are expected to be trained to evaluate, analyse, and program in Cobol.

Students at the end of the training unit must take a theory examination. However, each training unit has another assessment method, shown in figure 4.

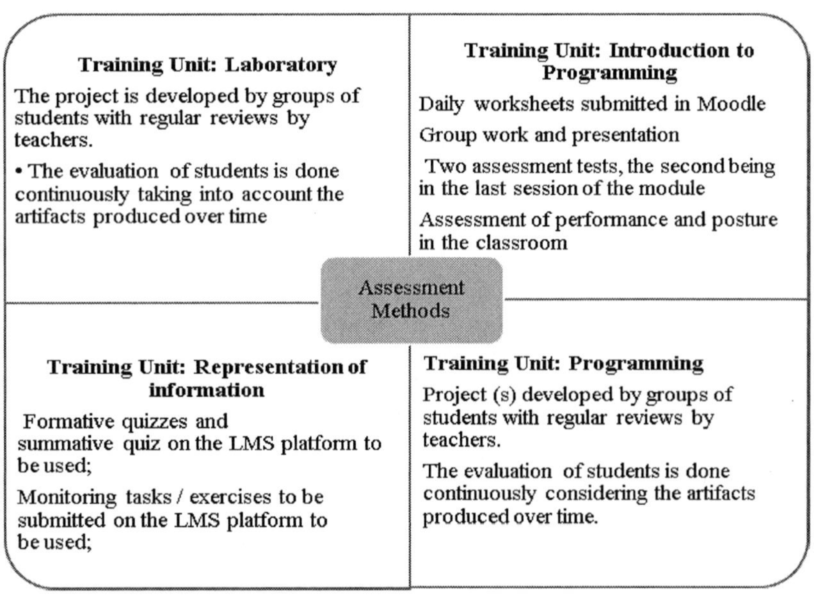

Figure 4. Assessment methods for each training unit

4.4 Learning Activities

A variety of in-class and online activities were used during the training. Some activities occurred in many of the units while others were specific to one or two units. For example, in the Introduction to Programming training unit, students developed a project in an iterative process where they applied all the learning concepts in unit. the iterative process was chosen because it is systemic. Each cycle follows a specific structure or guideline so that structural changes can be made in each cycle. This creates a gradual but constant improvement on each previous cycle, which means that each new cycle is one step closer to the final[1] goal. Other types of activities carried out in class and in online context were exercises, quizzes, online discussions, Q&A Blogs and Virtual Brainstorming Sessions.

Students developed questions to share perspectives or develop an argument to share with the class, engage in group discussions and collaborate on tasks as a group.

4.5 Evaluation of Training

At the end of the training, a questionnaire was applied to assess trainees' satisfaction and collect information that would help us identify whether the type of resources and strategies were the most appropriate.

The questionnaire was anonymous, and based on the objectives, it sought to highlight the trainees' reaction to the training action in relation to the pedagogical strategies, the trainers' performance, the resources, and the pedagogical material. It was also sought to highlight the perception of learning and involvement in the training, in relation to questions that led them to reflect on the level of learning achieved in each training unit. Finally, questions of an open nature were elaborated with the objective of seeking to involve the trainees in the process of improving the training, presenting related questions in which they are invited to point out the weak and strong points observed, especially to identify possible improvements in future editions.

As for the type of questionnaire, we considered the multiple-choice format, but most questions assume the degree of satisfaction/dissatisfaction and good/very good. For this reason, we used a Likert scale with 4 levels, which semantically indicates opposite positions, "Insufficient", "Sufficient", "Good" and "Very Good". This method allows obtaining complex and subjective information, such as perceptions, attitudes, representations, preferences, and opinions (Cohen *et al.*, 2007).

The matrix in Table 3 shows the structure and nature of the questionnaire, as well as the scales that were adopted for each theme.

Table 3. Structure and nature of the questionnaire

Dimension	Topics	Likert Scale
Speech by trainers	Mastery of the themes	Insufficient/Sufficient/ Good/Very Good
	Methodologies used	
	Language used	
	Commitment and support to trainees	
	Relationship with trainees	
Training Units	Suitability for the course	Yes or No
	Workload	Insufficient/ Inadequate/ Too much
	Methodologies	Not Adequate/Adapted
	Considerations about the training unit	Open response
Suggestions/criticisms	Themes considered most important Themes to be developed in greater depth Other topics to be included in the action Suggestion of training actions in which you would like to participate in the future	Open response

[1] https://businessterms.org/iterative-process/

4.5.1 Results of the Evaluation

Within the scope of this work, although giving an overview of the results obtained, we will focus our attention especially on the training component that took place in this environment. Thus, we will analyse aspects related to the intervention of trainers and training units because it allows us to characterise the group of trainers who carried out the training and to verify if the contents are adequate for the course.

Out of the 10 trainees, 10 responded to the questionnaire, which corresponds to 100% of the total number of participants in the training.

Regarding the face-to-face meetings, a good level of satisfaction was observed, with emphasis on the items "Effort and support to trainees" and "Relationship with trainees". Regarding the distance sessions, some dissatisfaction was pointed out at the level of interaction, which is explained from the open questions.

Graph 1 shows the results for each of the items evaluated in relation to the Intervention points of the trainers and, effort and support of the trainees and training units.

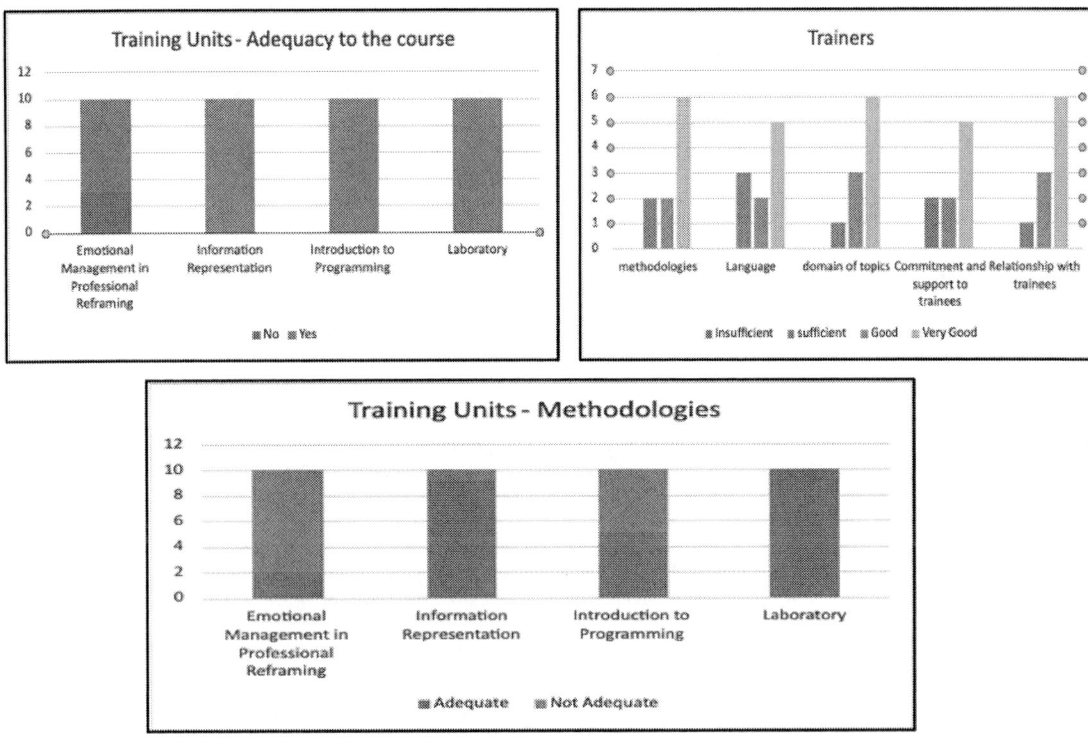

Graph 1. Results for each of the items assessed

The aspects related to the structure of the course, collaboration tools, and which competences acquired will be further analysed when the trainees are still doing internships in companies.

5. CONCLUSION

Despite the opinions that covid-19 and its restrictions brought only negative effects, it is also necessary to indicate the positive consequences of closing the negative effects. One such effect is related to the schools of the university. The new reality and unprecedented circumstances have forced a radical need to quickly introduce and use all available technologies and tools for distance work and communication. (Ozadowicz,2020). The learning system had to be restructured, both at the level of teaching technologies and various types of classes and student activities.

In this sense, we intend to demonstrate with this work that the design of courses should be thought considering these circumstances, because we believe that in the future teaching will not be the same, and that blended learning will bring more advantages. These bring benefits, both for the students themselves, who have grown up surrounded by technological innovations, especially mobile devices that they have been using daily, and for the teachers for whom new and better electronic tools and systems, LMS and other software platforms are being developed.

Considering all the benefits of blended learning, we believe that the proposed model described and substantiated with the case study, can help to better educate students in vocational education. Therefore, our intend that individual with academic qualifications at the 12th year and university level, at areas of competence different ICT, will be able to acquire competences in this area and may enter the professional milieu. We believe that having a partnership of several companies, where trainees in a first phase receive training in ICT and in a second phase enter into a professional internship, it allows easier their integration in companies with a need for staff in the programming areas. We emphasize that all trainees who attended these courses, during the year 2020-2021, are all already working in these companies, having signed an employment contract for 2 years and with a salary higher than the national minimum wage from Portugal.

In future work, the authors will improve the already developed methods of remote and hybrid work, mainly using the BL approach. According to Alqahtani *et al.* (2020), BL is one of the most popular and preferred e-learning models among teachers, professors, and students. In addition, more detailed surveys will also be conducted to collect students' opinions and reflections related to blended and hybrid learning approaches.

REFERENCES

Addis, A. (2009). A comparison of face-to-face and online learning environments to prepare teachers to use technology (Doctoral dissertation).

Alqahtani, A.Y.; Rajkhan, A. A. (2020). E-Learning Critical Success Factors during the COVID-19 Pandemic: A Comprehensive Analysis of E-Learning Managerial Perspectives. Educ. Sci. 2020, 10, 216.

Christensen, C. M.; Horn, M. B.; Staker, H. (2013) Hybrid Learning: a Disruptive Innovation? An introduction to hybrid theory. Clayton Christensen Institute for Disruptive Innovation. Translation Lemann Foundation and Peninsula Institute, 2013.

Cohen, L., Manion, L., & Morrison, K. (2007). Research Methods in Education (6th ed.). London and New York, NY: Routledge Falmer.

Evolve. (2020) Hybrid education: 5 things you should know, August 25, 2020. Online: interactive-teaching.co.uk/ensino-hibrido/, retrieved 13 May 2021.

Fagundes, G. D., Brod, F. A. T., Lopes, J. L. B., (2021) -O Ensino Híbrido nas aulas de Matemática do Ensino Fundamental. Brasília-DF, v. 10, n. 1, January-April 202, ISSN 2238-5630, revistaeixo.ifb.edu.br53I. Retrieved on 13 May, 2021.

Moran, J. (2015). Educacao híbrida: Um conceito-chave para a educacao, hoje. [A. of the book] Lilian Bacich, Adolfo Tanzi Neto and Fernando de Mello Trevisan. Hybrid Teaching: Personalization and technology in education. Hybrid Teaching: Personalization and Technology in Education. McGee, P., & Reis, A. (2012). Blended course design: A synthesis of best practices. Journal of Asynchronous Learning Networks, 16(4), 7-22.

Ozadowicz, A. Modified blended learning in higher engineering education during the case study COVID-19 lockdown-Building automationcourses.Educ. Sci.2020,10, 292.

Proença, P.; Marques, B. P.; Trainee Handbook, UPskill 2020-2021, Vocational training, APDC, IEFP and IPP, October 2020.

Ramos, O. (2018), - Lessons learned from creating b-learning training courses for engineering students TAC de Oliveira Ramos - Proceedings of the National Librarians' Congress, 2018 - www.bad.pt, retrieved 23 April 2021.

MANAGERIAL-LEADERSHIP COMPETENCIES FOR ENHANCING THE INTEGRATION OF INNOVATIVE TEACHING-LEARNING TECHNOLOGIES

Elizabeth Landa[1], Chang Zhu[2] and Jennifer Sesabo[3]
[1]Ph.D. student, [2]Professor, Vrije Universiteit Brussel, Belgium
[3]Senior Lecturer, Mzumbe University, Tanzania

ABSTRACT

The integration of teaching and learning technologies has been crucial catalysts for undergoing teaching and learning innovations. However, in many higher education institutions, these integration potentials have neither been consistently nor systematically used. The implementation of innovative teaching-learning technological change in higher education remains a significant challenge. Previous studies suggest that universities need to embrace the role of academic leaders for its effective implementation. We used 74 Mid-Level Academic Leaders (MLALs) from selected universities to show how MLALs attributes influence the managerial-leadership competencies for enhancing the influence the integration of Innovative Teaching-Learning Technological change (ITLTs). Our results suggest that MLALs have a relatively low competency level for motivating the adoption and execution of ITLTs change. Seemingly, the overall competency level for managing the integration of ITLTs change found to be relatively low. Furthermore, the results suggest that age, leader experience, leadership position and prior knowledge are essential factors influencing the managerial competency level for leading ITLTs change among mid-level academic leaders. Thus, this study recommends integrating ITLTS in higher to consider leaders' experience throughout the process.

KEYWORDS

Innovative Teaching-Learning Technologies, Managerial Competency, Academic Leaders, Higher Education

1. INTRODUCTION

Managing the execution of change is an essential task for improving the speed and intensification of the change in the organisation. (Bates,2000; Ghavifekr, Afshari& Salleh, 2012). In higher education, the fueled technological change in the education process is essential for universities to remain vital, relevant, dynamic and focused (Harshman & Phillips, 1995; Frost & Chopp, 2004; Tushman & Anderson, 2004; Ensminger etal, 2004, Gelaidan,2018). Despite the teaching-learning technological change in higher education for quite more than a decade, its implementation is either inconsistent or relatively low. (Bernad et al 2014; Zhu, 2015; Machumu et al,2018; Landa, Zhu & Sesabo, 2020). Scholars in change management provide over 50% of major changes implemented in various organisations worldwide fail, higher education in particular. Studies also show the relatively low implementation of e-learning technological change within higher education in Tanzania. Notwithstanding, to enhance the adoption of teaching-learning technological change, Bates (2012) suggest that universities need to embrace the role of academic leaders for its effective implementation. Sharma & Rai (2003) and Fullan (2011) argued that effective implementation of innovative technologies depends on leaders' initiatives. This further demands leadership abilities to meet technological transformations demand in higher education (Garrison & Kanuka, 2004). Besides, previous studies (Aitken &, 2014; Coetzee et al., 2013; Smit & Carstens, 2003) have pinpointed that leadership-change execution competencies assist in the smooth progress of any organisation towards a desired future state, whilst others have argued on its role in overcoming limitations during the change process. Though it has been noted that facing new changes, its implementation remains a critical challenge of leadership. Many of the change implementation failures relate to how leaders enforce it (Ashkenas,2013; Ghafikier, 2012). The available empirical literature relies on diverse leadership-strategic leverage for change implementation towards innovative teaching-learning technologies (ITLTs): For stance through exploring leadership roles (Betz,2003; Afshari etal., 2012, Ozcan,2017;

Zhu & Zayim, 2019), leadership styles (Schepers, Wetzels, de Recyter, 2005), leadership characteristics (Sharma & Rai,2002) and others on managing the design of the new change (Tushman,2007). Nonetheless, most of such studies have primarily neglected the exploration of leader-change execution competencies employed by meso level leaders to integrate Innovative Teaching and Learning Technologies (ITLTs) in higher education. Ensminger, (2004) provided that managing execution of change is relegated to middle-level managers.

In this study, we focus on examining Mid-Level Academic Leaders (MLALs)' managerial competencies for enhancing the integration of innovative teaching and learning technologies in the selected universities in Tanzania.

Objective

Assessing managerial competencies among mid-level academic leaders for enhancing the integration of innovative teaching-learning technologies in the selected Tanzanian universities.

Research Questions

1. What are the managerial competencies related to motivating the change, managing the transition, communicating the change and sustaining momentum for enhancing the integration of innovative teaching-learning technologies among mid-level academic leaders in the selected Tanzanian universities?
2. To what extent do the current levels of (perceived) managerial competencies are different to the required (desired) levels of managerial- competencies among mid-level academic leaders in the selected Tanzanian universities?
3. How do leadership attributes among mid-level academic leaders associate with the managerial competencies for enhancing the integration of innovative teaching -learning technologies in the selected Tanzanian universities?

2. LITERATURE REVIEW

2.1 Leadership Competencies and the Integration of ITLTs

From an organisation perspective, leadership is an essential attribute for driving change to achieve strategic goals (Garrison,2007). Scholars (Harigopal, 2006; Tushman & Anderson, 2004; Harshman & Phillips, 1995) emphasise the need for leadership, which is about facilitating the process of change and questioning the existing implementation practices. According to Garrison (2007), proper execution of any sector changes evolves on securing great leadership. When the organisation is coping /executing with new realities, it must look at what it stands for, the values being challenged and the new attitude, behaviours and competencies required to respond to new change needs.

Leaders in the educational context are known as academic leaders. According to Jing & Yao (2019), academic leaders are the personnel with formal managerial responsibilities who exhibit leadership in academic activities. They prevail as change agents who provide crucial insights that ultimately enhance instructors' motivation and capacitate the shift in teaching-learning practices with related change (Bisbee, 2007). Higher education contends on the effective-appropriate use of innovative teaching-learning technologies to meet the current demand of education. However, like in many other developing countries worldwide, higher institutions, Tanzania, in particular, are lagging behind in the execution of teaching and learning technological change as an alternative means of delivering education (Mwakyusa &Mwalyagile, 2016); Though the fact that some universities had adopted blended or online learning (Sharpe,2006; Almasi,2019).

Responding to those technological change challenges, academic leaders need relevant change management-execution competencies for enhancing the integration of innovative teaching-learning technologies. The competencies mainly employed by mid-level leaders provide diverse support towards implementing an inevitable change. The literature emphasises that every academic leader needs a couple of competencies to ensure the proper implementation of ITLTs. Likewise, there is a high demand for such academic leadership in higher learning institutions (HEIs) to set itself on a course of purposeful and sustained change (Les Bell & Middlewood, 2014; Khoshouei et al., 2013). Fullan (2009) argued that leader competency is critical to facilitate the moving stage. The employees will get into the move when leaders are well organised and facilitate their implementation support. The past studies by Baldridge & Burnham (1975) and Beatty

& Lee (1992) indicated that the role of individuals taking leadership might influence an institution's innovative behaviour.

However, the review of Bates (2012) of related literature shows that various studies have examined change execution competencies in various fields. These studies are limited to managerial competencies to execute innovative teaching and learning technologies employed by mid-level academic leaders in higher learning institutions. A study by Ashkenas (2013) and Lakshminarayanan (2016) noted that middle-level leaders lack essential managerial capabilities for managing innovative change.

2.2 Managerial Competencies for the Integration of ITLTs

Change execution competencies mean initiatives' ability for influencing the change. According to (Ashkenas 2013), leader competencies seize the opportunity to strengthen the ability to manage change. Competency allows leaders to spot indicators that lead to performance deficiency whilst speed up and aesthete the teaching-learning delivery in universities (Zhu & Kurtay,2018; Gelaidan,2018; Alshgeri, 2016).

Early studies (Miller & Snow,1978; Beatty & Lee,1992) identify basic leadership strategic-competencies related to general technological change adoption. Their emphasis based on prospectors, analyser, reactor and defender, though some scholars argued that their competencies could only be accomplished by superficial changes in the organisation. Nadler & Tushman (2006) identified three critical managerial competencies involving shaping political dynamics, motivating constructive behaviour and managing transition. Numerous scholars determine the replication of these competencies in a different context. For example, Sharpe, Benfield & Francis (2006) insist on obtaining the appropriate levels of participation in implementing change and using rewards system as necessary strategies for teacher-leader to enhance implementation of teaching-learning technological change. Based on the previous studies, literature suggests that managerial competency relating to technical- generic dimensions are vital in exerting influence in the implementation of organisation technological innovations (Wickramasinghe & Zoyza, 2008; Balyer & Ozcan, 2017).

Table 1. Managerial Competencies for Managing the technological innovations

Competencies	Literature	Findings
Ability to communicate the change	Tushman, (1997); Bordia etal,2004;	Provide direction for management of transition for reducing ambiguity
Ability to obtain feedback about the transition state: manage transition.	Tushman (1997)	Determine the progress of the transition, reduce dependence on traditional feedback processes.
Ability to reward desired behaviour in transition to future state	Tushman, (1997); Haas, (2016)	Use rewards system to shape behaviour to support the future state. Encourage the heart
Ability to obtain the appropriate levels of participation in planning/implementing change.	Tushman, (1997); Bordia etal, (2004);	Create opportunities for participation to obtain the benefits of participation such as motivation, better decision, reduce ambiguity, conflict and enhance better control.
Ability to demonstrate leadership support of the change	Tushman, (1997); Afshari *etal* (2012); Ghavifekr, Afshari & Salleh (2012)	Shape the power distribution and influence the patterns of behaviour through providing support/resources -remove roadblocks and maintain momentum.

3. METHODS

3.1 Research Design

A cross-sectional mixed research design was employed in this study, whereby the data was collected once at a time sequentially. Both qualitative and quantitative methods rely on the need for triangulation and seek elaboration for overcoming the weakness of one method on the other.

3.2 Participants

A total of 74 out of 150 mid-level academic leaders, including principals, deans, directors, Heads of Departments (HoDs) and Coordinators of the University of Dodoma and Mzumbe University in Tanzania, were involved. The participants were randomly selected, whereas the survey questionnaires were distributed using the drop & pick method and a shared link for the web survey. From 74 respondents, 7 participants were interviewed to get their deep insights on their competencies in managing the execution of change related to the integration of ITLTs.

Table 2. Demographic information of the participants

Variable	Categories	Measurement-variables	M	F	%
Gender	F	1=male; 0=female		25	33.3
	M			50	66.6
Academic position	Assistant lecturer	1=old career; 0=early career		19	23.7
	Lecturer			34	50.8
	Senior lecturer			15	16.9
	Associate Professor			6	8.5
Age		Years	42		
Academic leadership experience		Years of experience	5		
Leadership position	Principal	1=managerial leaders 0=supervisory leaders		4	6.8
	Dean/Director			9	15.3
	HoDs			25	25.4
	Coordinators			36	52.4
Prior knowledge	Yes	1=Training, 0=No training			
	Training			25	35.6
	Self-learning			35	42.5
	Colleagues			6	8.5
	No				

M=Mean; F=Frequency %=Percentage

3.3 Data Analysis

This study analysed quantitative data using SPSS version 26, involving both descriptive and inferential analysis. Firstly, one-way ANOVA was performed to check the significance of the means score among the managerial competencies employed. In contrast, post hoc analysis was conducted using Duncan multiple range test to check the means separation. Secondly, the influence of age, gender, academic leadership experience and managerial competencies were analysed using multiple-linear regression analysis.

$$Y = \beta 0 + \beta 1X1 + \beta 2X2 + \cdots + \beta 9X9 + \varepsilon$$

Where
Y= integration of ITLTs total score
$\beta 0$=Constant; $\beta 1$ to $\beta 9$=Coefficient of Xs, X1- X9=Independent variables (age, gender, academic leadership experience and MLALs managerial competencies)

Before performing multiple linear regression, we run the assumptions for the regression model, a normality check was performed $\rho \leq 0.05$, the collinearity/multicollinearity diagnostics test was done to detect whether there is a correlation among the independent (X1) variables. The results show that no variables had a tolerance value of VIF≤10 (Hair et al., 2010). This observation confirms that there was no violation of the multicollinearity assumption in this current study. In addition, the Durbin-Watson's d test was used to test for auto-correlations. The results showed that Durbin -Watson's is 1.51, which falls within the values of $1.5 \leq d \leq 2.5$ (implying that there is no auto-correlation) (Kutner et al., 2005). Hence, there is no auto-correlation in the multiple linear regression data.

The qualitative data obtained from the participants were reviewed and transcribed for accuracy. We used MAXQDA 2020 to support the thematic content analysis through the representation of coding schemes and visualisation. The qualitative data were used to support the quantitative results and was deductively analysed.

Table 3. Qualitative sample of MLALs

Participants	Age	Gender	Academic rank	Leader position	ITLTs-prior knowledge	Leader experience
Participant 1	47	M	Senior Lecturer	Coordinator	Yes	5^+ years
Participant 2	33	M	Assistant lecturer	Coordinator	Yes	2 years
Participant 3	56	M	Professor	Principal	Yes	8 years
Participant 4	49	F	Senior Lecturer	Dean	Yes	5 years
Participant 5	47	M	Lecturer	HoD	Yes	3 years
Participant 6	43	F	Lecturer	HoD	Yes	5 years
Participant 7	58	M	Professor	Principal	Yes	15 years

3.4 Validity and Reliability

We pre-tested our instruments to ten (10) mid-level academic leaders of the university who hold almost similar qualifications (Sokoine University of Agriculture). The split-half spearman alpha was conducted to perform the reliability of the instruments, and it was found highly reliable (0.9) according to Hair et al. (2010). The qualitative- pilot study involves an interview of 2 mid-level academic leaders at the same pilot university.

The exploratory factor analysis (EFA) was used to determine the validity of research items for each variable through principal component analysis (PCA). Principal Components Analysis (PCA) was carried out using an orthogonal rotation (Varimax rotation), which simplifies the factor structure by maximising the variance of a column in the pattern matrix (Osborne, 2015). The data was suppressed at 0.4 factor loading. Before proceeding with factor analysis, the Kaiser-Meyer-Olkin (KMO) measure and Bartlett's test (BTS) were conducted to determine whether it was appropriate to conduct factor analysis. The results show that KMO was 0.888, implying that the sampling procedure was adequate and (BTS; $\chi 2$=843.756; df=171, p=0.00) shows that the data for all variables were appropriate for factor analysis.

3.5 Measures

This study's managerial competencies of mid-level academic leaders' scale are based on Lewin's three-step model and literature about managerial competencies (Goleman,1998). This theory emphasises the driving and resisting forces associated with any change. It further argues that to achieve success in change implementation, its fact lies with ensuring driving forces outweigh resisting forces. Thus, middle leaders must have the managerial competence skills to reduce the resisting forces allowing movement towards the desired state without increasing staff tension. The managerial competencies for change execution were categorised as technical-generic competency needs (Martin & Staines, 1994). The technical-generic competencies based on the study of Cummings and Worley (2003) identified five activities of leadership in change process termed as managerial competencies for leading innovations. These include motivating change (MOTI), creating a vision (VISION), communicate the change (COMM), managing the transition (TRANSI) and sustaining momentum (SUSTAIN). This study adapted the list of generic-technical competencies from the frameworks proposed by Goleman (1998) and used nineteen (19) items, which adequately representing different aspects of technical- generic managerial competencies. The items scored on a five-point frequency rating scale ranging from "1" (low) to "5" (high). The required and the current levels of the mid-level academic leaders for each technical and generic competence were explored. The study used the self-administered questionnaire and web survey for data collection. It used a Likert scale to assess the current and future competency levels.

4. RESULTS

Given RQ1, Table 4 reveals the current level of managerial competencies. The results shows that the mean scores for the five dimensions are significantly different among MLALs. The current level competency with communicating the ITLTs change found a significantly higher mean score of 3.3(SD,0.1) $\rho \leq 0.05$ than motivating the ITLTs change with the lowest mean score of 2.1(SD,0.1). Generally, the results suggest for low-level competency related to the motivation for ITLTs change among MLALs.

Table 4. Descriptive statistics for the variables among ITLTs-change management competencies subscales

Current level	Mean	SD	Required level	M	SD
Motivating ITLTs change	2.1	0.1	Motivating ITLTs change	4.3	0.3
Managing the ITLTs transition	3.2	0.09	Managing the ITLTs transition	4.2	0.09
Sustaining momentum	3.2	0.1	Sustaining momentum	4.1	0.09
Creating vision for ITLTs	3.05	0.1	Creating vision for ITLTs	4.2	0.09
Communicating ITLTs change	3.3	0.1	Communicating ITLTs change	4.5	0.1

Means are significant at $p<0.05$.SD=Standard Deviation

Concerning the RQ2, the results reveal that the current managerial competence level for managing ITLTs change is relatively low with mean score of (2.9) among mid-level academic leaders in the selected Tanzania universities. While the required or desired competency level found quite higher with an average of (4.26). Generally, the results revealed the difference of an average of 2.17 competency level for the management of the integration of ITLTs among MLALs.

In view of RQ3, Table 5 presents the regression analysis results from the independent variable X (demographic characteristics of MLALs) which predict the results of dependent variable Y (managerial competencies for enhancing the integration of innovative teaching and learning technologies). Moreover, with regard to the contribution of the independent variables (age, gender, leadership experience, leadership position, and the prior knowledge) on the dependent variables (MOTI, TRANSI, SUSTAIN, COMM, and VISION), the results suggest a range between 12.6% and 17.2% as the contribution of MLALs-demographic characteristics to managerial competencies for the integration of ITLTs dimensions. For MOTI ($R=.355^a$; R2=.152; R2 adj=.025), with regard to TRANSI ($R=.364^a$; R2=.132; R2 adj=.032), similar for SUSTAIN with ($R= .341^a$; $R^2= .111$; R^2 adj = .015), VISION ($R= .415^a$; $R^2= .172$; R^2 adj = .076) and for COMM, ($R= .355^a$; R2= .126; R2 adj= .025).

Again, the results reveal that independent variables such as age, leadership experience and prior knowledge are a statistically significant predictor of managerial- competencies for enhancing the integration of innovative teaching and learning technologies. Age found to have a significant negative relationship with MOTI and TRANSI (-.041; -.039). This implies that adults' respondents had a low likelihood of possessing managerial competencies for enhancing the integration of innovative teaching and learning technologies than their counterparts, especially on how to motivate the ITLTs to change and manage the ITLTs transition. Leadership experience was found to have a significant relationship with MOTI and COMM (βMOTI =.076, p=0.043; βCOMM=.121, p =.001), signifying that MLALs with leadership experience are highly likely to possess managerial competencies for motivating and communicating the integration of innovative -learning technologies to their subordinates.

The results further show that prior knowledge acquired through [training, self-learning and colleagues] is a statistically significant predictor of VISION and COMM. The findings indicate (β_{VISION} =-.525, p=.026; β_{COMM}=-.489, p =.045), showing that MLALs with prior knowledge on the integration of ITLTs are less possessing competencies to create the vision and communicate ITLTs change among academic members of staff. With all the variables of demographic information, the only gender among MLALs did not significantly predict the five dimensions of managerial competencies for enhancing the integration of ITLTs change.

Table 5. Predictors of the constructs of demographic information in the integration of ITLTs change management competencies among mid-level academic leaders

Variables	MOTI		TRANSI		SUSTAIN		VISION		COMM	
	β	ρ	β	ρ	β	ρ	β	ρ	β	ρ
Age	-.041	*	-.039	*	-.027	ns	-.012	ns	-.003	ns
Gender	.122	ns	-.066	ns	-.076	ns	.069	ns	.024	ns
Academic Leader experience	.076	*	.023	ns	.025	ns	-.025	ns	.121	**
Academic rank	-.093	ns	.066	ns	-.192	ns	-.247	ns	.234	ns
Leader-position	-.186	ns	-.263	ns	-.309	*	-.240	ns	-.214	ns
Prior knowledge	.058	ns	-.204	ns	-.164	ns	-.525	*	-.489	*

*p<0.05; **P≤0.01; ns-non significant

Table 6. Themes, sub-themes emerged, code frequencies and participants' quotes for the qualitative results

RQs	Themes	Sub-themes emerged	Code frequencies	Participants quotes (sample)
RQ1.	Motivating ITLTs integration	Awards, token & Rewards; Recognition; ITLTs Training; Technical support	18	"We hardly emphasise ITLTs training to instructors. Training, in most cases, stand as extrinsic motivators for a person to use technology. One can not use technology if he or she misses the technological know-how part likely enough it may increase the chance of change resistance among staff." PARTICIPANT 5, Pos. 270
	Managing the ITLTs transition	Release of ITLTs-use trend reports; Compulsory use of ITLTs initiatives; Recognition of aspects needed for integrating ITLTs; ITLTs capacity building training, ITLTs policies; Leader willingness	43	"As a leader I must show a way to facilitate smooth use of educational technologies, I am supposed to present to the ICT boards, e-learning challenges let's say of internet connections, etc" PARTICIPANT 3, Pos. 337
	Communicating ITLTs change	Advocate ITLTs use through meeting, Awareness campaign via training/seminars;	44	"In fact, uuh.. sometimes we use platforms like departmental/faculty meeting to advocate the teaching - learning technological change..." PARTICIPANT 1, Pos. 401
	Sustaining the momentum for ITLTs	ITLTs policies; ITLTs capacity building training; managing attitudinal & cultural change; Top-level management support	39	People may tend to stay silence in terms of using ITLTs when there is no push mechanism. If we seriously need instructors to use and sustain the use of technologies, attitudinal change should be the first thing to address...". PARTICIPANT 3, Pos. 645

	Creating ITLTs vision	School/faculty strategic plans	18	"Any change implementation must have a vision, so even these technological change in teaching should be guided by a certain rule to provide us a direction" PARTICIPANT 3, Pos. 645
RQ3.	MLALs characteristics & managing integration of ITLTs	Age vs management of ITLTs change; ITLTs prior knowledge vs management of ITLTs change.	17	"...technologies are used mostly by youth…in fact you can't lead something you don't know, as a leader you firstly need to know the technology so as to direct your subordinates accordingly" PARTICIPANT 7, Pos. 705

5. DISCUSSION

This study devotes to examine the perceived managerial competencies associated with the integration of ITLTs change among mid-level academic leaders (MLALs) in higher education. The general results indicate a moderate managerial competencies level for enhancing the integration of ITLTs. However, mid-level academic leaders were found to have relatively low competency in motivating the integration of ITLTs by academic staff. These results are not due to chance; the majority of the MLALs participated in the interview, emphasising the means that could push extra support, is for them to have specific funds for implementing ITLTs change. "We have only recommendation role as meso level leaders. It is challenging to provide financial rewards to academic staff members who are extremely devoting to integrate ITLTs" (participant, 4).

The findings further indicate that age is negatively associated with competency in managing the transition and motivating the change. It implies that as age increases, the managerial competency for enhancing the integration of ITLTs change by mid-level academic leaders decrease. These results do not seem surprising since most scholars use technology to reveal that elderly hood negatively impacts ITLTs usage (Ke & Kwak, 2013), which can also be similar to its managerial-leadership competencies level. This is because adults are reluctant to learn new skills while young are energetic and eager to learn new knowledge.

According to this study, the leadership experience of mid-level academic leaders was an important factor in determining the competencies among MLALs for enhancing the integration of ITLTs in higher education. The results suggest a significant positive association with motivating the ITLTs to change and communicate the ITLTs change. It suggests that mid-level academic leaders with higher leadership experience are more likely to motivate and communicate the ITLTs change than their counterparts. The findings comply with the study by Weinberg, (2004), who also suggested that experience is a good teacher when it comes to technological change.

The study hypothesised that prior knowledge for ITLTs had a negative beta coefficient that statistically significant influence the managerial-leadership competency level for enhancing the integration of ITLTs. That means prior knowledge among participants do not determine competency level for creating a vision and communicating ITLTs change. The findings are a bit contrary to the scholars who suggest that ITLTs change is significantly associated with lack of training (Etmer,2012, Landa et al, 2020, Tyler- wood *et al*, 2018). The participants' acquisition of prior knowledge through self-learning could explain the contradiction (over 50%); that is, they lack knowledge on creating the vision for ITLTs change. One participant agreed with this, as he suggested training/workshop on change management competencies, especially in this fast pace of technology integration.

6. CONCLUSION

Generally, the study concludes that MLALs have relatively low competency level for motivating the adoption and execution of ITLTs change. Seemingly, the overall current competency level for managing ITLTs change found also relatively low. Furthermore, the results suggest that age, leadership experience, leadership position, and prior knowledge influence the managerial competency level for ITLTs change among mid-level academic leaders. The information generated from the results is crucial for designing the capacity building training programmes and strategies for integrating ITLTs. Since leadership experience significantly influenced managerial competency in the integration of ITLTs, therefore, this study recommends integrating ITLTs in higher education institutions to consider the leader experience throughout the process.

REFERENCES

Aitken, K. & von Treuer, K. (2014), Organisational and leadership competencies for successful service integration", *Leadership in Health Services*, 27(2),. 150-180

Ashkenas AM (2013) Needs assessment as a process for change management: Aligning organisational performance and human capital investment with strategic planning and change creation. *ProQuest Dissertations and Theses*: 122. Available at: https://search.proquest.com/docview/1816212520?accountid=26642%0Ahttp://link.periodicos.capes.gov.br/sfxlcl41?url_ver=Z39.88-2004&rft_val_fmt=info:ofi/fmt:kev:mtx:dissertation&genre=dissertations+%26+theses&sid=ProQ:ProQuest+Dissertations+%26+Theses+Globa.

Bates, A.W. (2000). Managing technological change: Strategies for college and university leaders. San Francisco, CA: Jossey-Bass. (Management_Strategies_for_E-Learning_Sys, P. 6: 4760).

Beatty, C. A., & Lee, G. L. (1992). Leadership among middle managers-an exploration in the context of technological change. *Human relations*, *45*(9), 957-989.

Betz, F. (2003). *Managing technological innovation: competitive advantage from change*. John Wiley & Sons.

Blieck Y, Zhu C, et al. (2019) Exploring technologies for Effective Institutional Continuous Quality Improvement of Online and Blended Learning in Adult Education Development and Validation of A Conceptual Quality Management Model Yves Blieck. (January). DOI: 10.13140/RG.2.2.15979.80160.

Bush T (2020) Managing a crisis: A contemporary challenge for all educational leaders. *Educational Management Administration and Leadership* 48(6): 959–963. DOI: 10.1177/1741143220951885.

Bush, T., Bell, L., & Middlewood, D. (Eds.). (2019). *Principles of educational leadership & management*. Sage.Coetzee, R., Visagie, J., & Ukpere, W. (2013). A proposed leadership competency model for effective organisational change intervention. *Journal of Social Sciences*, *36*(3), 247-253.

Bisbee, D. C. (2007). Looking for leaders: Current practices in leadership identification in higher education. *Planning and Changing*, *38*, 77-88.

Elizabeth Landa, Chang Zhu and Jennifer Sesabo (2020) Managerial Aspects for Deployment of E-Learning Technologies: A Literature Review of Selected Themes. *European Journal of Teaching and Education* 2(2): 107–121. Doi: 10.33422/ejte.v2i2.255.

Frost, S., & Chopp, R. (2004). The university as global city: A new way of seeing today's academy. *Change: The Magazine of Higher Learning*, *36*(2), 44-51.

Fullan M (2009) Large-scale reform comes of age. *Journal of Educational Change* 10(2–3): 101–113. Doi: 10.1007/s10833-009-9108-z.

Fullan M (2011) Whole system reform for innovative teaching and learning. *Microsoft-ITL Research (Ed.), Innovative Teaching and Learning Research* (October): 30–39.

Garrison, D. R., & Kanuka, H. (2004). Blended learning: Uncovering its transformative potential in higher education. *The internet and higher education*, *7*(2), 95-105.

Ghavifekr, S., Afshari, M., & Amla, S. (2012). Management strategies for E-Learning system as the core component of systemic change: A qualitative analysis. *Life Science Journal*, *9*(3), 2190-2196.

Gelaidan HM, Al-Swidi A and Mabkhot HA (2018) Employee Readiness for Change in Public Higher Education Institutions: Examining the Joint Effect of Leadership Behavior and Emotional Intelligence. *International Journal of Public Administration* 41(2): 150–158. DOI: 10.1080/01900692.2016.1255962.

Jing M and Yao X (2019) Academic Leaders in Leading Chinese Universities.: 18–32. DOI: 10.4018/978-1-5225-7441-5.ch002.

Khoshouei MS, Oreyzi HR and Noori A (2013) c r v i h o e f c f. 6(2): 131–152.

Kutner, M. H., Nachtsheim, C. J., Neter, J., & Li, W. (2005). Durbin-Watson Test for Autocorrelation. *Applied Linear Statistical Models. 5th ed. McGraw-Hill Irwin*, 487-490.

Lakshminarayanan S, Pai YP and Ramaprasad BS (2016) Competency need assessment: a gap analytic approach. *Industrial and Commercial Training* 48(8): 423–430. DOI: 10.1108/ICT-04-2016-0025.

Machumu, H., Zhu, C., & Almasi, M. (2018). Students' motivational factors and engagement strategies in constructivist-based blended learning environments. *Afrika Focus*, *31*(1).

Mwakyusa WP, Mwalyagile NV and Mwakyusa M (2016) Impediments of E-Learning Adoption in Higher Learning Institutions of Tanzania: An Empirical Review. *Journal of Education and Practice* 7(30): 152–160. Available at: http://search.ebscohost.com/login.aspx?direct=true&db=eric&AN=EJ1118921&site=ehost-live&scope=site.

Pandey R and Misra RK (2015) Identifying Managerial Competencies in the Indian Banking Sector. *Journal of Strategic Human Resource Management* 4(1): 1996. DOI: 10.21863/jshrm/2015.4.1.005.

Sharma, S., & Rai, A. (2003). An assessment of the relationship between ISD leadership characteristics and IS innovation adoption in organisations. *Information & Management*, *40*(5), 391-401.

Sharpe R, Greg B and Richard F (2006) Implementing a university e-learning strategy: levers for change within academic schools. *Alt-J* 14(2): 135–151. DOI: 10.1080/09687760600668503.

Smit, H., & Carstens, L. (2003). The influence of leadership role competencies on organisation change outcome in the manufacturing industry in South Africa. *SA Journal of Human Resource Management*, *1*(2), 45-52.

Tushman, M., & Anderson, P. (2004). *Managing strategic innovation and change: A collection of readings*. Oxford University Press, USA.

Uys, P., & Sieverts, S. (2001). Managing technological transformation in Higher Education: A Southern African perspective. In Proceeding of the 22nd World ICDE (International Council for Distance education) Conference Dusseldorf, Germany. Retrieved from; http://www.globe-online.com/philip.uys/www.globe- online.com, philip.uys,icde2001.htm.

Weinberg, B. A. (2004). Experience and technology adoption.

Wickramasinghe V and De Zoyza N (2008) Gender, age and marital status as predictors of managerial competency needs: Empirical evidence from a Sri Lankan telecommunication service provider. *Gender in Management* 23(5): 337–354. DOI: 10.1108/17542410810887365.

Zhou KZ, Tse DK and Li JJ (2006) Organisational changes in emerging economies: Drivers and consequences. *Journal of International Business Studies* 37(2): 248–263. Doi: 10.1057/palgrave.jibs.8400186.

Zhu C and Zayim-Kurtay M (2018) University governance and academic leadership: perceptions of European and Chinese university staff and perceived need for capacity building. *European Journal of Higher Education* 8(4). Taylor & Francis: 435–452. DOI: 10.1080/21568235.2018.1458636.

Zhu, C., & Zayim-Kurtay, M. (Eds.). (2019). *University Governance and Academic Leadership in the EU and China*. IGI Global.

E-LEARNING DESIGN THINKING AND DESIGN DRIVEN INNOVATION

Dalia Gallico
Università San Raffaele Roma, Italy

ABSTRACT

E-learning, knowledge sharing, design thinking education and design driven innovation innovation are all key elements of this case study.
The E-learning platform about Design Thinking is born as a result of the growing pervasiveness of this approach to innovation in different application contexts: from strategic consulting to digital transformation, from the design of digital experiences (UX / UI) to the development of new experiences. of consumption. The extraordinary amount of acquisitions in recent years of design firms by strategic consulting firms or major digital solution providers demonstrates the growing pervasiveness of Design Thinking. The phenomenon highlights the strategic value that the methodologies, approaches and tools of Design Thinking assume in different contexts.
In particular, the platform aims to be the reference point for the community of innovators who adopt pioneering approaches such as Design Thinking in creating value for their companies. The goal is to develop a group of actors interested in exchanging views on the latest developments in Design Thinking, analyzing both the strengths and weaknesses of this approach to become a solid and updated reference point for all Design Thinkers. Such roles are not always easy to explain, since they differ from case to case, but Design Thinking in Italy is – and will increasingly become – a definite value and a competitive tool. Design can and must be a fundamental part of every single company's production, communication and distribution strategy. The e-learning platform launched by Università Telematica San Raffaele Roma's "Design thinking innovation" is intended to demonstrate that design is neither a sole interest nor an exclusive prerogative of large companies or those operating in sectors that have traditionally been design oriented. In fact, design driven education and innovation is a basic lever for competitiveness and internationalization that is available in every sector.
Creating an e-learning platform is an important opportunity of building a new designing and community identity; a significant chance to meet and a landmark not only for professionals, but also for creative people working outside established enterprises (from every countries).
Conclusions are about Design Thinking education and possible future developments, the role of design as a key competitive variable for the system, the new professionals and the winning models.

KEYWORDS

Design Thinking, Elearning, Design Driven Innovation, Long Life Learning, Knowing How to Make System, Training Professionals

1. INTRODUCTION

In this particular historical moment where the subdivision of our days into deadlines, commitments and routines has definitely weakened, we have all had to reconsider and pay more attention to a fundamental aspect of our life, which has returned to be in our hands and that perhaps we had unlearned to manage time.

Time is a concept that we have always considered of fundamental importance. Each design methodology has its own particular interpretation of time: the Lean approach, the Agile one, etc. Today more than ever it is time for Design Thinking, a methodology to which we feel more connected and which in this period we have the opportunity to analyze with a different eye than usual.

Constantly working with this methodology has profoundly taught how important it is to know how to "live time" and respect it in the right way and above all to know how to listen to it, not only when I plan as a professional, but in general as an approach as a person. We therefore tried to try to analyze Design Thinking by separating only the concept of time in order to underline how important it is to understand the "breath of time" in order to face design and everyday life in the right way.

In the design approach of Design Thinking it is immediately clear how central the concept of time is: looking at the representations of the two main models - the 5 phases of Design Thinking and the Double Diamond represented below - one immediately perceives the clear division into phases (subdivision of time), their arrangement (chronological development) and the close relationship of connection they have (principle of consequentiality).

The first lesson that these models want to convey is in my opinion therefore precisely the importance of starting a design process trusting the process, not rushing and preparing to face each phase with the correct attitude.

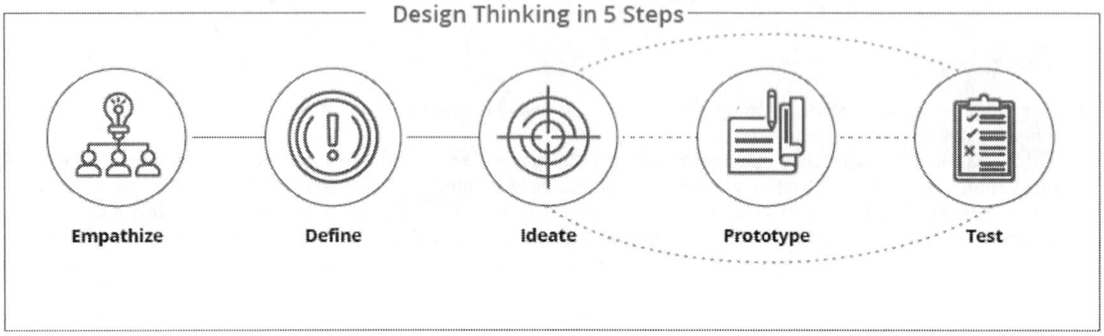

Figure 1. Design thinking: A 5 Stage Process – Stanford d. School

But how does time move within these phases?

1. Empathize

Get to know who you are planning for by entering "his shoes".

Empathize is the time of knowing and listening, you cannot think of being able to skip this phase and rush to the next phase; it is the time of research (qualitative and quantitative), it is the time to open your eyes, to be receptive, to ask questions, to explore in order to gather as much information as possible, it is not the time to sit, but the time to move within the design space with all the means we have available; it is the time of design curiosity and enthusiasm.

2. Define

Analyze all the information you collected in the first phase and formalize the question you want to answer, your point of view and your design direction.

Define is the time of interpretation and reflection, it is the moment when you stop looking and stop to look at everything from above. It is the time to put in order, to create connections, to select, to interpret, to discard. It is perhaps the time where attention is maximum because it is the time of choice, the time in which one's own design space is identified, decided which direction to take and which personal point of view to adopt.

3. Conceive

Propose as many solutions as possible to answer the design question identified above.

Ideate is the time of freedom, after the time of knowledge (Empathize) and the time of interpretation (Define) is the time to design. It is the most creative time of the whole process, the time of the "storm of ideas", of the "assault on the brains" (brainstorming); if in the Empathize phase we moved in the design space, here we move mentally to reach and formulate as many ideas as possible.

4. Prototype

Once you have selected the best idea, it is time to start making it concrete, or making part of it concrete.

Prototype is the time to do, the time to try, to compare, the time to question the ideas we have designed. In Design Thinking this time is anticipated compared to other approaches precisely because it is central to the importance of making concrete as soon as possible everything that until now has only been in our heads. It is the time when the idea opens up to the outside world for the first time, the time of confrontation, interaction and listening again to really understand what works and what doesn't.

5. Test Let the people for whom it was designed try the solution to see if it responds to the problem we wanted to solve.

Test is the time of testing, the time where the idea comes to life, where the static solution becomes fluid entering the real world. It is the time of attention and openness to see and receive all the feedback (direct and indirect) of those who interact with the solution.

So what did Design Thinking teach me as a designer, but above all as a person? It made me understand that in design, as in everyday life, there is a right time for everything.

What would happen if we immediately rushed to the Ideate phase, skipping the two very important phases of Empathize and Define? How many things would we risk losing?

If we put a solution on the market without having tested it, how much would we risk not knowing if it really meets the needs of the market?

This approach most of all shows us well how everything has its time, and every time needs to be faced with the right mental predisposition; even if we are all more comfortable in some phases of the process rather than in others, the important thing is to learn to trust the process itself, to live the moment without rushing ahead with the thought or without dwelling too much, to be able to adapt to time in a fluid and proactive way. We give things time and channel our thoughts into a project: it is the best way to satisfaction!

We can therefore commit ourselves to giving the right time to things, having time help us to channel our thoughts towards a goal, and knowing how to adapt to the time we are living by learning it to live in the right way.

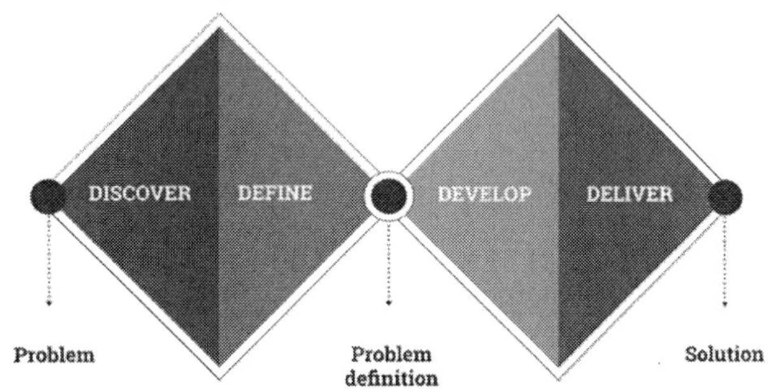

Figure 2. Double Diamond Design Thinking – Design Council

2. E-LEARNING DESIGN THINKING

Being able to understand, thanks to the ability to deal with and solve problems with the tools available, with the ability to ignite empathy and understand people's needs and desires, together with what is important and essential for them.

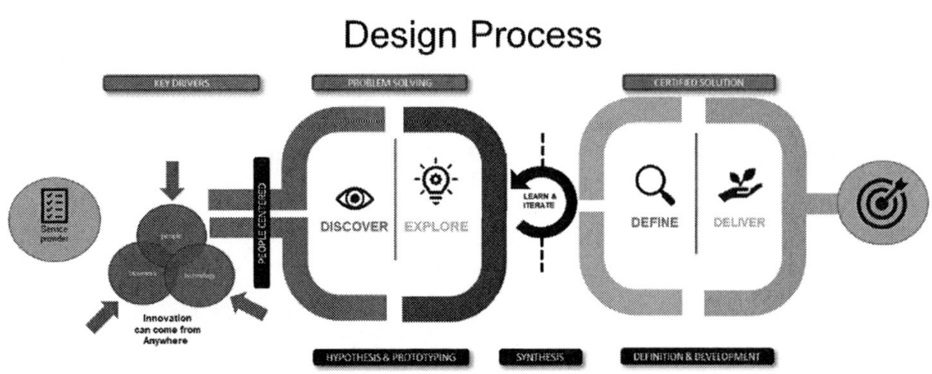

Figure 3. Design Thinking Process

Strategy is the ability to understand what is fundamental for your company starting from the point of view of the analysis of processes, models and who is running the game at that moment, to get to get a prototype, that is the ability to create, build and use our tools, with the intent to facilitate alignment and co-creation within the company. This is what design is all about:

- EMPATHY
- STRATEGY
- PROTOTYPING

this is called DESIGN THINKING

The word "Design" - in this specific context - refers to the ability to use the means that our community possesses and consciously manages: prototyping, manual activities in general, the visual arts, the creation of "things" (products, packaging, graphics, architecture, fashion, experiences, digital, etc.). What makes Design Thinking unique is the art of combining Human Empathy and Business Strategy with the ability to design and prototype.

Design Thinking has finally. Design Thinking has given value to Design by elevating it to something worthy of consideration, leveraging and investing in the entrepreneurial world and business leaders in each category, creating the opportunity to shift the attention of companies and the industry sector towards the world of Design. For this reason it must be promoted and made to grow, in order to put the world in a position to leverage the mentality, processes and knowledge of our design community and guide innovation, growth in the business world and above all evolution. Human.

All of the above, therefore, offers the possibility of creating value for the company, shifting the objective from companies that have focused on marketing (or tech-R & D) to companies that welcome creativity and design and that offer the possibility to create together for their target audience.

3. HOW TO CREATE SIGNIFICANT EXPERIENCES

How is it possible to design objects that are meaningful to people?
According to the interpretation provided by Donald Norman in his book "Emotional design", 3 levels of interaction occur every time we interact with a brand / product.

1. The VISCERAL RELATIONSHIP

can be identified with the so-called "WOW effect"; it is the same reaction that occurs when you see a beautiful woman / man or a beautiful landscape - it is a shopping experience that occurs when we feel butterflies in the stomach, it is something beyond rationality - we can love or hate a object, but in any case a reaction occurs. Whenever we design something, we build a co-system of stories by communicating and sewing mini-stories for the target in front of us. Heart and Brain are closely connected to each other; it is necessary to find a balance point between rationality and emotionality.

2. EXPRESSIVE / EMPATHIC RELATIONSHIP

We want to show, talk, inform and tell everyone about our experience. Social Media is the perfect platform to do this. Pride and Joy connect us with a particular experience.

Satisfaction & Emotional loyalty: this case, for example, is represented by the queue of people queuing in front of an Apple Store waiting to buy the latest model of mobile phone that they have never seen or tried before: this represents an emotional attachment and loyalty to brand. Spontaneous Communication & PR: the Public and Consumers become the Ambassadors of the brand & create communication around it.

- The VISCERAL effect translates into PURCHASE
- The INTERACTIVE effect translates into RE-PURCHASE
- The EXPRESSIVE effect means RECOMMENDATION, ADVICE

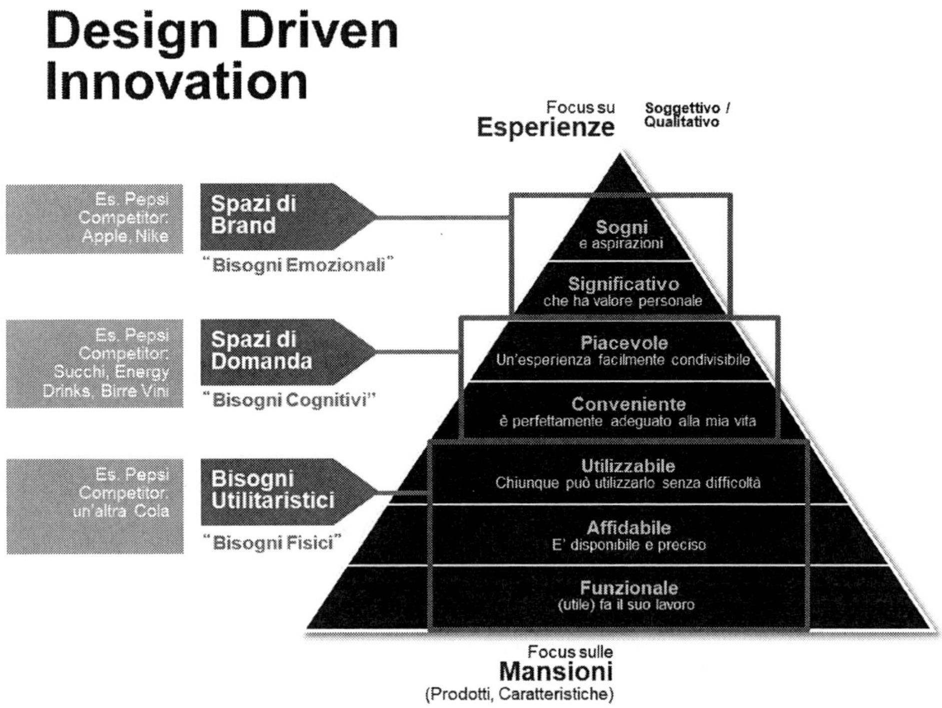

Figure 4. Design Driven Innovation- Jacob Nielsen

4. WHAT DOES IT MEAN TO THINK LIKE A DESIGNER? HOW TO LEARN?

The qualities listed above refer to the world of design, but not only. For designers, there are other qualities - additional capabilities that define the designer's philosophy. We can recognize them in people who are not designers but who belong to our world. These are the characteristics that identify the designer's philosophy:

Synthetic. Designers can immediately imagine the big picture. Their thinking is adductive and holistic.

Refined. Designers are refined - in the process as well as in the solutions.

Multilingual and narrator. Designers are able to convey understandable and important messages for different target audiences inside and outside the organization.

Intuitive. Designers do not stray from the magic of intuition. They recognize the role of the mysterious and visceral spark that the idea can play in the innovation process. And what is important is that they are able to manage intuition within business boundaries and processes.

Arguments. Designers are dialectical by definition. They easily move from one topic to another, from marketing to technology, from anthropology to communication and research. This ambiguity is part of their essence.

They are completely at ease in the face of the conflict between rationality and soul, between functionality and style, process and intuition. In fact, they always travel to the center of the storm! Looking for new solutions, designers comfortably navigate the line between what is feasible and what is not

Lovers. Designers are interested in the human being. They are not interested in consumer satisfaction but are in love with their customers. Try to transfer this concept into your personal life: when you want to please someone, do whatever it takes to satisfy their needs. But if you love someone - husband / wife, children, parents - you will do much, much more than they expect of you. You will surprise them by entering the sacred field of what is magical, extraordinary and unforgettable.

Design is at a crossroads. Companies try to understand how to welcome and use Design to their advantage.

We are creating a new role and a new space for design within the industrial society. It is a change that the new generations will be able to read in the history of design that has yet to be written.

Designers are in luck. As professionals, they are philosophers and thinkers but also actors.

They translate ideas into action. For the companies they work for, exploiting resources for the benefit of customers or companies, they also have the opportunity to shape the world.

They truly have the opportunity - and the responsibility - to shape the world better. Their mission is to "dream" of the things that can increase the practical, emotional and poetic value to the life of each individual - and not to create useless, unsustainable products that pollute our world both from an ecological and a visual point of view. They want to design meanings, not products.

5. DESIGNERS ARE PEOPLE WHO LOVE PEOPLE

Loving a person means taking care of them and their world. Therefore, design the environment that surrounds it, and make every interaction with it, every experience comfortable.

Designers have the wonderful opportunity to get in touch with everyone's life, every day, providing fun, convenience, safety, pleasure based on what they design. All these moments can become potential fragments of a broader social happiness only and exclusively if they are guided by a positive approach, with a positive purpose and intent and only and exclusively if they are designed with a view to sustainability thought at 360 °.

It must be done in accordance with nature and naturalness. Sustainably. Sustainability considered from an ecological and visual point of view, of beauty, without visual contamination; sustainability from a social, respectful perspective, which affirms everything that is user-friendly; sustainability from an emotional, engaging, stimulating point of view.

Our society is changing so quickly and on every front that it is essential to radically innovate even the world of design. Change takes place through technologies, techniques, tools and means that are increasingly effective and complex, but increasingly and better usable. The transparency of complexity is the trump card of our time, and the Designer can no longer create anything that goes beyond this principle. The creative process within large companies is closely linked to the transdisciplinarity aspect, which becomes indispensable to the creation project for overcoming the limits of the individual disciplines concerned. In this regard, it is important to remember that on 6 November 1994 the "Charter of Transdisciplinarity", drawn up by Basarab Nicolescu, Edgar Morin and Lima De Freitas, was signed in Arràbida (Portugal). According to its signatories, the Charter aims to be an expression of the attitude of the scientists of our time to lead science and its knowledge beyond the boundaries in which sectorialized knowledge tends to confine them. This also includes an ethical dimension, because, in an era of great advances in knowledge, the lack of dialogue and the circulation of knowledge increases the inequality between those who possess such knowledge and those who do not. These principles are applicable to different fields, not only to the human sciences but also to art, literature, poetry and the inner experience of each one. And also to Design. The human being is much more than a "complex structure" at the center of the various disciplines of study. Those who, like the designer, must be aware of their limits of knowledge, which can only be overcome through transdisciplinarity in the approach to the project.

Today young creatives should be prepared for everything: marketing, business, technical design, packaging, technologies, etc .: how can you have such a "holistic" preparation?

The world of education should change, and also the universities that prepare the talents of tomorrow, to offer a preparation that allows an "easier" integration of recent graduates into the world of work and companies. Companies themselves must know how to manage career development: how to train young talents and follow their path to success. The paradox of the modern era of education is that very often, the training process starts from elementary school education, which includes many generic "subjects", to evolve up to university level and then with masters, on increasingly specific topics. Where the "institutional" training stops, with the entry into the company, the company itself finds itself entrusted with the task of providing again a 360-degree training on the most disparate fronts, just as it happened in elementary and middle schools.

If the designer chooses the path of the independent profession, he himself will bear the weight of his own training, and establish its methods, times, areas and opportunities.

In both cases in Italy more than elsewhere the economic and social crisis involves scarce investments, if not real cuts, precisely in the fields of culture and education. Culture is now a luxury item. It is the economically most prosperous companies, and not the institutions, that can still invest in development and research. In science, as in design. But the 'raw materials' on which to invest, creativity and talent, are still many on the Italian territory.

6. TECHNOLOGICAL APPLICATIONS AND CHARACTERISTICS

As part of the project devoted to the dissemination of high quality material in Design, University San Raffaele Roma with the portal is designed to allow easy and flexible access to a big potential user arena. In this sense, the portal is based on some of the most widely used, reliable and functional tools in the field of content management, electronic commerce, and technology training. Inside the portal, the Joomla and VirtueMart platform is integrated in conjunction with Moodle for the sale and use of online courses. The implementation of the online sales system for the site is concerned with the Moodle, Joomla and VirtueMart platforms. The latter is an add-on for Joomla cms that allows you to extend its capabilities to create and manage an e-commerce portal. This tool, in conjunction with an API implementation, enables the integration of Moodle courses with the sale and purchase auto-subscription.

The basic component of VirtueMart covers the basic features of an on-line shop (online catalog submission, file download, cart), but add-ons that implement additional functionality such as product search or preview in. The shop management allows you to modify the seller and related product information by entering basic information (name, identifier), advanced (weight, unit of measure, size, related products) and images (Picture of the article).

Streaming video with Vimeo provider. To increase the portability of the contributions and to exploit the potential offered by streaming video, it has been chosen to use a professional broadcast service.

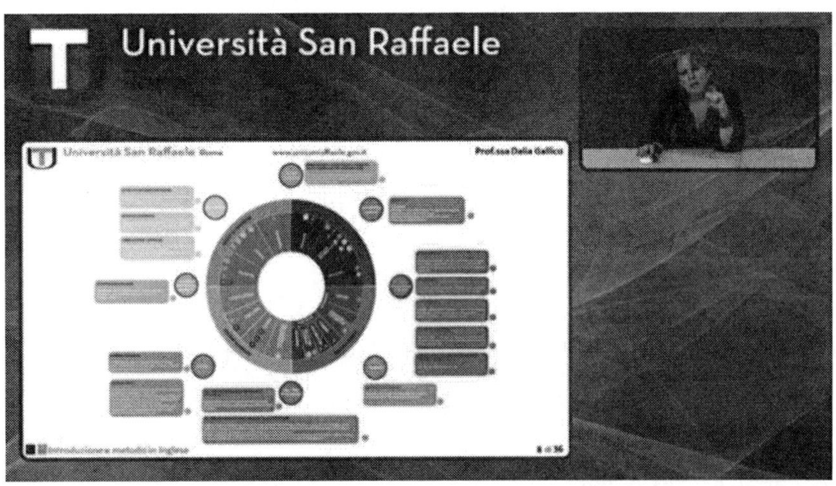

Figures 5. Screenshot E-learning Design Thinking lessons

7. CONCLUSION

The Design Thinking E-learning platform develops specific research lines that leverage the main results obtained in previous editions in relation to the role that Design Thinking can play in innovation projects.

Transformations in the way consultants interpret Design Thinking. The applications of Design Thinking by innovators: This line of research investigates the similarities and differences in the pioneering adoption of Design Thinking by innovators in different sectors (e.g. Finance, Energy, Information and Communication,

Public Administration) and professional roles (e.g. C-levels, Design, Research and Development, Marketing, IT);

The evolutions of Design Thinking enabled by emerging startups: this line of research identifies emerging startups that provide interesting technological solutions (for example, Artificial Intelligence, Big Data, Rapid Prototyping) to enhance Design Thinking processes.

The Design Thinking market: identification and measurement of established and emerging domains (sectors, types of projects and challenges) in which consulting organizations exploit Design Thinking;

Design Thinking in the digital age: role and adoption of digital technologies (artificial intelligence, big data, internet of things, augmented reality, additive manufacturing, etc.) able to enhance the approach to Design Thinking;

Transformations of Design Thinking: adoption of different types of Design Thinking (Creative Problem Solving, Sprint Execution, Creative Confidence, Innovation of Meaning) and complementary methodologies (Agile, DevOps, Inclusive Design, Speculative Design, etc.);

Design Thinking value: measurement of the value generated by Design Thinking (project results, radicalism, commercial success).

The Organization for Design Thinking: analysis of the organizational structures adopted by innovators to manage innovation projects based on Design Thinking; skills for Design Thinking: analysis of the skills and attitudes required of innovators to manage projects based on Design Thinking;

Design Thinking in the digital age: role and adoption of digital technologies (artificial intelligence, big data, internet of things, augmented reality, additive manufacturing, etc.) capable of enhancing the Design Thinking approach;

Design Thinking value: measurement of the value generated by Design Thinking (project results, radicalism, commercial success).

The classification of digital tools: identification and classification of digital tools capable of supporting Design Thinking processes;

global offer of digital tools to support Design Thinking: map and classification of digital tools based on digital technologies (such as artificial intelligence, big data, internet of things, augmented reality, etc.) capable of supporting Design Thinking processes ;

suppliers of digital tools to support Design Thinking: identification of start-ups and technology developers who enable Design Thinking processes;

pioneering adoptions of digital tools to support Design Thinking: development of case studies on pioneering adoption of digital tools capable of supporting Design Thinking approaches.

REFERENCES

Bentley, T. (1998). Learning beyond the classroom: Education for a changing world. London: Routledge.

Gallico D, (2016). Rapporto nazionale sul Design nelle imprese italiane (dalla A alla Z) isbn 9788868741518 Logo Fausto Lupetti editore

Gallico D (2013). Contam-Innovation Cinquecento icone tra design, cultura e innovazione. Bologna:Logo Fausto Lupetti editore

Guzzo T (2009). "Mobile Devices to support advanced forms of e-Learning" Handbook of Research on Multimodal Human Computer Interaction and Pervasive Services: Evolutionary Techniques for Improving Accessibility. Editor: Grifoni P., IGI Global

Dillenbourg, P., Baker, M., Blaye, A., & O'Malley, C. (1996). The evolution of research on collaborative learning. In E. Spada & P. Reiman (Eds.), Learning in humans and machine: Towards an interdisciplinary learning science. Oxford, UK.

Grew, P., & Pagani, E. (2005). Towards a wireless architecture for mobile ubiquitous e-learning. Workshop on Learning Communities in the Era of Ubiquitous Computing, Milan, Italy.

Norman D, A. "Emotional Design" – TLFeBook "Carta della Transdisciplinarità", Basarab Nicolescu, Edgar Morin e Lima De Freitas -http://disf.org/carta-transdisciplinarieta)

Porcini M "A Love Letter to Design" di, Design Management Institute Review – www.dmi.org

INTERNATIONALIZATION FOR ENHANCING THE EUROPEAN SECURITY AND DEFENCE HIGHER EDUCATION

Marina Marchisio[1] and Enrico Spinello[2]
[1]*Department of Molecular Biotechnology and Health Sciences, University of Turin, Via Nizza 52, 10126 Torino, Italy*
[2]*IT-Army Education and Training Command and School of Applied Military Studies, Via dell'Arsenale 22, 10121 Turin, Italy*

ABSTRACT

Internationalization of Higher Education is one of the key trends of development. Security and Defence Education aims to prepare highly specialized military (officers) and civilian personnel who are able to operate in national as well as international environments with colleagues and people of different nationalities and sometimes in a very complex context. For this reason, it is extremely important to strengthen the internationalization process in Higher Education, using traditional and virtual modalities, in order to allow students to develop skills, to create collaborations and networks. This paper answers to the research question what initiatives and policies of internationalization can be developed, and how, in order to enhance the European Security and Defence Higher Education, by analyzing and discussing the intensive internationalization experiences of the University of Turin with the Education and Training Command and School of Applied Military Studies in the last seven academic years at different levels: students, teachers and staff, Institutions. Several data collected during this period allow to understand how the direction of actions has changed, which difficulties were encountered, and which solutions can be found. This research can be considered a useful example for those who want to increase the internationalization of Security and Defence Higher Education especially in this new digital era.

KEYWORDS

Erasmus, Internationalization, Higher Education, Security and Defence Education

1. INTRODUCTION

Universities have always had international dimensions in their research, but less in their teaching. The increasing globalization of economies and societies, which started at the end of the previous century, requires a Higher Education (HE) with more internationalization programs, as a key change for a better insertion in the world of work for university graduates. In the past 30 years, internationalization education programs were inserted in the agenda of many institutions, and, in some cases, they became a business and an occasion to improve the reputation (Matei and Iwinska, 2015). English, as a globally recognized language, increased its dominance, and schools and universities had to also deal with this matter. In the period 2010–20 the number of international activities increased significantly and also many international bachelor's and master's degrees with double or joint titles were created and, in particular during the pandemic, online delivery of HE became important in order to allow these programs to continue as well. In 1987, the European Union (EU) in order to facilitate internationalization, started the ERASMUS Program, transformed into the ERASMUS+ Program in 2014, for sustaining and enhancing the mobility for students, teachers and staff. In 1988 EU approved the first directive to recognize the study abroad and in 1992, with the Maastricht Treaty, it recognized the competences in the field of education and culture at European level. In particular, the ERASMUS Program, among the various objectives, intends to offer added value to education and professional specialization provided by schools and universities, to prepare future citizens for mobility and professional career, and to encourage exchanges among students from different countries increasing the feeling of belonging to Europe. The European Commission (EC) has launched several impact studies on the topic. In the ERASMUS Impact Study (European Commission, 2014) the research, among 80.000 people, belonging to different groups such as students, teachers, staff personnel and enterprises, revealed that the so-called Erasmus generation acquires not only competencies in specific disciplines but also transversal competencies, very much in demand in the world of work. In 2019 a research conducted by the University of Turin on ERASMUS students (Roggero and Rabaglietti, 2019) demonstrates that the effects of the experience abroad represent an enriching moment for personal development and identity construction. The education in the field of Security and Defence aims to prepare highly specialized military (officers) and civilian personnel who are able to operate in national as well as international environments with colleagues and people of different nationalities and sometimes in a very complex context. Their education curricula require a solid and round theoretical preparation and participation to practical activities, obtained via specific traineeships. In order to allow them to learn how to work in cooperation with other colleagues, coming from other Member States (MS), since the initial and basic training period (university period), and to mature a European culture for Security and Defence in the changing international scenario, it becomes extremely important to create and develop a specific internationalization program for them. At the University of Turin, a dedicated university school, the Interdepartmental University School for Strategic Sciences (SUISS), was created in order to manage the education and training of officers and civilian students in the field of Security and Defence, in cooperation with the IT-Army Education and Training Command and School of Applied Military Studies (ETC&SAMS). It provides a Bachelor Degree (in cooperation with the University of Modena and Reggio Emilia) and a Master Degree, both reserved to the Army Officers, and in parallel a Bachelor Degree and a Master Degree for civilians, with a total of 350 officers and 240 civilians. They study together, cooperate and have international experiences. In the paper the intensive international program adopted is analyzed from when it started in 2012-13 to nowadays, in order to understand how it helps to reinforce the education in this specific area (Security and Defence) and how it is changing in the new digital era. In the section two, we describe the state of art, in the section three we explain the methodology used for the research and in the section four, we discuss the results from different point of view: students, teachers and institutions. We also try to outline how in this new post-pandemic period it is destined to change.

2. STATE OF ART

During the UNESCO World Conference on the HE in 2009, globalization was defined as "the reality shaped by an increasingly integrated world economy, new information and communications technology, the emergence of an international knowledge network, the role of the English language, and other forces beyond the control of academic institutions" (Altbach et al., 2009). In this context, the universities cannot avoid dealing with the international comparison in compliance with national legislation and with the peculiarities of the various bachelor's and master's degrees. Globalization and internationalization are two distinct processes. The former intends to ensure competitiveness in the HE field and its tools are international rankings, marketing techniques and the establishment of branches of the same university in different countries, such as campuses abroad, while the latter follows the logic determined by political, academic (rather than economic) and cooperative incentives. Knight (Knight, 2008) defined the internationalization as "the process of integrating an international, intercultural or global dimension into the purpose, functions and delivery of post-secondary education". The Italian universities have participated actively in the ERASMUS Program since the very beginning, and mobility is always identified as a fundamental tool in order to realize the internationalization of the university. As an example, in 2012-13 in terms of external mobility, Italy ranked fourth, with a percentage of 9,62 outgoing students, and at fifth place for the incoming mobility with 7,99% of European students. The University of Turin, one of the largest Italian universities, contributes actively to the Program, for example in 2018/19, with 1.687 outgoing and 857 incoming students. The Security and Defence Education differs a lot from other disciplinary areas, because it does not prepare students for future professions who are in competition among them - at least, this is evident for military students - but professionals who have the necessity to learn to cooperate with civilians as soon as possible, and to be integrated in international theatres of interoperability. Until 2008, every EU MS, as responsible for the education of their officers, had made decisions in total autonomy, and even the international process was a national issue. However, in 2008, during the 2903rd External Relations Council Meeting, the EU Ministers of Defence decided to establish an Implementation Group for the "European Initiative for the exchange of young officers inspired by ERASMUS" (shortly "Military Erasmus"), in order to ease the internationalization process. This Initiative has created a network of all EU Basic Officers' Education Institutes (BOEIs) and launched a short term mobility in addition to the medium-long term mobility (ERASMUS). The short mobility is simpler to realize than the ERASMUS (minimum of two months for traineeships and three months for a study program). In the report of 2018/19 (European Security and Defence College, 2019) Romania, Austria, Greece, Poland and Italy are indicated as the MS more active inside the Military Erasmus Initiative. In some MS the short and long mobilities of the officers are very few. Moreover Greece, Poland and Italy involved in this program civilians students too. In order to satisfy all these specific needs, the SUISS decided to adopt an intense internationalization program regarding exchange and cooperation, peace and mutual understanding, human capital development, solidarity and service to society. The definition of internationalization given by de Wit (de Wit et al. 2015) as "intentional process of integrating an international, intercultural or global dimension into the purpose, functions and delivery of post-secondary education, in order to enhance the quality of education and research for all students and staff and to make a meaningful contribution to society" was adopted with the perspective to contribute to the creation of a European identity and promote a European Security and Defence culture. Moreover, it is important to mention that a certain number of international officer students who attend the Bachelor's and Master's Degrees in strategic sciences comes from extra-EU countries in accordance with the Ministerial Cooperation Plan (from Europe, Asia, Africa and South America). This contributes to create an even more international environment in the education field.

3. RESEARCH QUESTION AND METHODOLOGY

In this paper we want to answer the following research question: What initiatives and policies of internationalization can be developed, and how, in order to enhance the European Security and Defence HE? The methodology adopted in order to answer is to analyze the experiences of the University of Turin in the last seven academic years using both quantitative and qualitative data. In particular, we study separately the actions introduced based on the level of the main actors involved: students, teachers and staff, institutions. The initiatives are discussed describing the type, the duration, the objectives, the effects, which tools require implementation, what kind of risks or difficulties were encountered and in which way they change in this digital era. Several data collected are used together with the answers to the questionnaires filled by the participants to the international activities at the end of each event, to collect feedback, critiques, suggestions, strong points and weakness. In 2019-20 the COVID-19 pandemic obviously had a deep impact on the internationalization: as a consequence, new solutions needed to be found, with an open mind to new prospects.

4. RESULTS

4.1 Actions for Students: From Abroad to Home

The first internationalization initiatives adopted by SUISS involving military and civilian students are those of outgoing and incoming mobility within the Erasmus + which allow them to achieve ECTS (European Credit Transfer and Accumulation System) during their stay abroad. Table 1 shows the numbers of incoming and outgoing students.

Table 1. Military and civilian students outgoing and incoming

Erasmus	2013-14	2014-15	2015-16	2016-17	2017-18	2018-19	2019-20
Outgoing	2 C	2 M + 3 C	2 M + 5 C	7 M + 7 C	7 M + 6 C	8 M + 23 C	8 M + 20 C
Incoming	2 M	2 M	6 M	5 M + 2 C	4 M + 4 C	3 M + 5 C	7 M + 2 C

It can be observed that incoming students are decidedly fewer than the outgoing ones, since the courses offered by SUISS are almost all in Italian; only since 2019-20, four university modules entirely taught in English have been made available in online version, covering an entire semester (Marchisio et al, 2019). The percentage of outgoing students of SUISS is higher than the average of the University of Turin. This can be explained in different ways: most of the destinations chosen for Erasmus are destinations reserved for SUISS students and offer a training course lasting one semester that integrates well within the Bachelor or Master

Degree; moreover, a group of teachers and staff of SUISS offers a support service for the preparation of the Learning Agreement and for the search for accommodation abroad. The number of military students participating in Erasmus exchanges is decidedly lower than the number of civilian students, and concerns only the Master Degree. It is more difficult to fit the training officers activities during the exchanges since their education follows, in each MS, national protocols that differ from one another. Moreover the mobility cannot be placed during the external training or specific military training. Officers who spend an entire semester abroad certainly have the opportunity to have a very formative experience in a European key that allows them to develop teamwork skills with peers from other MS, very useful when they will be deployed in international operational theaters, where they have to work with other colleagues form different countries. These medium and long-term mobilities (3 months up to 1 year) were immediately accompanied by short mobility in the context of Military Erasmus because, in addition to being more easily feasible for officers, it allows to involve a greater number of students also at home. Short mobilities are international training modules lasting three weeks, two remote and one face-to-face, involving about 40 civilian and military students from different armed forces and from different EU MS. The face-to-face activities are intensive, in English, and involve active participation in group works, workshops and discussions. The professors and tutors of these modules are teachers from the University that organizes the module but also from other universities within the EU, mainly BOEIs. The SUISS, in collaboration with the ETC&SAMS, since the academic year 2013-14, has decided to organize two international modules CSDP (Common Security Defence Policies) and LOAC (Law Of Armed Conflicts) in Turin to further expand the number of students involved in short mobilities, to increase collaboration between teachers, and to strengthen the network between EU institutions. Tables 2 and 3 show the numbers of military students involved in incoming and outgoing short mobilities. The number of outgoing SUISS students in the span of 6 years has increased tenfold and in the academic year 2018-19 the number of students who attended a common module in Italy, represents a fifth of the officers who attended courses abroad and it can be said that internationalization has spread from abroad to home. Starting from the academic year 2020-21 SUISS offers also the international module Biosafety and Bioterrorism and moreover, in this pandemic crisis, decided to deliver the international modules completely online by exploiting the digital learning environment that it has developed for e-learning activities.

Table 2. Military and civilian students in incoming short mobilities

Year	CM	IT Officers	EU & US Officers	Civilians	Total
2013-14	2 CSDP	20 Army 6 Air Force	19 EU	15	60
2014-15	CSDP – LOAC	26 Army 6 Air Force	23 EU	22	77
2015-16	CSDP – LOAC	20 Army 9 Air Force	16 EU	25	70
2016-17	CSDP – LOAC	23 Army 2 Air Force	11 EU 3 US	20	58
2017-18	CSDP – LOAC	20 Army 7 Air Force	17 EU 4 US	33	81
2018-19	CSDP – LOAC	16 Army 8 Air Force	27 EU 4 US	30 (2 PL)	85

Table 3. Military students in outgoing short mobilities

Year	2009-10	2010-11	2011-12	2012-13	2013-14	2014-15	2015-16	2016-17	2017-18	2018-19
Officer	2	2	0	3	7	20	17	29	55	68

Other mobilities, semi-short, lasting 2 months, were organized with the aim of having the degree thesis carried out and/or for an international traineeship. For these mobilities, as part of the Erasmus program, financial support is granted to participants to cover travel and accommodation expenses. To participate in the various mobilities, students make an application in a call that takes into consideration the evaluation of career, language skills and motivations that lead to participate in the proposed initiative. The number of applications to participate is always much higher than available places. This pushed SUISS to expand the available places and denotes a strong desire to be involved in an internationalization experience. Among the most frequent motivations of applicants there are: to get to know and collaborate with peers from other foreign countries, to enrich their curriculum, to broaden their cultural horizon, to strengthen their linguistic skills, to test themselves, to get a better preparation for a work in multinational contexts at the end of the university course, to develop soft skills useful to face the insertion in the world of work. One of the major difficulties encountered in increasing the flow of incoming civilian students is the lack of accommodation and support facilities for reception. For the military, there are reciprocal agreements between Academies that facilitate the logistic matter. One of the most interesting effects of having officers involved in mobility activities is the creation of informal networks among peers operating in the ward. This confirms how the Europeanization process in the field of Security and Defense starts during HE. There are also international initiatives with non-European countries such as USA, but at the moment, they are reserved for an elite of particularly good students. Table 4 below shows, on a Likert scale from 1 to 6, the average overall satisfaction of the participants to the short mobilities organized in Turin. The comments collected in the questionnaires are all extremely positive and all the participants say that they recommend the experience to a colleague and would like to repeat a second one during their university path.

Table 4. Overall satisfaction of participants to the short mobilities organized in Turin

Year	Common module	Feedback	Common module	Feedback
2013-14	CSDP	5.34	CSDP	5.10
2014-15	CSDP	5.00	LOAC	5.10
2015-16	LOAC	5.10	CSDP	5.20
2016-17	CSDP	4.80	LOAC	5.00
2017-18	CSDP	5.00	LOAC	5.40
2018-19	CSDP	5.10	LOAC	5.20

Table 5 shows an overview of the proposed opportunities and services for students.

Table 5. Overview of the proposed service mix for students

Scope and objectives	Recommended actions and initiatives	Expected benefits
Create new opportunities of mobility for students.	Hosting Common Modules with international students, teachers and staff.	Having an international experience at home for national (fits for all kind of students) and receiving more international students who participate in short mobility.
Develop digital skills and support learning activities during the mobility.	Implementation of online Courses.	New kind of exchange plus digital skills. It can be used to complement residential program for internationals while helping national students after mobility in order to recover part of the program. Increasing of obtained ECTS.
Facilitate participation to international activities.	Creation of support group of teachers who helps students before the mobility for logistic and admin activities	Increase the number of participants to short, medium, long and virtual mobilities.
Increase the exchange.	Integrate different kind of mobilities in the curricula and offering new activities abroad.	Engaging more students with more topics.
Create a network of EU partners.	Selection of specific partner with the same topics (BOEIs).	Enhancing the quality of academic activities.
Increase the number of ECTS gained abroad.	Supporting students for academic issue.	Increasing the ECTS per students and the number of students who obtained ECTS abroad.

4.2 Actions involving Teachers and Staff: Curriculum and Collaborations

The internationalization initiatives in which the teachers and staff of SUISS are involved and committed have two objectives: the construction of more international curricula and the creation of collaborations, including research. For the first objective, two visiting professors from foreign universities are invited every year for the provision of two courses entirely in English: teachers are asked to adopt in their teachings the CLIL methodology (Content and Language Integrated Learning). The Erasmus program is used for incoming and outgoing mobility for educational activities of teachers and staff within the international modules. Teachers have also implemented four open online courses held in English among the compulsory modules of the curriculum, both to facilitate the recovery of teachings by outgoing students and to offer training activities in English to incoming students. To facilitate the participation of officers in the mobilities, an immersive week is organized at the beginning of each semester on military English. Civilian students, on the other hand, can attend a cultural intercomprehension course which aims to develop the ability to integrate into different cultural contexts. For the second objective, teachers and staff participate periodically to international conferences and meetings on Security and Defense HE to share experiences and initiatives, to discuss and to implement common activities together. In the period 2014-20 several European Erasmus+ Key Action2 Strategic Partnership among Higher Institutions which deal with Security and Defense education were funded. They reinforce the research and facilitate the spread of good practices. The SUISS participates in two of these: MGS – Military Gender Studies on gender gap and DIGICODE – Digital Competences for Improving Security and Defence Education to develop teachers' digital skills.

Table 6 shows an overview of the proposed opportunities and services for teachers and staff.

Table 6. Overview of the proposed service mix for teachers and staff

Scope and objectives	Recommended actions and initiatives	Expected benefits
Increase the research and cooperation.	Participation to all international activities (In & Out) and create a network of researchers with similar interests in Security and Defence Sector.	Having an international experience at home for national (fits for all kind of students) and receiving more international students who participate in short mobility.
Enhance the possibility to lecture abroad.	Creation and implementation of a Pool of Lecturers.	Receive more lecturers and participate to modules abroad.
Improve digital skills.	Create new digital contents.	Possibility to share more contents with other teachers and improve didactic.

4.3 Actions of the Institution: e-Learning, Nets and New Scenario

The SUISS and the ETC&SAMS have taken various actions to support this internationalization process. First of all, they invested in e-learning as a winning tool to facilitate mobility. It reduces costs, increases participation at a distance, in presence and in hybrid mode (students in presence and at a distance at the same time). Since 2016, they developed and adopted a digital learning environment, enhanced the infrastructure, trained many teachers and put available content also in English (Marchisio et al, 2017 and Spinello et al., 2017). Thanks to this huge investment, the internationalization process has been only reduced but not interrupted by the pandemic (Spinello et al., 2021). Much attention was given to organize meetings with outgoing students to present the initiatives and incoming to welcome and support them also with peer-to-peer initiatives. Secondly, 17 bilateral agreements were signed with other European Institutions/Universities dealing with Security and Defense Education. During the pandemic, a virtual mobility agreement was also signed with the Military University of Technology - Warsaw to involve Polish students in the didactic activities in e-learning offered in Turin. For the next few years, also in the light of the COVID experience, the University of Turin intends to further invest in the production of content on Security and Defense in English as micro-credentials that are more easily usable than other modules, also in a lifelong learning perspective. Furthermore, according to the new Erasmus+ Programme (European Commission, 2021) opened on 25 March 2021, SUISS intends to increase the virtual mobility, not to replace the one in presence, but to integrate it. It will be helpful also in a lifelong learning perspective (Spinello et al., 2019 and 2020). The virtual mobility paradigm will transform the mobility into a blended mode. In this new scenario SUISS intends organize Blended Intensive Programmes (BIP) that also allow in addition the acquisition of digital competences.

Table 7 shows an overview of the proposed services for Institutions.

Table 7. Overview of the proposed service mix for Institutions

Scope and objectives	Recommended actions and initiatives	Expected benefits
Facilitate and increase the exchange.	Adoption of Legal Framework. Creation of dedicate staff for international activities	Admin procedure simplified. Task oriented personnel and increased numbers of mobility.
Enhance the quality of Education and be able to face new challenges.	Participation to international fora and meetings. Integrate a Learning Management System in support of didactic activities.	Best practices sharing and adoption of new ideas and procedures. Possibility to adopt e-learning contents created by partners.

4.4 Lessons Learned and Suggestion for Guidelines

The internationalization process adopted by the SUISS and the ETC&SAMS represent an interesting case study inside the Security and Defence Higher Education for the number of actors involved, for the variety of actions adopted, for the investment made in terms of personnel and financial resources. Its analysis makes it possible to help the institutions that deal with training in the field of Security and Defense to have the right approach and avoid mistakes. First of all, it suggests that adopting an internationalization process is important because it allows the development of a European culture of security and defense and to enable officers to operate more easily in international operational theaters. The analysis of the Case Study suggests that the process is now ahead not only in terms of mobility, but also in terms of curricula. It also shows how important it is to trigger the process which then in a few years became scalable at the level of students and teaching staff and staff involved. To avoid failures and practice sustainable internationalization, it is necessary to have a good e-learning service, digital learning environments that integrate presence and distance. To undertake a process of internationalization in the field of Security and Defense, a good organization of educational activities and training programs and a certain flexibility are required. As regards the internationalization of curricula, it is important to incorporate new methodologies in the didactic such as the use of resources in different languages, collaborative and cooperative learning, role play, simulations, different forms of evaluation such as peer evaluation that allow collaboration between students also from different countries also according to (Taalas et al., 2020). The development of an internationalization strategy is subject to many influences both from outside as well as within the institution. The primary drivers are the motives that an institution has, but which may not always be expressed, to engage with this process. This article looks at the internal organization and structures that are pertinent to the development of such a strategy, and provides a range of options which can be used by institutions. Finally, the development of an internationalization strategy needs an engagement at institution level. The institutions need internal organization and structures that are pertinent to the development of a strategy of internationalization and a good internal quality monitoring system. In case of risks the Institutions must think to a number of possible responses as happened in the case of the Covid pandemic.

5. CONCLUSION

In the paper we answered the research question: What initiatives and policies of internationalization can be developed, and how, to enhance the European Security and Defense HE: we analyzed the experiences of the University of Turin, through the SUISS and ETC&SAMS, in the last seven academic years. This research can be considered a useful example for those who want to increase the internationalization of Security and Defence Higher Education, especially in this new digital era. The internationalization process intended not as a globalization but as a European educational training is absolutely crucial to create a European spirit and, in the field of Security and Defense HE, it is even more so for the type of complexity of the organizations in this sector. This change of spirit during the HE helps the creation of collaborations that continue throughout the career path. The actors involved in this process are students, teachers, staff, and the institutions themselves, which must adopt strategic policies to ensure that also those who, for any reasons, cannot physically move, can still be involved in this process. The EC's Digital Education Action Plan 2021-27 (European Commission, 2020) published in September 2020 indicates three main directions that will certainly facilitate the internationalization process: the development of infrastructures in terms of connectivity, devices and technologies, the enhancing of educators' digital competences and the creation of open quality content. It is important that all MS and all Institutes dealing with Security and Defence Education invest in digital education (Spinello et al. 2018) within a common framework to boost internationalization process that represents a great challenge for the future.

REFERENCES

Altbach P.G. et al., 2009. Trends in Global Higher Education: Tracking an Academic Revolution. Retrieved from http://unesdoc.unesco.org/images/0018/001831/183168e.pdf

de Wit H. et al. (Eds) 2015. *Internationalisation of higher education: A study for the European Parliament*. http://www.europarl.europa.eu/RegData/etudes/STUD/2015/540370/IPOL_STU(2015)540370_EN.pdf

European Commission, 2014. *The Erasmus Impact Study*. DOI: 10.2766/75468.

European Commission, 2020. *Digital Education Action Plan 2021-2027*. https://ec.europa.eu/education/education-in-the-eu/digital-education-action-plan_en

European Commission, 2021. *Erasmus+ Programme Guide*. https://ec.europa.eu/programmes/erasmus-plus/resources/programme-guide_en.

European Security and Defence College, 2019. *GAREA 2018-19. Promoting the Common Security and Defence Culture*. Brussels, Belgium. http://www.emilyo.eu/sites/default/files/GAREA/2019%2010%2023%202019-195%20REV%204%20GAREA%202018-19%20annexes%20included.pdf

Knight, J., 2008. *Higher education in turmoil: The changing world of internationalization*. Sense Publishers.

Marchisio M. et al., 2017. Advanced e-learning for IT-Army officers through Virtual Learning Environments. In *Journal of e-Learning and Knowledge Society*, vol. 13(3), 59-70.

Marchisio M. et al., 2019. Start@unito: Open Online Courses for Improving Access and for Enhancing Success in Higher Education: *Proceedings of the 11th International Conference on Computer Supported Education*, 639–646. https://doi.org/10.5220/0007732006390646

Matei L. and Iwinska J., 2015. National Strategies and Practices in Internationalisation of Higher Education: Lessons from a Cross-Country Comparison. DOI 10.1007/978-3-319-08054-3_11. In Curaj A. et al. (eds). *Higher Education Reforms in Romania*, 205-226.

Roggero, A. and Rabaglietti, E., 2019. *Generazione Erasmus Piemonte*. Università di Torino. https://www.unito.it/sites/default/files/generazione_erasmus_piemonte_30anni_2019.pdf.

Spinello E. et al., 2017. E-learning as winning tool for supporting teaching and for enhancing the internationalization processes. DOI:10.12753/2066-026X-17-015. In *Elearning and Software for Education*. Bucharest, Romania. ISSN: 2066-026X vol. 1,101-108.

Spinello E. et al., 2018. The COMFOR-SA Virtual Learning Centre becomes a Special Hub for gaining new modern standard for the IT-Army E-learning Programmes. DOI:10.12753/2066-026X-18-068. In *Elearning and Software for Education*. Bucharest, Romania. ISSN:2360-2198 vol. 1, 479-486.

Spinello E. et al., 2019. A Full Spectrum Lifelong e-Learning Project for the Army. In *Elearning and Software for Education*. Bucharest, Romania, vol. 1, 152-158.

Spinello E. et al., 2020. The E-learning project for institutional learning. In *Elearning and Software for Education*. Bucharest, Romania, vol. 1, 147-121.

Spinello E. et al., 2021. Security and Defence Higher Education in pandemic times: measures adopted and new perspectives for the future. In *Elearning and Software for Education*. Bucharest, Romania, in press.

Taalas P. et al., 2020. Internationalisation in learning and teaching - Thematic Peer Group Report. In *Learning and Teaching Paper 9*. European University Association. Brussels, Belgium.

E-LEARNING CHALLENGES USING ZOOM AND APPLICATION OF ARTIFICIAL INTELLIGENCE TO IMPROVE LEARNING IN AUSTRALIA HIGHER EDUCATION INSTITUTES

Raj Sandu, Shakir Karim and Mahesh Kayastha
CQUniversity, Sydney, Australia

ABSTRACT

The advancement of information technology in learning has prompted the development of the new teaching and learning strategies at academic institutes. E-learning has become a need in higher educational organizations and is employed in educational institutions around the globe. Zoom is one of the emerging technologies of e-learning. Analysts have made a lot of emphasis on its advantages however very little is examined on the drawbacks of the e-learning innovation. This paper investigates the challenges of zoom innovation that learners are confronted with and recommendations for an effective e-learning result using Artificial Intelligence (AI). AI based e-learning frameworks can be utilized by educational institutes to assure better educating and learning experience of a learner.

KEYWORDS

E-learning, Zoom Technology, Online Learning Challenges, Artificial Intelligence (AI)

1. INTRODUCTION

While the expression "e-learning" has been tossed around a considerable amount in these years, many are yet uninformed of what it really means and how it can assist them with accomplishing achievement in both their personal and professional lives (Mishra, Gupta et al. 2020) . Learning with the help of electronic revolutions to get hold on academic plan outside of a traditional/regular classroom is termed as e-learning. It refers to a course delivered entirely on the web (Lenkaitis 2020). There are countless expressions used to describe knowledge that is delivered on the web i.e., distance education, advanced electronic learning, web-based learning etc. This is a type of learning system based on systematized teaching that uses electronic sources (Sayem, Taylor et al. 2017).

E-learning has been carried by many methods or applications i.e., LMS, SCORM, xAPI, and Zoom etc. Among all these, zoom is the widely used application for the purpose of trainings, and academia etc. (Lowenthal, Borup et al. 2020). Zoom is a video conferencing tool that has many features like screen sharing during the call, recording of call etc. Moreover, one can arrange meetings with many persons at time and meeting analytics such as joining time and duration of members are also available. Especially in this period of COVID-19, when all educational institutes are closed, a rapid growth is seen in the use of this application. Students are engaged by their respective institutions through zoom to complete their syllabus and credit hours. Moreover, this application is cost effective and poses lower environmental impacts. Thus, zoom has proved to be really helpful in this current situation of pandemic (Reimers, Schleicher et al. 2020).

Zoom gives Breakout Rooms, which is not accessible in other video conferencing tools. This component empowers the teacher to separate the members into smaller class groups. This component is useful in delivering lecture and presentations (Nadezhda 2020). The teacher can look in on each class to examine the situation of introduction and the discussion among the members. Following the completion of meeting according to the organized time, the members will ultimately be driven back to the "main room" (Dharma, Asmarani et al. 2017). This paper demonstrates the challenge using zoom by students and propose application of AI to improve learning in Australia higher education institutes.

2. LITERATURE REVIEW

Numerous colleges are preparing learners to incorporate innovation like zoom applications to be utilized during training since individuals are quickly adjusting to getting to these advancements to encourage correspondence which prompts the far and wide prevalence of online learning (Ali, Naeem et al. 2020). This comes as an answer for educational researcher who are continually attempting to create innovative means to improve the intuitiveness of the learning cycle to animate learners' motivation and commitment in conversations for information, which like acquiring knowledge that prompts creating overall learning. An research was directed that centered on coordinated systems, for example, chat bot and video conferencing like zoom to begin subject conversations utilizing the English language (Chamekh and Hammami 2020). Additionally, researcher discovered the utilization of chatting in online meetings and expressed that it yielded positive effects on understanding among the students (Radha, Mahalakshmi et al. 2020).

Different researcher recommended that a zoom meeting (a simultaneous learning methodology) can have an immediate connection with positive effect on learners' scholarly exhibition and inspiration towards the learning cycle (Gupta, Shrestha et al. 2020). It was accepted that utilizing zoom meetings can encourage understating of syntactic and semantic perception through the way toward composing and modifying before sharing these communication because of the sentiment of weakness of imparting them to their colleagues and educator which urges them to structure right explanations (Molchanova, Kovtoniuk et al. 2020). Studies found out on how learners show better understanding when utilizing an innovative method through the learning cycle, for example, giving additional time and flexibility in delivering their works. With all the attention and rapid growth in its use, zoom is facing many security issues that pose a serious threat to its popularity. Security specialists and even the FBI caution that Zoom's default settings aren't sufficiently secure (Wagenseil 2020). Analysts have discovered that the secret IDs provided to join the meeting can be predicted effortlessly, permitting anybody to enter the meeting. Part of this usability has prompted the "Zoom bombing" marvel, where comedians get into Zoom calls and broadcast offensive material like pornography (Aliyyah, Rachmadtullah et al. 2020).

Zoom's default settings do not ask for a secret key to be set for these video conferences and permit any members to mirror their screen. Zoom balanced these default settings for the purpose of learning of educators, with an end goal to expand security and protection for gatherings (Verawardina, Asnur et al. 2020). For every other person, you will have to change your Zoom settings to guarantee this never occurs. The usage of free Zoom version is restricted to 40 minutes at once for meetings, you must restart another meeting. Likewise, for the free account, the absolute number of members who can be associated at once in a meeting is restricted to 50 people. Moreover, many technical challenges are also faced by zoom users especially by those who live in remote areas. The hindrance of Zoom, as indicated by those clients, is the eccentric and poor video quality. Video is frequently foggy and pixelated. This mostly happen in those areas where poor quality internet connections are available.

There is no training provided to the teachers and students of small towns and villages especially in developing countries, that is why they are not aware of the benefits and risks associated with this application. display of this app is viewed as somewhat confounded; in this way there are a few features which are elusive. At the very start, even the teachers face troubles in discovering a few features. To address many of this learning problem of Zoom, AI is suggested as discussed below.

Artificial intelligence and its use to improve learning: While the debate concerning how much screen time is suitable for adolescents is increasing among instructors, and guardians. It's another emerging revolution as artificial intelligence is setting up to revamp training gadgets and organizations and is transforming what the future may look like in the field of education (Wang, Minku et al. 2014) . US Education Sector report indicates that it is normal that AI and machine learning in U.S. training will grow by 47.5% from the last four years. Regardless of the way that most pros acknowledge the essential presence of teachers is key, there will be various movements to an educator's action and to enlightening recommended rehearses. Numerous analysts guarantee that AI and Machine Learning can expand the educational standards (Perozzi, Al-Rfou et al. 2014).

AI innovation carries a great deal of advantages to different fields and software like chatbot is used in higher education (Sandu and Gide 2019). A chatbot can create chats or discussions with a learner or user in common language. For what rationale are chatbots noteworthy? A chatbot is normally portrayed as one of the most growing and promising communication of joint effort among individuals and machines. Notwithstanding, from a mechanical viewpoint, a chatbot just addresses the general improvement of a communication framework. The benefit AI provides to students and teachers are as discussed below.

The benefits students get from these AI-based technologies are as following:

• Youngsters invest a great deal of time on learning. Artificial Intelligence based technologies give a likelihood to focus on spare time, using 10 or 15 minutes. Moreover, they can get feedback from mentors in a constant manner (Molnár, Szűts et al. 2018).

• These arrangements can be revamped by learners' degree of information, interesting themes, etc. The system will usually assist learners with their weak points (Sapkota and Narayangarh 2020).

• Simulated intelligence-based phases offer virtual instructors to note the learners' improvement. Obviously, only human instructors can efficiently address the learners' needs; anyway it's satisfactory to get second input through virtual tutor (Song, Oh et al. 2017).

Teachers also get benefited through these technologies. Some of those benefits are quoted below:

• Distinctive instructional sessions allow seeing the shortcomings in learners' knowledge and understanding. For occasion, the Coursera platform can inform the instructor if a huge number of learners picked off false reactions to a specific question. Therefore, the teacher has a possibility to concentrate on the requested point (Wei, Yu et al. 2018) .

• Various AI-empowered platform can check the students' knowledge and interests and provide more related knowledge and learning programs (Sandu, Gide et al. 2019).

• Educators get an exceptional benefit by AI improvement. These days, they do not need to make an instructive arrangement without any planning. Appropriately, teachers contribute less in searching for crucial educational materials (Smutny and Schreiberova 2020).

Educational platforms have a huge number of educators, so the learner has likelihood to speak with experts from different continents. One of The World Bank reports (2020) expressed that few nations had executed unique learning frameworks as schools were shut because of the COVID-19. For instance, toward the beginning of February 2020, China actualized an internet learning framework concerning concurrent web based learning activities to guarantee that was not intruded for learners (Pantano and Pizzi 2020). This idea is described by a mix of numerous characteristics, for example, an AI associated with an organization (zoom application), is an appropriate tools for both the educators and learners, through ongoing correspondence, using video, voice or text between members (Villegas-Ch, Arias-Navarrete et al. 2020). The AI based academic platform present the instructor, with great learning experience. Thus, Learning can be improved by using Artificial intelligence technologies.

3. METHODOLOGY

This research used quantitative methodology for the collection of data. Students from different localities and countries studying online using zoom or other applications were surveyed using questioners on Google Form. The variables which were considered were age, gender, area/country, field of study. Most of the data was collected from the students from India, Nepal, Pakistan, Zambia, Australia, and China studying in Australia higher education institute. The age of the students was mostly in range of 18-30 years. They were presented with different hypothesis to ask the reliability of zoom technology for the purpose of online learning and how learning can be improved through artificial intelligence. Some of those hypotheses are quoted below:

• Is online learning feasible during this situation of COVID-19 pandemic?
• What do you think about zoom? Is it easy to use?
• How was your interaction with the teachers during online sessions through zoom?
• Does lecture delivered through zoom make better understanding?
• How was the video and audio quality during your sessions on zoom?
• What source do you prefer to use this application i.e., mobile phone, laptop etc. which one is more suitable?
• Is this application easy to use or work?
• What improvements you think should be made in this application?
• Can artificial intelligence tools like Chabot improve online learning?

4. DATA ANALYSIS

Quality assertion of learning and training measures is significant for any education organization to be successful. For instructors, it is likewise essential to convey great learning techniques. Current innovation has given fundamental help to accomplish the necessary norm of nature of learning tools. Table 1 shows response of learning using Zoom application during online classes by the survey students.

Table 1. Response frequency of learners using zoom application during online classes

	Response frequency (%)			
Queries	Disagree	Neutral	Agree	Extremely agree
E-learning during COVID-19 is best solution.	11.6%	16.28%	4.7%	67.4%
Experience with zoom is great.	32%	5%	10.5%	52.5%
Interaction with teacher is good.	2%	17%	35%	46%
Delivery of lecture content make better understanding.	2%	18.6%	58%	21%
Teacher always asks about screen.	2%	11.6%	46.5%	39.5%
No background noise during class.	7%	9.4%	62.8%	20.8%
Good audio quality.	0	9.4%	51.1%	39.5%
Good video quality.	2%	13.9%	53.5%	30.6%
Online classes are easier to attend than face to face classes.	16.27%	18.6%	23.25%	41.86%
Application is easy to use.	11.6%	4.7%	13.95%	69.77%
Laptops are easier to use than other sources for zoom meeting.	16.3%	4.6%	9.3%	69.8%
Everything is good. No improvements are needed in the application.	16.34%	7%	0	76.7%
Artificial Intelligence tools like chatbots on e-learning platform would improve learning experience and standard of education.	20.93%	0%	0	79.07%

In 2020, because of instructional meetings being offered by zoom, the teachers' burden decreased by around 25%. The presentation of zoom additionally brought about a negligible increment in the level of HD grades granted. Evaluations were not altogether transformed over this period; this is proof that zoom instructional exercises may likewise permit students to acquire further knowledge. What is more, while joining zoom instructional exercise meetings, studies demonstrated their enthusiasm about the zoom communitarian device for giving compelling effects on accomplish the objectives of the subject. There has been a constructive impact of zoom innovation in the learning cycle. Further online system for zoom has been expended in year following 2019 to 2020 due to pandemic COVID-19 and need of hour. Descriptive statistics was used for analysis based on questioners which were filled earlier and showed that most of the percentage was female student's i.e.,73% and remaining 36% were male. Most of the participant students were either secondary school, graduated or undergraduate students. Elementary school students may deliver invalid surveys because of their troubles in text perception. As indicated by the review on the terminal kinds of internet instructing stages utilized by members, cell phones represented 84.62%, followed by PCs tablet PCs. Students faces many challenges while learning online such as insufficient learning resource, live interactive chat, network congested among the major ones.

Figure 1 shows the problem faced by students learning through the online platform. Moreover, 11 types of errors were seen in online system which was included in online education system. Major issues apart from technical issues was communication, and support provided to the students. These issues can be solved by improving their communication functionality, quality of system and enhancement of network capacity.

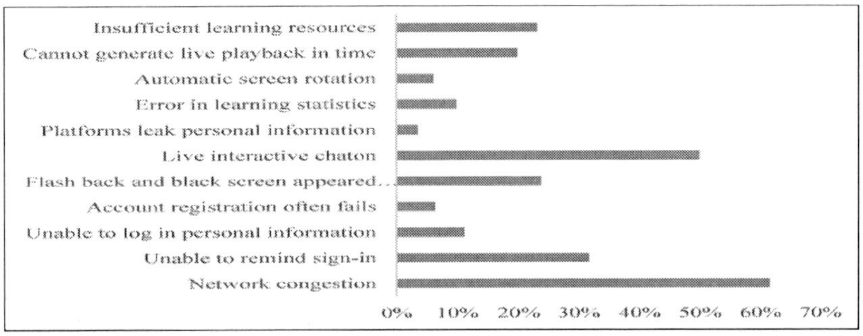

Figure 1. Percentage of challenges faced by student learning online

So, from analysis it can be inferred that most of the students about 85% having age range between 18-30 gives the positive rating to online system using zoom and preferred the system using laptops PC's and mobile phones as we go through the data available through questioners present in excel sheets. Although they also face few issues with the Zoom. Most of the students agreed that using AI such as Chatbot will enhance their learning.

5. CONCLUSION

E-learning is an effective approach in the current era of technology. The standard of education is raised due to the emerging use of these applications for the purpose of e-learning. In this period of COVID-19, high growth in the usage of zoom technology has been observed especially in education sector. The current study shows that zoom is an effective tool for the purpose of education through home and the data collected in the study reveals that most of the features of zoom are satisfying. But there are some challenges especially the security backlashes, which should be improved by the education institutes. Moreover, use of artificial intelligence tools like chatbots can improve the standard and quality of e-learning. Immediate responses through virtual instruction by the software can save the time of the learners and make e-learning more attractive and appealing. Future research will focus on different type of AI technologies that can be used to improve students learning.

REFERENCES

Ali, M. Y., S. B. Naeem and R. Bhatti (2020). "Artificial intelligence tools and perspectives of university librarians: An overview." *Business Information Review*: 0266382120952016.

Aliyyah, R. R., R. Rachmadtullah, A. Samsudin, E. Syaodih, M. Nurtanto and A. R. S. Tambunan (2020). "The Perceptions of Primary School Teachers of Online Learning during the COVID-19 Pandemic Period: A Case Study in Indonesia." *Journal of Ethnic and Cultural Studies* 7(2): 90-109.

Chamekh, Y. and M. A. Hammami (2020) Ways Artificial Intelligence Will Shape eLearning, *International Journal of Sciences: Basic and Applied Research ISSN 2307-4531.*

Dharma, H. R. C., D. Asmarani and U. P. Dewi (2017). "Basic Japanese Grammar and Conversation e-learning through Skype and Zoom Online Application." *Procedia computer science* 116: 267-273.

Gupta, A., R. M. Shrestha, S. Shrestha, A. Acharya and N. Pandey (2020). "Perception of BDS students of Kathmandu University on online learning during COVID-19 pandemic." *Orthodontic Journal of Nepal* 10(2): 20-28.

Lenkaitis, C. A. (2020). "Teacher candidate reflection: Benefits of using a synchronous computer-mediated communication-based virtual exchange." *Teaching and Teacher Education*: 103041.

Lowenthal, P., J. Borup, R. West and L. Archambault (2020). "Thinking Beyond Zoom: Using Asynchronous Video to Maintain Connection and Engagement During the COVID-19 Pandemic." *Journal of Technology and Teacher Education* 28(2): 383-391.

Mishra, L., T. Gupta and A. Shree (2020). "Online Teaching-Learning in Higher Education during Lockdown Period of COVID-19 Pandemic." *International Journal of Educational Research* Open: 100012.

Molchanova, E., K. Kovtoniuk and O. Savych (2020). "Covid-19 Presents New Challenges and Opportunities to Higher Education." Revista Romaneasca pentru Educatie Multidimensionala 12(2Sup1): 168-174.

Molnár, G., Z. Szűts and K. Biró (2018). "Use of augmented reality in learning." *Acta Polytechnica Hungarica* 15(5): 209-222.

Nadezhda, G. (2020). "Zoom Technology as an Effective Tool for Distance Learning in Teaching English to Medical Students." *Бюллетень науки и практики* 6(5).

Pantano, E. and G. Pizzi (2020). "Forecasting artificial intelligence on online customer assistance: Evidence from chatbot patents analysis." *Journal of Retailing and Consumer Services* 55: 102096.

Perozzi, B., R. Al-Rfou and S. Skiena (2014). Deepwalk: Online learning of social representations. *Proceedings of the 20th ACM SIGKDD international conference on Knowledge discovery and data mining.*

Radha, R., K. Mahalakshmi, V. Sathis Kumar and A. Saravanakumar (2020). "E-learning during lockdown of Covid-19 pandemic: a global perspective." *International journal of control and automation* 13(4): 1088-1099.

Reimers, F., A. Schleicher, J. Saavedra and S. Tuominen (2020). "Supporting the continuation of teaching and learning during the COVID-19 Pandemic." *Oecd* 1(1): 1-38.

Sandu, N. and E. Gide (2019). Adoption of AI-Chatbots to Enhance Student Learning Experience in Higher Education in India. 2019 18th International Conference on Information Technology Based Higher Education and Training (ITHET), *IEEE.*

Sandu, N., E. Gide and S. Karim (2019). Improving Learning through Cloud-based Mobile Technologies and Virtual and Augmented Reality for Australian Higher Education. Proceedings of the 2019 *International Conference on Mathematics, Science and Technology Teaching and Learning.*

Sapkota, P. P. and C. Narayangarh (2020). Determining Factors of the Use of E-learning during COVID-19 Lockdown among the college students of Nepal: A Cross-Sectional Study, A Mini Research Report, Balkumari College, Narayangarh, Chitwan, Nepal.

Sayem, A. S. M., B. Taylor, M. McClanachan and U. Mumtahina (2017). Effective use of zoom technology and instructional videos to improve engagement and success of distance students in engineering. *28th Annual Conference of the Australasian Association for Engineering Education (AAEE 2017), Australasian Association for Engineering Education.*

Smutny, P. and P. Schreiberova (2020). "Chatbots for learning: A review of educational chatbots for the Facebook Messenger." *Computers & Education*: 103862.

Song, D., E. Y. Oh and M. Rice (2017). Interacting with a conversational agent system for educational purposes in online courses. *10th international conference on human system interactions (HSI), IEEE.*

Verawardina, U., L. Asnur, A. L. Lubis, Y. Hendriyani, D. Ramadhani, I. P. Dewi, R. Darni, T. J. Betri, W. Susanti and T. Sriwahyuni (2020). "Reviewing Online Learning Facing the Covid-19 Outbreak." Talent Development & Excellence 12.

Villegas-Ch, W., A. Arias-Navarrete and X. Palacios-Pacheco (2020). "Proposal of an Architecture for the Integration of a Chatbot with Artificial Intelligence in a Smart Campus for the Improvement of Learning." Sustainability 12(4): 1500.

Wagenseil, P. (2020). "Zoom security issues: here's everything that's gone wrong (so far)." Tom's Guide 11.

Wang, S., L. L. Minku and X. Yao (2014). "Resampling-based ensemble methods for online class imbalance learning." *IEEE Transactions on Knowledge and Data Engineering* 27(5): 1356-1368.

Wei, C., Z. Yu and S. Fong (2018). How to build a chatbot: chatbot framework and its capabilities. *Proceedings of the 2018 10th International Conference on Machine Learning and Computing.*

ONLINE WRITTEN EXAMS DURING COVID-19 CRISIS: AN UPDATE AFTER ONE YEAR

Goffredo Haus, Yuri Benvenuto Pasquinelli, Daniela Scaccia and Nello Scarabottolo
Università degli Studi di Milano, Milan, Italy

ABSTRACT

The paper discusses what happened since May 2020 up the end of April 2021 regarding online written exams at the University of Milan, where the solutions identified during first pandemic lockdown (and described in a paper presented last year at e-Learning 2020) have been applied.
In particular, the paper shows how the different envisaged scenarios have been perceived and applied by the teachers. Presented data clearly show the large adoption of the scenarios self-handled by the teachers with respect to costly and complex proctoring platforms, used only when numbers of students in a single exam are too large to be self-handled.

KEYWORDS

Written Exams, Closed Answer Exams, Open Answer Exams, Online Student Monitoring, Proctoring

1. INTRODUCTION

The lockdown imposed by the Covid-19 pandemic around the end of February 2020 forced Italian Universities to transfer suddenly online all the teaching activities normally carried on with students physically present in classrooms.

Due to the urgency requirements, the implementation of online lectures has been left to the personal initiative of teachers, without the possibility of significant methodological guidelines, as the ones discussed, e.g., in Troussas et al. (2020), Xiao et al. (2020), Troussas et al. (2021). A similar approach has been followed to allow the thesis discussion of graduating students: the web conference platforms used for lectures have also been adopted to connect these students from home with the teachers evaluating their final exam.

On the contrary, particular attention has been paid to the management of exams evaluating the knowledge and the competences acquired by students at the end of each single course present in their study curriculum.

Among the various references in literature regarding online exams, it is worth mentioning Truszkowski (2019), Ardid et al. (2015) and Weiner & Hurtz (2017). In the first two, some comparisons between proctored and non-proctored tests are made, clearly showing that in the absence of some form of proctoring the final grades are higher, due to usage of unauthorized support and cheating. In the third one, a comparison between online and onsite proctored exams shows, on the contrary, no significant differences in final grades, allowing to state that the level of student behavior control can be satisfactory both online and onsite.

To allow proctoring of written exams online, the authors of this paper from the University of Milan:

- the Deputy Rector for Digital Innovation, ICT Services, Strategic and Special Projects;
- the Director of the ICT Division;
- the Director of CTU: the Teaching and Learning Innovation and Multimedia Technology Center of the University;
- the Rector Delegate to ICT infrastructures coordination;

identified during Spring 2020 possible scenarios to carry on online written exams, allowing teachers to avoid the limitations of oral exams while still guaranteeing a reasonable level of reliability in their evaluations. These scenarios have been described deeply in Haus et al. (2020), a paper presented in last year's e-Learning conference. In this short paper, we report and discuss some results after one year of application of these scenarios.

The following section summarizes the impact of exams in our University, in terms of numbers of students and distribution over the year. Section 3 recalls the different scenarios identified by the authors. Section 4 gives some data about exams from May 2020 up to April 2021.

2. ANALYSIS OF EXAM SESSIONS

To better understand the different scenarios described in the following sections of this paper, it is worth remembering that in our University:

- each course must propose to students at least six different exam dates every academic year;
- a student can decide her/his first exam date after the end of the course lectures, but in case of failure or unsatisfying result, she/he can reapply for the same exam in the following dates;
- there is no penalty for students that, after application, do not show up at the exam date: they are simply considered absent, and they can reapply whenever they want.

Thus, each teacher has to plan for at least six exam sessions every year, with a number of participating students known only a few days before each session, i.e., after the closing of the student application period for each exam date.

A comparison between the situation before and after Covid-19 pandemic can be found in Table 1, where data referring to the last "normal" academic year (2018-19) and to the pandemic one (2020-21) are given. From Table 1 it is possible to see that:

- the highest numbers of exam sessions are located at the end of the winter and summer semesters, during breaks between lecture times (i.e., January-February and June-September, with August being the traditional vacation month in Italy, thus omitted in the Table);
- the average number of students applying for each exam session is reasonably limited, but:
  - there are exam sessions characterized by large numbers of students;
  - there are evident effects of the pandemic in terms of reduction of the number of exam sessions (-16.3% between 2019-18 and 2020-21) as well as the number of examined students (-20.3%). The main reason for these reductions is the significant increase of oral exams, more straightforward to perform online and initially suggested by the University governance as the only acceptable way.

Table 1. Written exam sessions in 2018-19 and 2020-21

Month	Exam sessions		Examined students		Avg studs per session		Max stud per session	
	2018-19	2020-21	2018-19	2020-21	2018-19	2020-21	2018-19	2020-21
January	2'116	2'500	45'617	45'396	21.6	18.2	309	358
February	2'868	502	54'806	12'089	19.1	24.1	353	298
March	471	767	8'998	17'466	19.1	22.8	275	452
April	838	15'337	18'255	272'105	21.8	17.7	214	588
May	1'102	1'032	25'677	19'115	23.3	18.5	302	272
June	2'477	1'923	51'301	34'691	20.7	18.0	428	226
July	3'197	2'518	49'074	39'949	15.4	15.9	206	251
September	3'043	2'556	39'083	31'067	12.8	12.2	223	269
October	497	428	5'533	3'863	11.1	9.0	245	96
November	896	702	19'780	13'233	22.1	18.9	545	285
December	827	680	23'464	18'098	28.4	26.6	401	377
Total	**18'332**	**15'337**	**341'588**	**272'105**	**18.6**	**17.7**	**545**	**588**

Table 2 shows the differences in terms of the number of enrolled students, the number of written exam sessions and the number of examined students among the various faculties present in our University. It interesting to note that:

- the largest number of exam sessions is organized by the faculty of Medicine, far above the faculty of Science and Technology, which has the largest number of examined students;
- Humanities, i.e., the faculty where the highest number of students are enrolled, usually adopts oral exams. Thus the number of written sessions is quite limited;

- the total number of examined students during pandemic shows a 20.3% reduction with respect to the previous situation, but with significant differences among the various faculties; however
- despite the pandemic and the troubles expected in distance learning, the total number of enrollments increased last year by 4.8%.

Table 2. Distribution of students and sessions per faculties in 2018-19 and 2020-21

Faculty/School	Enrollments		Exam sessions		Examined students	
	2018-19	2020-21	2018-19	2020-21	2018-19	2020-21
Agricultural and Food Sciences	3'431	2'893	1'613	1'113	27'462	15'256
Exercise and Sport Sciences	1'398	1'294	349	127	9'518	5'993
Humanities	14'878	15'298	1'037	1'036	32'633	28'965
Language Mediation + Interfaculties	4'737	6'941	1'115	688	32'394	22'221
Law	6'748	6'672	397	233	10'696	5'881
Medicine	7'682	7'665	5'494	4'316	62'523	45'702
Pharmacy	3'075	2'948	1'161	969	24'286	18'678
Political, Economic and Social Sciences	7'708	8'022	2'614	2'406	53'776	48'653
Science and Technology	8'450	9'643	3'823	3'794	75'325	70'411
Veterinary Medicine	1'836	1'469	729	655	12'975	10'345
Total	**59'943**	**62'845**	**18'332**	**15'337**	**341'588**	**272'105**

3. DIFFERENT SCENARIOS FOR MANAGING WRITTEN EXAMS

3.1 Monitoring

A first discriminating aspect considered in Haus et al. (2020) in defining the different scenarios has been the possibility for the teacher to monitor in real-time the behavior of the whole set of examined students or of a limited number of student groups through some web conference platforms.

After some tests, it has been seen that a reasonable number of students that can be monitored by a single person was in the range of 20-30, and that it was not worth asking teachers to split students into more than 4 to 5 groups, to be monitored in parallel, with the help of some collaborators. Then, we decided to consider 100 students applying for the same exam date as the limit for exam sessions monitored under the teacher's responsibility and exams sessions requiring external support. Monitoring of a group of 20-30 students by means of a web conference platform (e.g., Microsoft Teams, Zoom, etc.) has been performed asking the student to position her/his smartphone behind her/his shoulders. This allowed the teacher to control student behavior and to see the screen of her/his computer during the exam.

When 100 or more students apply for a single exam session, we decided to adopt a proctoring system offered in the market. After some initial tests with two proctoring platforms, Respondus and Proctorio – described in (Respondus 2020) and (Proctorio 2020) – the second one was selected, mainly due to the more straightforward setup of the student computer and the reduced amount of frames stored during recording.

3.2 Types of Supported Exams

Besides identifying the most suitable ways usable for monitoring student behavior, we had to take into account the nature of the exam each teacher may decide to use. The most common type of written exams is constituted by open answer tests, for which two solutions have been proposed:

- for limited numbers of students – i.e., groups that can be monitored by the teacher – we used the exam.net platform, described in (Exam.net 2020) and implemented by the Swedish company Teachiq AB. The main characteristics of the platform are very easy teacher interface, support for real-time monitoring of student work, the possibility for students to include pictures of hand written work. Moreover, the scenario adopts the safer approach proposed by exam.net and based on the usage of the Safe Exam Browser SEB software – described in (SEB 2020) – that turns any computer temporarily into a secure workstation.

- for larger numbers of students, requiring proctoring, Proctorio has been integrated with the Moodle LMS (Learning Management System) already adopted by CTU, where several types of exam questions can be defined and submitted to students.

Some teachers prefer to adopt in some cases closed answer quizzes instead of open answer written exams. Since the exam.net platform cannot be easily used for this kind of exams, closed answer quizzes for limited numbers of students have been implemented by directly integrating SEB with the Moodle LMS. Sometimes, however, teachers asked to avoid the usage of SEB, whenever the proposed questions did not require to hide any application from the student computer. For large numbers of students, quizzes were handled through proctoring platforms.

4. EXAM SESSIONS

Table 3 and Table 4 show the results after the first month of applying the scenarios described above and after the first complete academic year (May 2020 through April 2021).

As it can be seen from both Tables, the scenario based on the exam.net platform (i.e., open answer questions or quizzes with few questions, for groups of students directly monitored by the teacher) shows a huge number of sessions and the largest number of examined students. The average number of students per session was very small during the test phase and in line with the forecasts during the following academic year. It is clear that such a way of examining students has been greatly appreciated by our colleagues: in fact, it allows teachers not familiar with Moodle to submit written exams also to very small groups of students, exploiting all the facilities and friendliness of that platform.

Moodle was initially used by only a few teachers: the number of sessions and students during the test phase was definitely smaller. During the academic year the situation has changed, even because some tests for evaluating basic student competences in using a PC have been moved to Moodle.

As already said, proctoring has been limited to sessions with large numbers of students, growing from 76.2 during the test phase to 99.8 during the academic year, perfectly in line with the expected usage of such a (costly) solution.

Table 3. Summary of first month of online written exams

Scenario	# of sessions	% of sessions	Average # of students per session	# of examined students	% of examined students
Exam.net	1'333	93.7%	9.5	12'673	74.0%
Moodle with SEB	55	3.9%	32.6	1'793	10.5%
Proctoring	35	2.5%	76.2	2'668	15.6%
Total	**1'423**	**100.0%**	**12.0**	**17'134**	**100.0%**

Table 4. Summary of the complete academic year of online written exams

Scenario	# of sessions	% of sessions	Average # of students per session	# of examined students	% of examined students
Exam.net	7'630	80.8%	21.2	161'598	66.9%
Moodle with SEB	1'190	12.6%	27.6	32'883	13.6%
Moodle without SEB	184	1.9%	19.3	3'542	1.5%
Proctoring	436	4.6%	99.8	43'498	18.0%
Total	**9'440**	**100.0%**	**25.6**	**241'521**	**100.0%**

5. CONCLUSION

Our study analyzed different exam sessions at the University of Milan to assess the efficacy of the proctoring scenarios for online written exams identified during the first lockdown phase of the pandemic. The presentation is limited to a short paper, since this is a follow-on study referring to the application of the scenarios already presented in Haus et al. (2020).

However, the findings are useful: like Wibowo et al. (2016), we are definitely satisfied about the online management of exams during the pandemic: numbers of examined students are not dramatically lower with respect to the normal situation before pandemic, and success rates seem in line too, even if some deeper investigation is required. Of course, more longitudinal studies along with cross-institutional and cross-country comparisons are necessary to fully assess the methods so far described.

As a conclusion, we can state that we will adopt online exams for particular situations (as, e.g., exams for full time employed students) even when our University will reopen.

REFERENCES

Ardid, M, Gómez-Tejedor, JA, Meseguer-Dueñas, JM, Riera, J & Vidaurre, A 2015, 'Online exams for blended assessment. Study of different application methodologies', Computers and Education, vol. 81, pp. 296-303.

Exam.net 2020, A robust, easy-to-use and secure exam platform, viewed June 10th 2020, < https://exam.net/>.

Haus, G, Pasquinelli, YB, Scaccia, D & Scarabottolo, N 2020, 'Online Written Exams during Covid-19 Crisis', Proceeding of the Intl. Conf. e-Learning 2020, pp. 79-86.

Proctorio 2020, A Comprehensive Learning Integrity Platform, viewed June 10th 2020, < https://web.proctorio.com/>.

Respondus 2020, Assessment Tools for Learning Systems, viewed June 10th 2020, < https://web.respondus.com/>.

SEB 2020, Safe Exam Browser, viewed June 10th 2020, < https://safeexambrowser.org/>.

Troussas, C, Krouska, A & Sgouropoulou, C, 'Collaboration and fuzzy-modeled personalization for mobile game-based learning in higher education', Computers & Education, Volume 144, 2020.

Troussas, C, Krouska, A & Sgouropoulou, C, 'A Novel Teaching Strategy Through Adaptive Learning Activities for Computer Programming', IEEE Transactions on Education, vol. 64, no. 2, pp. 103-109, May 2021.

Truszkowski, D 2019, 'Proctored Versus Non-Proctored Testing: A Study for Online Classes', Dissertation of the Doctoral Program of the American College of Education.

Weiner, JA & Hurtz, GM 2017, 'A Comparative Study of Online Remote Proctored versus Onsite Proctored High-Stakes Exams', Journal of Applied Testing Technology, vol. 18, no. 1, pp. 13-20.

Wibowo, S, Grandhi, S, Chugh, R and Sawir, E, 2016, 'A Pilot Study of an Electronic Exam System at an Australian University', Journal of Educational Technology Systems, vol. 45, no. 1, pp. 5-33.

Xiao, C & Li, Y, 'Analysis on the Influence of the Epidemic on the Education in China', 2020 International Conference on Big Data and Informatization Education (ICBDIE), 2020, pp. 143-147.

LOSING THE ELEARNING SAFETY NET: TEACHING AN MBA CLASS WITHOUT AN EDUCATIONAL TECHNICIAN

Gerald E. Evans, Daniel C. Evans and Michael V. Harrington
College of Business, University of Montana, 32 Campus Dr. Missoula, MT 59812, USA

ABSTRACT

The forced transition caused by the safety lockdowns associated with the COVID-19 pandemic imposed "emergency eLearning" on many university faculty members. This transition had many facets including moving away from face-to-face instruction to fully online and hybrid or blended forms of eLearning. For programs that were already leveraging blended teaching, using simultaneous synchronous and asynchronous teaching in the same classroom, the major change was the loss of an educational technician to operate and monitor the technology used for these hybrid teaching models. This paper outlines some of the changes required to navigate this transition and the positive and negative consequences associated with this forced move to eLearning.

KEYWORDS

Educational Technician, COVID-19, Emergency eLearning, Blended eLearning

1. INTRODUCTION

The COVID-19 pandemic was a significant disruptive event that affected every institution and the way of life for the general population. Although college-age students were at a lower mortality risk, government and institutions forced a transition from face-to-face to various modalities of eLearning using the theory of securitization (Murphy, 2020). This transition, termed "emergency eLearning" (Murphy, 2020, p 492), was sudden and caught many members of the university faculty unprepared.

Müller et al. (2021) catalogued and analyzed the experiences of 14 faculty in medical disciplines at a large university in Singapore. A high level of stress and anxiety was noted as well as the necessity of adjusting expectations. Key opportunities observed included reduced apprehension toward eLearning, greater flexibility allowing learning independence for students, reflection and examination of the teaching process, and reduction of barriers to faculty-student interaction. The challenges were more psychological than technical and included creating engagement at the social, emotional, and cognitive levels, addressing diverse student needs, and providing a holistic learning experience. Kalogiannakis et al. (2015) reported on eLearning experiences that promoted positive emotions and mitigated negative ones.

One aspect of best practice in eLearning is the use of instructional technicians to facilitate the educational process mediated by technology. The term educational technologist has changed in the past 50 years from denoting educators skilled in instructional development (Mager, 1967) to educators who are skilled in educational foundations, instructional systems development, and instructional development (Tennyson, 2001). Current thinking is that instructional technologists must be competent in the three areas denoted by Tennyson (2001) as well as being effective coaches or mentors (Sugar, 2005). The benefits of having a technology coach to assist in integrating information technology into the instruction process are well documented (see Cole et al., 2002; Smith, 2000; and Smith and O'Bannon, 1999). Chuang et al. (2003) expanded the application of instructional technologists to higher education where an individual is assigned to a faculty member to support and integrate technology into the instructional process. More recent work has focused on the role of instructional technologists in fostering a more learner-centered instructional environment (Campbell, 2008). Educational technologists also help instructors take full advantage of eLearning platforms and the flexibility such technologies afford (Papachristos et al., 2010).

This paper describes the experience of a seasoned educator in a college of business who had to transition from eLearning supported by an educational technician to both teaching and running the technology after the supporting technician was no longer able to assist in the learning process. The change was abrupt and came with little warning and required significant adaptation for an educator experienced in the eLearning environment. The methodology used is similar to that used by Laskaris et al. (2017) used to interactively evaluate an eLearning course.

2. PROCEDURES AND RESULTS

2.1 Procedures

This case study describes the adaptations required of a professor of business by the forced lockdown precipitating from the COVID-19 pandemic. This professor had significant experience in eLearning in an accredited MBA program. Over 30 years ago, the program was taught using closed-circuit television to a statewide audience. The instruction transitioned to bi-directional compressed video and audio on a dedicated educational network. When sufficient bandwidth was available on the internet, the eLearning migrated to that channel using Blackboard, Adobe Connect, and finally Zoom. The constant feature of this three-decade adventure in eLearning was the direct participation of an educational technician to provide operational support for the process by managing the technology during each instructional session. The professor had to merely show up and teach.

When the pandemic emerged in late winter of 2020, campus was shut down and the faculty had to transition to forced eLearning without the support of an educational technician. Instead of instruction originating from a well-designed "Zoom room" with electronic smart boards, multiple monitors, ceiling microphones, and an educational technician, instruction moved to a home office without all the supporting infrastructure and personnel. The internet and Zoom were still there, but the technical and moral support provided by an educational technician was gone.

A grounded theory methodology was employed (see Glaser and Strauss, 1967), using as the primary questions: "What were the primary challenges in teaching without an educational technologist?" and "What were the outcomes?" A qualitative methodology like grounded theory attempts to develop a theory as opposed to traditional quantitative research where theories are tested with empirical data.

2.2 Results

The results are a set of observations and reflections from the individual making the transition enlightened by the observations of colleagues making similar transitions. The loss of the educational technician required significant adjustments to simultaneously teach and run the technology. However, because the actual educational content remained unchanged, the emotional and cognitive resources used for instruction were redirected toward mastering the capabilities of the technology to make the eLearning experience as good as or better than the face-to-face instruction prior to the pandemic. Several factors made this possible.

First, this professor also taught pre-licensing for real estate professionals and that instruction had to move online as well. Because of statutory regulations, this professor had to become certified by a national association to move the required pre-licensing education to online synchronous instruction. The content of this training provided valuable insight into some of the issues and adjustments necessary for eLearning. Additionally, some available capital from this business was used to purchase a Microsoft Surface Studio, a 27" tilt-screen computer with both pen and touch capabilities. This workstation, along with a second monitor, replaced the campus "Zoom room" and made the technological transition much easier. Zoom still had to be mastered but that infrastructure includes many training videos, and the college provided some training sessions as well.

Second, since students had planned their lives around the face-to-face class schedule, the move to a blend of synchronous and asynchronous eLearning presented no scheduling difficulties. Zoom meetings could be convened during the regularly scheduled times and students could participate synchronously since they had been attending class at these times earlier in the semester. The Zoom sessions could be recorded and watched asynchronously by students who lacked the bandwidth or technical infrastructure to attend synchronously. By fall of 2020 and spring of 2021, the university schedule was built around online or blended eLearning, and MBA students used this new flexibility to participate either synchronously or asynchronously as their preferences dictated. The university and the college, desperate to maintain enrollment, allowed students to choose their attendance modality, making each class both a blended classroom and an online offering. This maintained enrollment and provided a roadmap for more online education.

In addition, the recording capabilities of Zoom provided a convenient platform for recording software demonstrations, in-depth help sessions, and supplementary material without the use of sophisticated video recording studios. The fact that both students and faculty were accustomed to the less polished content produced in Zoom paved the way for additional content development that may not have been pursued under the expectations of professional video standards.

Finally, as familiarity with the technological capabilities of Zoom increased, enhanced features were incorporated into the eLearning experience. Simple things like virtual backgrounds obscured the office clutter that is often a distracting feature of video conferences originating in home or university offices. The chat feature was used to encourage collaboration during the lecture and to require students to ask questions that encouraged engagement while monitoring attendance. Breakout rooms provided the capability to discuss issues or case studies and further encouraged engagement and participation. With a little practice, these new eLearning venues became as interactive and engaging as the face-to-face classrooms they replaced.

3. CONCLUSION

First, the technological capability to support eLearning must be present to provide the foundation for these new teaching modalities. Low computing workstations will not support eLearning at a level necessary to produce an adequate educational experience. This is vital for both the faculty originating the broadcast as well as for participants in the virtual classrooms. The cameras and microphones necessary for engagement in the educational process must be part of the hardware requirements for students. Colleges and universities could not add this requirement on students during the emergency transition to eLearning but, going forward, students must have the technical capabilities necessary to engage in the elearning process. The specifications for required student computers must include cameras, microphones, and computing power sufficient to participate in video conference sessions.

Universities have important decisions to make on how they will support eLearning in the future. Most faculty workstations have limited capabilities so investment must be made in this critical infrastructure. The most likely path forward will be to invest in classrooms dedicated to eLearning either for fully online or blended hybrid instruction. The price point of these technologies is coming down and the investment must be made. For fully online instruction, faculty must be provided the computing and video conferencing resources necessary to support eLearning.

Second, there must be significant collaboration among faculty, educational technologists, and students on best practices. Simple things like having cameras on to foster a collaborative environment and proctoring software to facilitate secure testing are mandatory. In the transition from having an educational technologist prior to the pandemic to going it alone after the lockdown, several collaborative sessions among faculty and educational technologists were provided to share best practices and successful implementation. Using the transition mandated by the pandemic as a social experiment led to the discovery of best practices. In the face-to-face environment, faculty rarely share their classroom management techniques, perhaps assuming that such things are too pedestrian for faculty conversations or too obvious, making collaboration unnecessary. True or not in the face-to-face classroom, in the eLearning environment such collaboration is vital. Those resources are available on most campuses, but faculty have shown a reluctance to have educational technologists tell them how to teach. This must change for successful eLearning.

Finally, and perhaps most importantly, the emergency eLearning mandated during the pandemic taught us that instruction did not have to be perfect for it to be useful and serviceable. Everyone has experienced the loss of internet service in the middle of a Zoom session or an accidental termination of a meeting. Everyone has learned to be patient, reconnect, and resume the meeting. A video conference does not need to be seamless and polished to convey content, engage students, and create an effective eLearning environment. Recorded content does not need to be professionally produced video in order to engage students and communicate content effectively. This was one of the barriers to broad migration to eLearning prior to the pandemic, and the forced transition to eLearning taught us that the instructional production does not have to be perfect to be effective.

Perhaps the disruption caused by the pandemic has broken the barrier to more extensive use of eLearning. Additionally, as the pandemic begins to fade into an historic event, most university faculty have a year or more experience in eLearning. Most have taught multiple classes either fully online or as a blend of synchronous video conferences and asynchronous recorded content. The transition now will be going back to face-to-face instruction. Most universities will probably require that at least one section of each required class be taught online. In addition, perhaps student demand will require that all classes be taught in multiple formats to accommodate work schedules, living situations, military deployments, and educational preferences. To paraphrase the lyrics of Young and Lewis (1919) "How you gonna keep them content in the classroom once they've seen eLearning"?

REFERENCES

Campbell, T. (2008). The capacity of instructional technologists to provide systemic support for science education reform. *Teacher Development*, 12(1), 67-83.

Chuang, H. H., Thompson, A., & Schmidt, D. (2003). Faculty technology mentoring programs: Major trends in the literature. *Journal of Computing in Teacher education*, 19(4), 101-106.

Cole, K., Simkins, M., & Penuel, W. R. (2002). Learning to teach with technology: Strategies for Inservice professional development. *Journal of Technology and Teacher Education*, 10(3), 431-455.

Glaser, B., & Strauss, A. (1967). *The discovery of grounded theory: Strategies for qualitative research*. Chicago: Aldine.

Kalogiannakis, M. & Touvlatzis, S. (2015). Emotions experienced by learners and their development through communication with the tutor-counsellor. *European Journal of Open, Distance and E-learning*, 18(2) 36-48.

Laskaris, D., Kalogiannakis, M., & Heretakis, E. (2017). 'Interactive evaluation' of an e-learning course within the context of blended education. *International Journal of Technology Enhanced Learning*, 9(4), 339-353.

Mager, R. F. (1967). The Instructional Technologist. *Educational Technology*, 7(9), 1-4.

Müller A. M., Goh C., Lim L. Z., & Gao X. (2021). COVID-19 Emergency eLearning and beyond: Experiences and perspectives of university educators. *Education Sciences*, 11(1), 19. https://doi.org/10.3390/educsci11010019

Murphy, M. P. (2020). COVID-19 and emergency eLearning: consequences of the securitization of higher education for post-pandemic pedagogy. *Contemporary Security Policy*, 41(3), 492-505.

Papachristos, D., Arvanitis, K., Vassilakis, K., Kalogiannakis, M., Kikilias, P., & Zafeiri, E. (2010). An educational model for asynchronous e-Learning. A case study in a higher technology education. *International Journal of Advanced Corporate Learning (IJAC)*, 3(1), 32-36. https://www.learntechlib.org/p/45622/.

Smith, S. J. (2000). Graduate students mentors for technology success. *Teacher Education and Special Education*, 23(2), 167-182.

Smith, S. J. & O'Bannon, B. (1999). Faculty members infusing technology across teacher education: A mentorship model. *Teacher Education and Special Education*, 22(2), 123-135.

Sugar, W. (2005). Instructional technologist as a coach: Impact of a situated professional development program on teachers' technology use. *Journal of Technology and Teacher Education*, 13(4), 547-571.

Tennyson, R. D. (2001). Defining core competencies of an instructional technologist. *Computers in human behavior*, 17(4), 355-361.

Young, J. & Lewis, S. M. (1919). How ya gonna keep 'em down on the farm (After they've seen paree)? Waterson, Berlin & Snyder Co, New York, Music by Donaldson, W.

DESIGN-BASED LEARNING IN TEXTILES FOR HIGHER EDUCATION

Benny Malengier[1], Ion Răzvan Rădulescu[2], Mirela Blaga[3], Radek Polanský[4] and Zoran Stjepanović[5]

[1]*Ghent University, Technologiepark-Zwijnaarde 70A, Ghent, Belgium*
[2]*INCDTP, Str. L. Patrascanu 16, Bucharest, Romania*
[3]*Technical University "Gh. Asachi" – Iași, Str. D. Mangeron 29, Iași, Romania*
[4]*University of West Bohemia, Univerzitni 2732/8, 301 00 Pilsen, Czech Republic*
[5]*University of Maribor, Smetanova 17, Maribor, Slovenia*

ABSTRACT

Jobs in design and development of textiles require high end software and techniques, and higher education has problems providing adequate training for this, as the possibilities are large, and institutions don't have experts on hand for all options. Distributed design-based learning (DBL) can aid in this, as the experts can come from a larger group, and the focus is on the output, not the specific software used. Design-based learning (DBL) is a modern concept of education for technical disciplines. The learner starts the educational process using end-user applications, and gains understanding of the theory by conceiving projects and solving real-life situations. We present a tool developed for textiles, OptimTex, where 5 modules have been worked out in which textile design software tools are used: weaving, knitting, virtual prototyping of clothing, embroidery and experimental design. Each module tackles 4 to 5 cases, each divided in a four element structure: example, theory behind the example, software, and quiz. Each module was developed by a different group of experts, and follow up of students is done distributed by each group.

KEYWORDS

Textile, Design-Based Learning, e-Learning

1. INTRODUCTION

There has been a shift to a wider use and an increased importance for E-learning and Open Educational Resources (OER) in all fields of education (Grosseck 2020). The need of online education has accelerated the development of new concepts and practices in e-learning. One of the significant improvements is the shift from OER to Open Educational Practices (OEP). Several educational processes have been enhanced by OEP during the pandemic restrictions in 2020-2021. OER is a content centered approach, with focus on creation and re-(use) of resources, while OEP is a practice centered approach, with focus on interaction between teachers and learners using OER for education (Ehlers 2011).

Another modern educational concept is Project-Based Learning (PBL) and Design-Based Learning (DBL). With PBL, students start learning an educational theme and include the achieved investigation and results into a project. This concept is focused on the students, not on the curriculum, and relies on authenticity of real-life applications of research (Markham 2011, Blumenfeld 1991). DBL on the other hand, implies understanding and application of knowledge in constructing a device or output, often based on STEM disciplines (Darling-Hammond, 2008).

Modern textile applications integrate multiple functionalities as well as electric conductive components. The so-called wearables or smart textiles represent a growing niche of products, able to provide to the textile producer competitive advantages. However, the design of such textile products requires an interdisciplinary approach (textile science, electronics, informatics etc.), as well as appropriate numerical software. Numerical software for textiles have gained in the last decades a great significance, enabling estimation of the fabrics properties in the design phase, such as: drape, mechanical properties (bending, tensile strength), electric conductivity and even ageing. As such, the use of software supports the manufacturing of a smart textile product, with saving of resources, energy and time, needed to test the properties of the real manufactured products. Moreover, the use of applications for design in textiles is a highly demanded skill within the world-of-work, offering to the skilled worker better prospects for employment.

Considering textiles education at higher education institutes, a limitation in the courses is training with state-of-the-art software tools and production machines, while industry has a high need for profiles with these skills. Often this training is limited due to teachers being only fluent with one or two of these tools. Combining skills of different institutions, and gathering the knowledge in an online e-learning tool can offer a solution. PBL or DBL are very suited for this, as the aim is to obtain practical knowledge to use the software tools. PBL is more suited when only one or two applications are considered, while for a broad training, DBL is ideal, as students can aim to obtain outputs with all software covered. The scientific literature suggests that students learn more deeply and perform better on complex tasks, if they are challenged with real-life projects and activities (Darling-Hammond, 2008). The concept of DBL for engineering education is characterized by opening up the space for multiple and non-unique answers in providing engineering design solutions (Gomez Puente 2014). Solving of engineering design problems includes analyzing, abstracting and synthesizing knowledge in order to achieve innovative solutions by integrating knowledge from various disciplines.

Main aim of this paper is to present the ongoing work in creating an e-learning course with DBL suited for textile engineering students aiming to support training with state-of-the-art textile applications.

2. OPTIMTEX APPROACH TO DBL

As most higher education institutions specialize only in some of the tools textile students should be fluent in, an Erasmus+ strategic partnership was set up between research and educational providers in textiles on European level, *Software tools for textile creatives - OptimTex*, with the aim to prepare HEI students in design software for various textile disciplines: weaving, knitting, virtual prototyping of clothing, embroidery, experimental design and a guide on how to apply this knowledge into enterprise practice. This partnership is ongoing, and the OER e-learning instrument will be fully available in 2022.

Training within the field of textile software gains a lot of importance nowadays, and, as the software solutions and textile technology are continuously evolving, adaptation of training materials is an underling need. Regarding the training methods, a common established concept - especially during current pandemic times, are the blended courses, which combine classroom courses with e-learning courses. By combining the advantages of both methods, a more efficient learning process is ensured (Grosseck 2020, Radulescu 2017). Classroom courses have as main advantages the close connection between the tutor and the trainee with direct contact and consulting availability, motivation within the learner's community and deep studying. On the other hand, e-learning permits consulting of the educational materials in proper timeslots, with 24h access and at any location with internet connection. Moreover, e-learning has some special features, such as easy access to multimedia content, for explaining the functioning of the textile machinery or the use of design software for a smart garment.

Interactivity in e-learning between tutor and trainees is ensured by synchronous and asynchronous communication instruments, such as chat or forum. E-learning also enables self-assessment of the acquired knowledge by quizzes and offers the possibility of generating mathematical equations with changing parameters for endless versions of tests, such as the WIRIS add-on in Moodle.

As indicated, our tool is aimed at textile creatives, which includes both HE students and young professionals in the industry. This target group aims to upscale their skills in order to become competitive in the world-of-work, and having a broad understanding of software for textile design offers an excellent opportunity in this regard. Not only students require more training of this kind, there is also a tremendous need within the textile industry for highly qualified personnel who has mastered textile design software. While students of one Faculty of the partnership have as learning focus only one textile technology domain, creating a joint e-learning instrument with educational content in all of the five textile technology domains (weaving, knitting, virtual prototyping of clothing and experimental design), the students will have the possibility to learn from each of these domains, and to benefit from the expertise of other partners.

2.1 The e-Learning Instrument

Within OptimTex, five educational modules are being developed which cover the main textile technologies to design and manufacture e-textiles, smart textiles, and technical textiles with support of software programs. These are joined with e-learning methods, see Fig. 1. The educational modules, consisting of text, pictures, graphs, and videos, are going to be implemented in e-learning format, by two formats: as e-learning content on the Moodle platform (www.advan2tex.eu/portal/), and as a special instrument including a HTML5 navigation button for quick and illustrative access to the structured content (http://www.optimtex.eu/instrument.php), see Figure 1.

As the covered subjects are very broad, a careful selection is done of the material to include, so as not to overwhelm students, limiting a full module to 20-25 pages of text. The decision was taken to further divide each module in 4-5 design cases. These are then worked out in depth, and they are chosen so as to cover an as broad as possible subject area of the topic. Next, each design case was structured on four elements, in a design-based learning approach (Radulescu 2021): 1/ Example of a special e-textile product, requiring design by software; 2/Theory behind the example one must master to execute the use case; 3/ Applications supporting the design process; and 4/ A Quiz consisting of multiple choice tests for self-assessment.

With this strict structure, the material can be presented to the students in a very organized way, making use of e.g. a HTML5 navigation button. The teacher, or student, can create their own learning path in this way, considering only the use cases relevant for a specific course, or only the use cases of interest for a job application. This approach was introduced to help the trainees understand the theory by real examples. The approach illustrates very well the practical meaning of theory, supports easy understanding, and is in line with the modern concept of DBL (design-based learning).

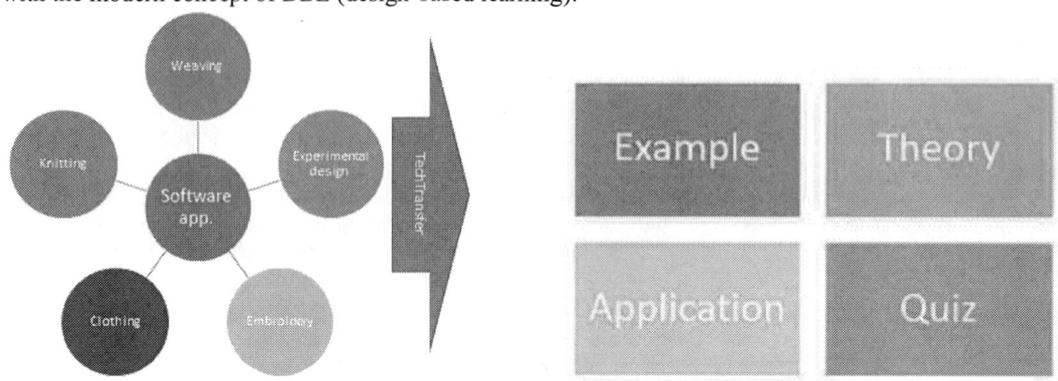

Figure 1. Left: concept of the modules in the project, Right: Structure of a module

The application part is structured in such a way that the students must perform specific tasks with the application in order to master it. The teacher can then link the content to a creative design the students must create. During the first year the proposed e-learning solution envisages support for three Intensive Study Programs (ISP), to be organized within the project. For one week, one of the partner Universities will host a group of 20 students (with 12 mobility students) and one tutor from each partner. Focus will be shared on the specific expertise of the host University, while practical work on the specific textile domain will be organized. As such, the e-learning instrument is specially conceived to support the DBL approach within these three ISPs, to be completed by the practical work in creating technical textiles or e-textiles. The output of these ISPs will serve as examples to other lecturers who want to use the e-learning instrument.

2.2 The e-Learning Content

The content is divided in 5 modules, each divided in 4-5 use cases. Each use case again divided in 4 parts. For the part of using the applications to obtain a design output, extensive use is made from video resources. This is done as learning a software via text is complicated for students, and would make the OER very page heavy. A hard limit on 20-25 pages of text for a module can be kept like this, allowing to keep the material manageable for the teachers and students. As example of the build up of the content, we present briefly the content of two of the modules.

2.2.1 Weaving Module

The weaving module starts with applying basic weaving theory to create uniform woven fabrics. In this the TexGen software (Brown 2021) is used to create a draft plan and a visual representation. In this way all the standard weaving terminology is trained. As TexGen is open source, this software is ideal for use in an OER. The second use case is the addition of special yarns into woven structures, like conductive yarns, or hairy yarns, with the possibility to create visualizations of the resulting structure. In this way students learn how yarn properties will influence the final fabric structure, and obtain a glimpse of large variety in yarns.

The complexity of the use cases increases gradually, with the third use case covering 3D woven structures, for example the structures created to obtain non-crimp composites, see Figure 1. The aim of creating these structures is to perform engineering simulations, for example with a Finite Element Analysis Software like Abaqus, so the fourth case covers the simulation of a woven structure with Abaqus. In this, the student edition version of the software is used, allowing all students to perform their own experimentation. Finally, to train actual design for a woven structure, the creation of a Damask woven structure is considered as last case, where demo versions of ArachWeave are used, or the new open source online tool AdaCAD.

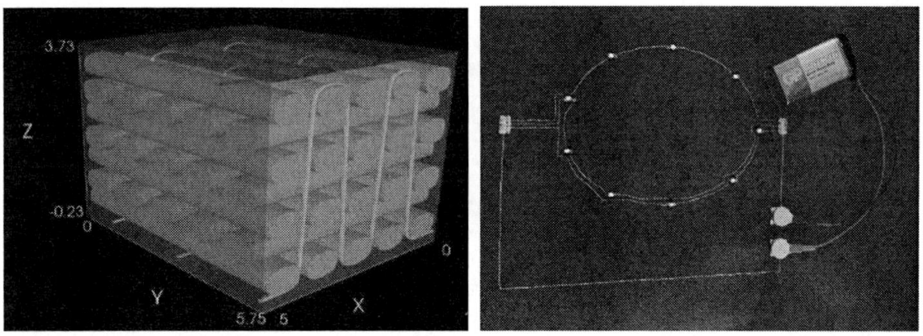

Figure 2. Left: 3D woven structure as generated by TexGen; Right: Embroidered illuminated fabric

2.2.2 Embroidery Module

The embroidery module focusses on intelligent textiles. Also here, fully open source software is used so the module is accessible to all students: Inkscape and its extension Ink/Stitch, inkstitch.org, which can generate output files that embroidery machines can use. First, conductive paths are considered together with patches where electronic elements can be soldered. As next case, textile-based heating elements are designed, followed by illuminated fabrics, see Figure 2. Finally, a textile-based water sensor is considered as use case, explaining all steps to design, and create this electronic component with textiles.

2.2.3 Promotion of the Content

The content as created will be applied in 3 ISPs, with a total of 36 mobilities for students. Apart from this, multiplier events with participation of 115 young professionals in textile are going to be organized in the second project year, in order to support textile creatives and to demonstrate our innovative approach for textile software training through DBL. All content will be made available through www.advan2tex.eu/portal/ where already different OER in the field of textiles are available. One of these is an OEP created during the Skills4Smartex project (www.skills4smartex.eu). The DBL created in the current OptimTex project will complement the content available, and offer extra possibilities to young textile creatives to improve their skills under the guidance of the lecturers with up-to-date software in design of technical and e-textiles.

3. CONCLUSION

OERs and OEPs have gained a lot of importance in the last decade, and certainly during the pandemic restrictions. Apart from allowing to reach a diverse group of students, OER also allows to collaborate over institutions, pooling resources and experience, so as to improve the education. When considering the training with state-of-the-art textile software tools, hands on experience is very important. Design-Based Learning is a modern educational concept which is ideal for software tool training, with focus on creating practical output. In order to support OEP and DBL for students in technical fields, an e-learning instruments is under construction, which links practical use cases of software tool use with textile theory knowledge. The DBL approach is meant to drive the educational process complementary to the official curricula. The students are required to perform the example designs through the application use-cases given under expert guidance (live or through the videos accompanying the content), to do the quizzes to test their theory, and then to build on the skills they learn to create their own designs.

ACKNOWLEDGEMENT

This project has been funded with support from the European Commission under the Erasmus+ Programme. This publication reflects the views only of the author, and the Commission cannot be held responsible for any use which may be made of the information contained therein. The authors would like to acknowledge the support of the Erasmus+KA2 projects, "Software tools for textile creatives", acronym OptimTex, grant agreement number 2020-1-RO01-KA203-079823.

REFERENCES

Blumenfeld et al, 1991. Motivating Project-Based Learning: Sustaining the Doing, Supporting the Learning, *Educational Psychologist*, 26(3&4), pp 369-398.

Brown L.P. et al, 2021. Modelling the geometry of textile reinforcements for composites: TexGen, Chapter 8 in *Composite reinforcements for optimum performance (Second Edition)*, Woodhead Publishing Ltd,

Darling-Hammond, L, et al, 2008. *Powerful Learning: What we know about teaching for understanding,*John Wiley&Sons, San Francisco, USA.

Ehlers, U., 2011. From Open Educational Resources to Open Educational Practices, *eLearning Papers*, 23/2011.

Gomez Puente S-M, et al, 2014. Exploring the effects of design-based learning characteristics on teachers and students, *International Journal of Engineering Education*, Vol. 30, No. 4, pp. 916–928.

Grosseck, G. et al, 2020. *Ghid pentru aplicarea Practicilor Educaţionale Deschise în timpul pandemiei de coronavirus. Utilizarea Resurselor Educaţionale Deschise în conformitate cu Recomandările UNESCO*, Smart Learning Institute of Beijing Normal University (SLIBNU), Bejing, China

Markham, T., 2011. Project Based Learning. *Teacher Librarian*, 39(2), pp. 38-42.

Radulescu, I.R. et al 2017. Blended Learning for innovation in textiles, *International Conference on Intelligent Textiles and Mass Customisation (ITMC2017): proceedings.*Ghent, Belgium

Radulescu, I.R. et al, 2021., E-Learning instruments for design based learning in textiles, *ELSE2021 international conference in e-learning proceeding*, Bucharest, Romania.

DEVELOPMENT OF A MULTI-USER VR ENVIRONMENT FOR TRAINING ELECTRICIANS TO WORK ON ELECTRIC POWER DISTRIBUTION NETWORK

Eduardo H. Tanaka[1], Tiago Z. Paula[1], Alisson F. Silva[1], Guilherme S. F. Gouveia [1], Lucimara de Almeida[1], Leonardo R. Domingues[1], Alex H. F. Alves[1] and Roberta R. Oliveira[2]
[1] *Eldorado Research Institute, Brazil*
[2] *Companhia Paranaense de Energia Elétrica, Brazil*

ABSTRACT

Formal education and corporate trainings have adopted immersive virtual reality environments for a while. These environments are great tools to represent real world situations, conditions and scenarios that may be dangerous or not easily reproducible on classrooms, laboratories or formal trainings. That is exactly the case of the electric power distribution network in Brazil, as the electricians take formal trainings but usually do not experience the real conditions of the network and the several risks involved with it during these trainings. As a result, the electricians may not be confident to work on the network and may eventually harm themselves or take longer than expected to find and fix problems on the network. Thus, this paper presents the development of a virtual reality environment for training electricians to work on the distributed network, considering the safety procedures, the proper usage of equipment and the collaboration with other electricians. With the proposed environment, it is expected to enhance the knowledge and the skills of the electricians and, therefore, have better professionals working on the distribution network.

KEYWORDS

Corporate Training, Virtual Reality, Simulator, Multi-User

1. INTRODUCTION

Virtual reality (VR) has been utilized in professional trainings and several educational activities, especially because it provides free interaction with realistic 3D objects with no risks while it can also promote active practices that, quite often, are not possible in regular classes (Mikropoulos, et al., 1997). According to Mikropoulos et al. (1997) and Pantelidis (1994), the usage of VR in a teaching and learning context is adequate when the users:

- Can't make mistakes in the real environments, because they can harm themselves or other people or even cause damages to the environment;
- Are not allowed to practice in the real environments;
- Are motivated to interact with simulated objects;
- Need to view, manipulate and organize information to acquire a specific knowledge;
- Develop or practice activities that are only possible in a virtual environment;

Additionally, by practicing in VR environments, users can try different approaches to solve problems as many times as they want, with no pressure of a classroom or a formal assessment (Patel, et al., 2006). Therefore, these environments encourage users to lead their own learning (Mikropoulos, et al., 1997).

Some VR environments for educational purposes are stand-alone experiences, designed for a single user. However, many of these environments allow collaboration and cooperation among users. That is the case of the EcoMUVE (Grotzer, et al., 2011), a set of virtual reality environments developed for high school students to learn about ecosystems and complex causal patterns. In addition, medical courses are continually adopting multi-user VR environments, especially to visualize 3D models representing parts of the human body and organs. One of the greatest advantages of this kind of VR environment to view medical models is to allow a collaborative analysis of these models with tools such as voice communication, pointers to highlight specific areas and to rotate and resize the models (Silverstein & Dech, 2005).

In professional trainings, multi-user VR environments have been adopted as well. Passos et al. (2017) developed a VR environment for training security agents in very large events such as the Olympic Games and the World Cup, as it is not easy to simulate emergency or critical situations in the real world environments. In the proposed VR environment, security agents need to collaborate and communicate with each other to identify potential security risks or suspects, guide the public and, eventually, isolate and/or eliminate the risks. According to the authors, the results of the user tests showed that the security agents were able to develop a sense of collaborative actions.

Other example of a multi-user VR environment for professional training is from Le et al. (2015). The proposed VR environment aimed to educate construction professionals about safety work. Using realistic scenarios, users need collaborate to inspect risks and share with others their findings.

One of the potential fields of usage of multi-user VR environments is in the electrical distribution system. During the current trainings, many of the electricians in Brazil have only formal classes (in a classroom) and some practices in special training centers that usually represent some parts of the electrical distribution network and contain poles, cables, distribution transformers, switches and other equipment. However, these training centers often do not have all equipment that the electricians can find in the distribution network. Moreover, they do not represent the real environment and conditions that the electricians will face when going to the field: high traffic streets, trees that conflict with the distribution network cables, consumers that may not be satisfied with the service, dogs and other animals that may be a threat, different weather conditions (wind, heavy rain, fog, and others).

Considering the gaps present in the current trainings for electricians to work on the distribution system, this paper presents a multi-user, VR simulator that aims to offer realistic scenarios and situations that can not be easily reproduced in the training centers. With the proposed simulator, it is expected that the electricians learn the safety procedures and best practices, the correct usage of Personal Protective Equipment (PPE) and Collective Protective Equipment (CPE), in addition to enhance the sense of collaboration among them.

The next sections present some related work, the development of the simulator and the results for far.

2. RELATED WORK

Due to the complexity and the risks involved with the electrical distribution system, an effective and efficient training for electricians is a key factor to achieve safety, reliability and quality of the services. Additionally, when these professionals need to work on any maintenance on the distribution network, if they were effectively trained, the chances are high that they will adopt the best practices and the most appropriate PPE and CPE and, consequently, decrease the risk of accidents.

Thus, simulators for training electricians to work on the electrical distribution system in Brazil have been proposed since the last two decades as tools to enhance their knowledge and prevent accidents. Some of them focus only on the visualization of the installations and/or equipment whereas others encourage and require that users interact with the equipment and explore the environment to solve problems. Additionally, a few of them adopted VR to promote immersion and give to the users a realistic and immersive experience.

STOP (de Castro Silva, et al., 2011) is one example of a simple simulator for the electrical system. In this simulator, electricians must analyze and interact with single-line diagrams of electrical systems and configure their equipment such as relays, circuit breakers and transformers. Also, it is possible to simulate faults in the systems. One of the drawbacks of STOP is that, as the electricians only interact with 2D diagrams of the electrical system, they do not have the experience of interacting with all the equipment present in the system – for example, a user may not be aware of how to operate a circuit breaker present in the real life.

An example of more realistic simulator is Virtual Substation (Silva, 2012), which uses 3D models to represent an electrical substation and its equipment. Although it is possible to interact with these 3D models using joysticks and VR goggles, the look and feel of the equipment is not realistic.

A more recent project also to simulate an electrical substation using VR is from Paludo et al. (2017). In this simulator, all equipment were 3D modelled according to a real substation in Brazil. Also, panels, buttons, switches and disconnectors are interactable through motion controllers and the electrician must select PPE according to the tasks he/she will perform. Moreover, the stress level is monitored using biometric data acquired from a smart band (Paludo, et al., 2017).

Despite the benefits to the trainings, it is interesting to notice that neither of these simulators are focused on the objective of this research and development project: a multi-user, VR environment to simulate scenarios and conditions that the electricians face when working on the electrical distribution network.

3. MATERIAL AND METHODS

The major objective of this project is to create a multi-user, VR simulator to enhance the knowledge of electricians to work on typical services on the distribution network, allowing them to practice tasks that, typically, are not possible in current trainings. An electrical distribution network usually includes several equipment and structures such as switches, isolators, cables, distribution transformers and poles. In addition, different elements that may conflict with the network or compromise the work of the electricians may be present, for example, a tree whose branches are in contact with the cables or a hive that is on the top the pole. Moreover, as most of the tasks of an electrician are performed on top of a ladder or in a truck with elevator bucket, these services may also have a risk of falling.

Unstructured interviews with electricians, safety specialists, instructors and engineers took place at the beginning of the project to gather details about the most relevant exercises to include in the proposed simulator, the equipment that electricians used to work, how they communicate with each other and work as a team. During the interviews, it was clear that, given the inherent risks, all initiatives to prevent accidents and to educate electricians about the recommended safety procedures are fundamental. After the interviews, a focus group was also conducted with the participants to raise the pros and cons in the current trainings. Furthermore, to understand how electricians work together and how the training classes take place, the researchers went to a training center and attended a training class (as observers) with a group of electricians.

After the interviews, focus group and the attendance of the training class, it was decided to have in the simulator exercises related to services and tasks that, usually, have a high rate of accidents, harming the electricians or causing damages to the distribution network. Moreover, as a result of the focus group, the major recommendation was to start with a tree pruning exercise using a chainsaw and a truck with elevator bucket to reach the higher branches.

The proposed simulator has been developed using the Scrum framework. And, to provide the basic functionality and VR support, the simulator is developed using Unity 3D (Unity, 2021) and the SteamVR plugin (Valve Corporation, 2021). Also, to create a realistic 3D scene, a specialized 3D modelling team has been assisting the project, producing the equipment and all other 3D objects based on technical specifications and documentation, photos and videos. Additionally, all the 3D objects related to the environment have been modeled: streets, sidewalks, vehicles, trees, grass, buildings, houses and road signs.

To create a more realistic and immersive experience, gestures similar to the real ones to manipulate the equipment were implemented in the simulator using motion controllers. For example, to start the chainsaw, a user needs to pull the engine's crank and, to cut some branches of a tree, a user must move the chainsaw to hit the branches. There are also other gestures to manipulate the hot stick: to expand or collapse it and to open and close fuse switches attached to the poles from a safe distance.

Another finding from the interviews, focus group and attending the training class was that, most of the time, electricians work in pairs when performing their tasks and have specific roles: one of them is the executor whereas the other is the supervisor, who must assist the executor and assure his/her safety and other people around. For instance, if a task needs to be performed on the top of the ladder or the elevator bucket, the supervisor must remain on the ground, preventing strangers to get close of the working area. Therefore, the electricians must talk to each other, so that a radio communicator (through voice) was also implemented to coordinate the execution of the tasks in an exercise.

For each task performed by electricians, there are formal procedures that describe a step-by-step of actions and the required PPE and CPE to mitigate or eliminate risks. Then, in the simulator, the exercises were created based on these step-by-step guides. If an incorrect action is performed in an exercise, it is registered in the exercise log so that instructors can review later. The same happens if the required PPE and CPE were not used. To assist the electricians during the tasks, the documents containing the safety procedures as well as some helpful tutorial videos were included into the simulator and are accessible through a virtual tablet.

As some users may have motion sickness when wearing VR goggles, the simulator can be used without the VR goggles. In this case, users can interact with an ordinary monitor, keyboard and mouse or a gamepad.

To evaluate the development of the simulator, some usability tests were conducted, especially to verify the locomotion. The major results can be found in Tanaka et al. (2020). Also, reviews with electricians, instructors and safety specialists have been conducted during the development of the simulator to validate the step-by-step of the exercises, the required PPE and CPE in the exercises and the equipment in the distributed network included in the scenario. Results from this review will be covered in the next section.

4. RESULTS

Figure 1 shows some screenshots of the proposed simulator. (a) the inventory system, which allows the electricians to pick up PPE, CPE and other equipment; (b) an electrician's avatar wearing safety glasses, gloves, helmet is equipped with the chainsaw, which is required to perform a tree pruning; (c) the first-person view of an electrician pruning a tree; and (d) the supervisor's view (on the ground) of the scene.

Figure 1. (a) Inventory system; (b) Electrician wearing PPE and equipped with chainsaw; (c) Using the chainsaw to prune some branches of the tree; (d) supervisor's view

Currently, there are three different exercises in the simulator. The goal of the first exercise is to prune a tree whose branches conflict with the low voltage network and is expected that the electricians perform the following actions:

1. Wear the appropriate PPE: helmet, safety glasses, face shield, hearing protection and gloves.
2. Isolate the working area with signaling cones.
3. The executor goes up with the elevator bucket and use the chainsaw to select the region of the tree to prune, while the supervisor remains close to the truck to assist the executor.
4. Collect the signaling cones back to the truck.

The goals of the other exercises are to open and close fuse switches in the poles and follow a similar procedure, except that, instead of the chainsaw, the electricians use the hot stick to reach the fuse switches on the top of the pole.

The feedback from the reviews with electricians, instructors and safety specialists was positive so far. According to them, the proposed simulator has a high level of immersion and a detailed representation of the components of the distribution network (poles, cables, switches, isolators, and others). Moreover, one common comment was that, with the simulator, it is possible to verify if the electricians are aware of all required PPE and CPE for the tasks they perform day-to-day and if they are following the safety procedures.

As enhancements, the reviewers suggested to include into the simulator a specific form to be filled by the electricians prior to do any task on the simulator to check the risks of the environment, on the network, and others, as this form is mandatory in the real life work.

5. CONCLUDING REMARKS

This paper presented a multi-user, VR simulator to enhance the current trainings of electricians to work on the electrical power distribution network. Given its potential, the simulator can enhance the quality of the service of the electricians, promote safety in their jobs, as well as their motivation.

As future work, it is planned to add more complex exercises to the simulator and develop a management system to allow the instructors to organize the exercises in the simulator and analyze reports of the exercises performed by the electricians. Also, the authors are investigating gamification mechanics to improve the engagement (for example, implementing scores, rankings, badges, and others). In order to do that, a study is on going to identify the gamer style of the electricians (Kumar, et al., 2020) as well as the feasibility of some of the existing gamification mechanics listed by Mambo.io (Kanazawa, 2020) to the project.

REFERENCES

de Castro Silva, C. H. et al., 2011. Desenvolvimento de um Laboratório Virtual para Capacitação Tecnológica à Distância em Proteção de Sistemas Elétricos. Revista Novas Tecnologias na Educação, July.

García, A. S. et al., 2019. Collaborative virtual reality platform for visualizing space data and mission planning. Multimedia Tools and Applications, 12, 78(23), p. 33191–33220.

Grotzer, T. et al., 2011. Helping Students Learn More Expert Framing of Complex. Orlando, FL, s.n.

Kanazawa, M., 2020. 108 Gamification Elements and Mechanics to Encourage Engagement. [Online] Available at: https://mambo.io/blog/gamification-elements-and-mechanics [Acesso em 30 04 2021].

Kumar, J. M., Herger, M. & Frii, R., 2020. Bartle's Player Types for Gamification. [Online] Available at: https://www.interaction-design.org/literature/article/bartle-s-player-types-for-gamification [Acesso em 30 04 2021].

Le, Q. T., Pedro, A. & Park, C. S., 2015. A Social Virtual Reality Based Construction Safety Education System for Experiential Learning. Journal of Intelligent & Robotic Systems, 08, 79(3-4), p. 487–506.

Mikropoulos, T., Chalkudis, A., Katsisis, A. & Kossivaki, P., 1997. Virtual realities in environmental education: The project LAKE. Education and Information Technologies, Volume 2, pp. 131-142.

Paludo, J. A. et al., 2017. Plataforma Virtual Interativa para Capacitação de Eletricistas em Subestações. P&D: Revista Pesquisa e Desenvolvimento da AneeL, pp. 58-61.

Pantelidis, V. S., 1994. Suggestions on when to use and when not to use virtual reality in education, s.l.: s.n.

Passos, C., da Silva, M. H., Mol, A. C. A. & Carvalho, P. V. R., 2017. Design of a collaborative virtual environment for training security agents in big events. Cognition, Technology & Work, 09, 19(2-3), pp. 315-328.

Patel, K. et al., 2006. The Effects of Fully Immersive Virtual Reality on the Learning of Physical Tasks. Cleveland, Ohio, USA, s.n.

Silva, R. C., 2012. VIRTUAL SUBSTATION um sistema de realidade virtual para treinamento de operadores de subestações elétricas. Uberlândia, MG: UFU.

Silverstein, J. C. & Dech, F., 2005. Precisely Exploring Medical Models and Volumes in Collaborative Virtual Reality. PRESENCE: Virtual and Augmented Reality, 2, 14(1), pp. 47-59.

Tanaka, E. et al., 2020. Evaluation of immersive virtual reality locomotion mechanisms. Diamantina, Association for Computing Machinery.

Unity, 2021. Unity Real-Time Development Platform | 3D, 2D, VR, AR.... [Online] Available at: https://unity.com/ [Acesso em 30 04 2021].

Valve Corporation, 2021. SteamVR Plugin. [Online] Available at: https://assetstore.unity.com/packages/tools/integration/steamvr-plugin-32647 [Acesso em 30 04 2021].

TEACHER ASSESSMENT OF ONLINE INSTRUCTION

Cecilia B-Ikeguchi
Ph.D., Tsukuba Gakuin University, Japan

ABSTRACT

As the world grappled with the unprecedented challenges brought about by the spread of the virus and where a state of emergency has been in place worldwide (Roshan, et al, 2021), a shift to digital forms of instruction was imperative. Japan was no exemption. The rushed implementation of remote instruction brought to light the enormous issues regarding online instructions not only in the country (Obe & Okutsu, 2020), but worldwide as well. There is a need not only to holistically understand learning and teaching in contexts where technology mediates learning, but also to understand the immense complexity of effectively assessing learning results in such context.

KEYWORDS

Online Instruction, Virtual Learning, Assessment and Evaluation

1. INTRODUCTION

Assessment and Evaluation has been an area of numerous discussions and research in the past (Lynch, 2020). However, assessment of student language learning in an emergency online situation is a different and difficult situation. This paper aims to review practical issues that address language educators' common question today "How can teachers effectively evaluate how much students learn from their online classes?"

Before proceeding with the discussions, it is imperative to clarify differences between synonymous concepts that have been interchangeably used with regard to online instruction and e-learning. A review of literature suggests that terms sharing common characteristics but with differing definition include, but are not limited to ①digital learning, ②online learning, ③e-learning, ④virtual learning, ⑤distance learning, ⑥blended learning. But the education world does not seem to universally agree on what each term means. Learning online is a vast landscape. Educators would usually describe learning online in one specific way: learning on a computer. How then can online learning be differentiated from e-learning and all other synonymous concepts in the field? In this section, I take two major instructional concepts discussed above and highlight their contrast as well as the aspects they share as they relate to the concepts of online evaluation discussed later.

First a clarification of the basic differences between e-learning and online learning. E-learning, which is usually home-based, usually contains soft copy materials such as PowerPoint slides and/or Word Documents and/or pre-recorded video lectures. Teaching materials are stored in a set of either hard or soft files, and students have to sit through a huge chunk of information by themselves. Lectures are pre-recorded; there is hardly any interaction. In case of question, students post on the platform or email the teacher. E-learning structure is rigid and standard. It does not cater to individual learners; all students go through the same set of materials.

Online learning, as the word suggests, is like conventional learning style, but is conducted entirely online. Lessons are conducted at the comfort of student's homes, except the student is not alone. The student participates in a class taught live by the teacher. Live online lessons usually require both students and teachers synchronically – at the same time. Lessons are conducted real-time, and both students and teachers communicate with each other using the same platform like an audio, a video or an interactive whiteboard. There is a lot of interaction involved and guidance is provided as instruction proceeds. While the structure of e-learning is rigid and standard, online learning is customized to help students in the learning process. The relationship between these concepts is summarized below using ConexED's definition.

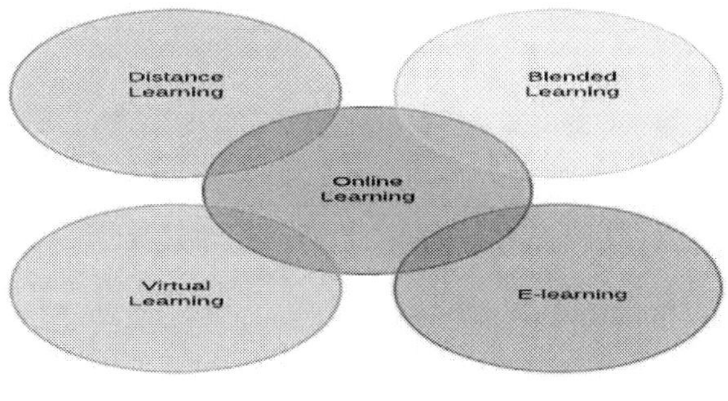

Figure 1

As educators, we do not and cannot teach in a vacuum. Our practices are supported somehow in one way or the other by one or some existing theories of ESL investigations which in turn determine the learning outcome we expect out of our teaching. In the following section, I will summarize some of the earlier and recent contemporary ESL theories on second language acquisition research that have guided ESL instruction and are relevant to the discussions.

1.1 Earlier ELT Methods and Models of L2 Language Acquisition

1. **The Audio-lingual Method** was probably one of the earliest methods of instruction and learning. The goal of instruction is to enable students to respond quickly and accurately in any given communication situation. It is based on the idea on English Language Development (ELD) of the four language skills. It focuses on the development of oral communication skills using dialogues, pattern drills and carefully ordered structures. It is an offshoot of the behaviorist theory which postulates that humans, like other living creatures, could be trained through a system of reinforcement.
2. **The Behaviorist Model Theory w**as first proposed by John Watson in the early 20th century based on the idea that "the mind is a blank slate" and behaviors are learned from environment. As indicated earlier, the theory postulates that human beings could be trained through a system of reinforcement. Skinner later argued that in terms of language acquisition, infants learn to speak a language by imitating human role models through a process involving imitation, rewards and practice. The need for a "learning model" is a key word in this concept.

1.2 Recent and more contemporary theories of Language Acquisition

1. **Interactionist theory**. The Interactionist theory suggests that one of the most salient and significant modes of discourse is conversation. Children learn language out of a desire to communicate with the world around them. Language therefore emerges from, and is dependent upon, social interaction. Children learn languages more easily than adults, and they are able to grasp grammatical structures without formal education, suggesting an innate or native ability for language. The Social Interactionist emphasizes lots of meaningful language use in the classroom.
2. **Krashen and Second Language Acquisition Theory**. Krashen's theory suggests that students learn a language through predictable five stages, and language instruction needs to provide a positive affective domain. This means that learners with high motivation, self-confidence, a good self-image, a low level of anxiety and extroversion determine success in second language acquisition. Classroom instruction therefore should build an accepting, encouraging environment, providing activities that allow student-student interaction.
3. **The Feedback model.** One of the most recent and widely discussed concepts in ESL instruction is the feedback model proposed by Hattie & Timperlery (20017). The concept suggests that using feedback with instructional content at the process level when learners are actively learning, helps the learners focus on information processing, which can be more effective. How and when can feedback be useful in the online classroom? Hattie & Timperley suggest that elaborate feedback in instruction is more effective in retention of knowledge and skills rather than in formal assessment.

The universal and unchanging rule of assessment is that we assess what we teach; how can this be done? Assuming that assessment of student language learning in an emergency online situation is a different and difficult situation, how can we accomplish this goal? This paper suggests a clear understanding of the characteristics of online learning is the first step in achieving this goal.

2. CHARACTERISTICS OF ONLINE LEARNING

Although the universal and unchanging rule of assessment is that we assess what we teach, assessment of language learning in an emergency online situation is an entirely different and difficult situation. This section focusses on the unique characteristics of online instruction which calls for a unique set of assessment tools to effectively measure how much learning took place. There is a need to holistically understand learning and teaching in contexts where technology mediates learning. The need for schools to turn to online instruction has shown a shift from an elitist mode of instruction to a mass and egalitarian education. The schools saw it imperative to create more structured and planned course programs and the challenge of uniformity in the delivery of those programs.

1. The most common general advantages attributed to online language learning include space and time saving, lower costs, flexibility in time and location, standardization in educational programs, improvement of instruction through using the class time efficiently, and providing immediate feedback. In addition, online instruction can offer numerous advantages including flexibility, accessibility, independency, interactivity, multimodality, cost-effectiveness, ubiquitous learning, convenience, and learner-centeredness (Moore, 2013).
2. The use of technology-enhanced language learning environments has facilitated interaction, collaboration, and communication with a wider audience. Butler and Wilburg (2003) proposed twelve attributes on how technology enriches language learning online and suggested that by providing comprehensible input; online instruction develops cognitive abilities and offers task-based, problem-solving and student-centered activities.
3. Mehran (2017) assessed Japanese students' readiness for online learning and suggested that by helping Japanese learners who feel anxious or shy by allowing them to personalize their learning in their own way and at their own pace, online instruction allows flexibility, accessibility, independency, interactivity, multimodality, cost-effectiveness, ubiquitous learning, convenience, and learner-centeredness and enhances out-of-class learning.
4. Ikeguchi (2017) discusses the use of computer-mediated learning in terms of the degree of student-teacher interaction during instruction. The report differentiates between teacher-mediated instruction wherein the teacher plays a role in the delivery of online learning in the classroom using maximum student-teacher interaction, and total computer use by students independent of the teacher. The former has been labelled teacher assisted language learning (TALL), while the latter has been identified as technology assisted language learning (tall), arguing that although computer use in the acquisition of language in the classroom has become imperative, the teachers' role in language instruction cannot be eclipsed by technology.

The innate characteristics of online instruction in terms of technical requirements, skills requirements, the breadth and use of different media, the dynamic interaction between learners and instructors seem to be its strength and its weakness at the same time. As in ordinary situations, testing online learning requires us to ask "how well the standards have been met? With a better insight on online learning environments, we realize that assessment and testing of language instruction online using ordinary face-to-face assessment methods based on the available theories needs a different set of approach, as will be seen in the following section.

2.1 Specific Issues and Challenges in Testing and Evaluation of e-Learning

1. The one-size fits all instructional pedagogy found in asynchronous online courses results in significantly less knowledge retention than does the personalized instruction in face-to-face course (Lindsey et al, 2014). The task becomes more profound when we think about testing and assessment in asynchronous online courses.

2. The problem of readiness. We often fall prey to the oft repeated fallacy that assessment begins when instruction ends. With online classes, however, assessment is necessary before instruction begins – to be able

to measure student readiness. To set the stage" for online course designers and teachers this refers to the need to evaluate students' online needs and technical skills before starting instruction. (Aisami, 2009). While the benefits of student readiness cannot be underestimated face-to-face instruction, they help redefine and raise student achievement in e-learning situations.

3. "Accountability issue. Accountability in e-learning is required both from teachers and students alike. For the former, assessment of student learning solely for accountability does not necessarily lead to learning. (Zeliff, 2000). The past few months saw teachers submitting evaluation reports and grades using the same unchanged evaluation criteria used in ordinary situation. Assessment only at the end of a course is what has been called "autopsy evaluation". Besides a mere obligation to stamp students a PASS or FAIL after completion of a course, it behooves the language teacher to gauge the extent to which students comprehend, remember and apply the results of instruction. For an online learning course to succeed, students must be held accountable for engaging in all essential and required course requirements.

4. The difficulty of feedback. The importance of feedback in instruction cannot be underestimated, but the online learning situation is different. Instructors should be reminded that while online learners are able to regulate and monitor their own learning (Bocchi, Eastman, & Swift, 2004) and assess their own progress student performance must, nevertheless, be carefully monitored, because instructors are unable to communicate with their students as quickly, easily, and fully as in traditional settings. Although feedback plays a significant role in learning, providing elaborate feedback during instruction is limited in online instruction. For this to be even more effective, students need to be empowered through constant feedback and reinforcement.

5. Academic honesty. A closer look at the situation gives an honest assessment of the practicalities we deal with regarding testing students' learning online. Despite remote proctoring platforms that can monitor behavior during online tests, online assessment represents a greater challenge (Fodor, 2003) because no existing technology can ensure academic honesty (Scanlon, 2003).One view stresses that online tests should be viewed as take-home tests, because there is very little to catch cheats other than trust on student's sense of personal integrity at a time when academic dishonesty is rampant.

6. Timing and frequency of tests. Language is a complicated component requiring a complicated set of assessment tools. There are several language tests, each measuring different skills. Language tests are conducted in several stages of language acquisition. Online assessment, however, requires a more ongoing, systematic approach than that of traditional instruction (Robles & Braathen, 2002). Assessment methods must match the level of desired competencies, online assessment requires educators to modify their methods of instruction. Assessment only at the end of a course is what has been called "autopsy evaluation"; assessment of online learning should be ongoing.

3. EVALUATION AND ASSESSMENT OF ONLINE INSTRUCTION

1. Retrieval Practice Learning. Retrieval practice is a recent instructional approach that emphasizes bringing information to mind to enhance and boost learning (Ding, 2017). The theory claims that by deliberately recalling information, learners are forced to pull knowledge "out" and examine what is already know. In terms of testing, the strategy calls for constant and repeated testing. Testing students immediately a material learned, and repeated testing conditions allow students to retrieve information learned and incorporate these ideas to current experiences, thereby retaining long-term memory and making possible the transfer of learning. When assessment becomes a consistent part of teaching, it helps consolidate language learning (Firth, 2017).

2. The Skills Acquisition Approach. Deeply rooted in Cognitive Science original experiment suggested that games are a great source for practicing recently learned ideas and apply knowledge in practical solutions. Besides overcoming learning problems like frustration, gamification was found to foster more positive learning outcomes and helps transfer of skills learned. It combines both the elements of traditional learning and online learning. SHIFT (2018) provides interesting insights with regard to testing students in an online learning situation. Based on the Skills Application theory, the method suggests some of the best instructional tools teachers can use to assess students throughout online instruction including quizzes at the onset of the course, T-F exercises, self-assessments, case studies and problem-solving questions, scenario-based questions. These are summarized below.

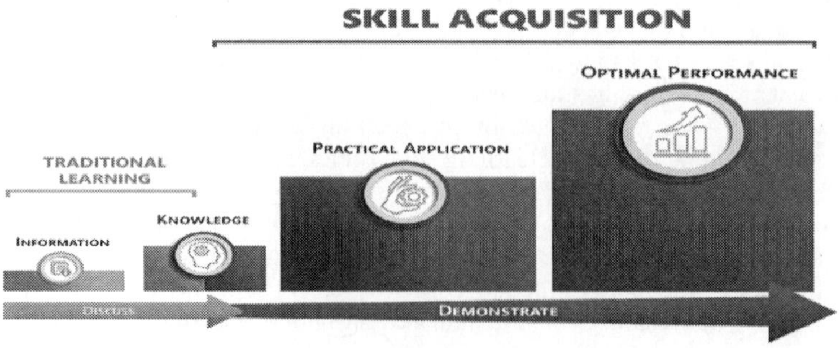

Figure 2

3. Ongoing Assessment. To effectively measure online learning, assessment should be ongoing. I would call this formative assessment. Frequent assessment during instruction determines how well a student has learned the required material. This can be done by collecting data such as content and quality of student posts on discussion board, feedback that students are required to give to each other on peer-reviewed assignments, open-ended responses or tasks that the instructors deems necessary to the course or alignment of teaching goals and learning needs. The results of periodic tests explain to students where they are and provide feedback of their learning. One ways summative evaluation of both traditional instruction and online learning can be done is summarized in the form of RDP, described below.

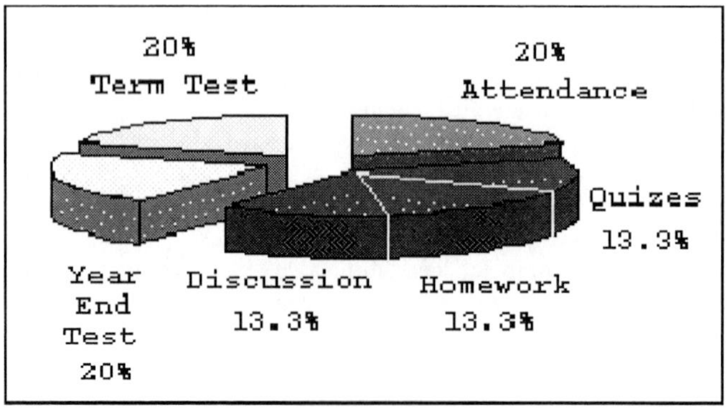

Figure 3

4. Use of Classroom Technology. While teachers scramble to learn how to use technology to deliver online classes, testing becomes a secondary priority and concern. To address this issue, Kohler and Mishra (2009) propose that teachers consider using technology together with pedagogy to deliver content learning in the online classroom. Readily available online quizzes, for instance, can tremendously help build understanding, alongside flashcards that assist student to commit to memory more permanently (Roediger, Mc Daniel and Brown, 2014).

4. SUMMARY AND CONCLUSION

The shift to online instruction as a temporary substitute for traditional instruction in times of pandemic has posed a new set of challenges. Information must be provided from research data to instantly inform education policy and practice. This paper discussed the unique character of online learning and suggested practical strategies for teachers to bridge theory and practice to address learning needs in online instruction.

REFERENCES

Aisami, R. S. (2009). Planning and teaching online courses. In P. L. Rogers, G. A. Berg, J. V. Boettcher, C. Howard, L. Justice, & K. D. Schenk (Eds.), *Encyclopedia of Distance Learning* (2nd ed., pp. 1628–1638).

Bocchi, J., Eastman, J. & Swift, K. (2004). Retaining the Online Learner. *Journal of Education for Business*, 79 (4). 245-253.

Butler-Pascoe and Wiburg (2003). Technology and Second Language Learning. *The Electronic Journal for English as a Second Language*.

Ding, Lu. (2017). Studies of Student Engagement in Gamified Online Discussions. *Computers and Education. 115*(10).

Firth, J. (2017). Assessment as Learning: The Role of Retrieval Practice in the Classroom. *Journal of Experimental Psychology, Memory, and Cognition, 36*(5), 1118-1133.

Fodor, P. (2003). Fundamentals of Software Development. Systematic program design, coding, and testing. *Computer Science III*. 2013-2015.

Hattie, J. & Timperley, H. (2007). The Power of Feedback. *Review of Educational Research*, *77*(1). 81-112.

Ikeguchi, C. (2017). Teacher Assisted Language Learning and Technology Assisted Language Learning. International Academic Forum (IAFOR). ISSN: 2186-4691.

Kohler, M., Mishra, P. (2009). What is Technological Pedagogical Content? Contemporary Issues in Technology and Teacher Education. 9(1). 60-70.

Krashen, S.D. (1987) Principles and Practice in Second Language Acquisition. Prentice-Hall International.

Lindsay, G., Cullen, S.S., Cullen, M.A. (2014). Universal Program Provision in England. Children and Society. Wiley Online Library. P. 2012-2014.

Lynch, M. (2020). Revisiting Accountability in Online Learning. Online Learning. E-learning. The Tech Advocate. June 3, 2020.

Mehran, P. (2017). Are Japanese Digital Natives Ready for Learning English Online? *International Journal of Educational Technology in Higher Education*. Springer: Open Access.

Moore, L. (2015). A Rich Environment for Active Learning (REAL): A Model for Online Instruction. Heather Robinson. IGI Global online.

Obe, M., Okutsu, A. (2020). Corona Virus Forces Japan to Grapple with Online Education. Mikkei Asia. March 9.

Brown, P., Roediger, H., Mc Daniel, M. (2014). Make It Stick. The Belknap Press. London.

Scanlon, P. (2003). Student Online Plagiarism: How Do We Respond? *College Teaching*, *51*(4). 161-165.

Ravidchandran, P., Shah, A. (2021). "A Literature Review on Impact of COVID on Teaching and Learning.*" ERIC. Higher Education for the Future*, *8*(1), p133-141.

Watson, J. (2008). *Behavior: An Introduction to Comparative Psychology*. Kessinger Publishing. 454 pages.

Zeliff, N. (2000). *Alternative assessment*. National Business Education Yearbook 2000, pp. 91-102.

SELF-PRESENTATION AND LIABILITY WITHIN E-LEARNING ENVIRONMENTS

Stella J. Phipps[1], Michael V. Harrington[2], Gerald E. Evans[2] and Daniel C. Evans[2]
[1]*Office of Institutional Effectiveness, University of Montana, 32 Campus Drive, Missoula, MT 59812, USA*
[2]*College of Business, University of Montana, 32 Campus Drive, Missoula, MT 59812, USA*

ABSTRACT

This paper outlines some of the implications of delivery and participation within e-Learning courses and explores whether awareness of these implications may affect the behavior of participants in these courses.

KEYWORDS

Data, e-Learning, Surveillance, Online, Tracking

1. INTRODUCTION

The COVID-19 pandemic resulted in a pronounced shift to e-Learning, but the use of web-based lecture technologies to supplement or replace face-to face modalities had been steadily increasing in higher education well before the onset of the pandemic (O'Callaghan et al., 2017). Courses have become increasingly supplemented by web-based learning platforms such as Moodle and Blackboard, utilizing these tools to encourage student engagement and simplify administrative course management. It is now customary, in an effort to support students who may be uncomfortable with online modalities, to provide recorded lectures of both synchronous and asynchronous courses. Students can access and replay them at their leisure to prevent missing valuable content and to enhance comprehension (DeNeui & Dodge, 2006). Features such as these heighten the convenience of online courses and increase the likelihood of students enrolling and successfully completing an online course (von Konsky et al., 2009), but also present implications for the participants that would not typically arise in a traditional face-to-face setting.

Self-presentation is a term used in the behavioral sciences that refers to how individuals choose to present themselves to a wider audience, in light of how they want to be perceived by that audience. This is related to the concept of impression management, which entails controlling information about oneself to create a desired impression on others (Baumeister & Vohs, 2007). Self-presentation may be deliberate and potentially deceitful, but it may also be an entirely unconscious act. Self-interest of individuals and their awareness and understanding of their social environment determines the amount and type of effort they put forth toward creating their desired impression on others or, more broadly, the "public sphere".

Rauchfleisch and Kovic (2016) and Mahlouly (2014) explored Habermas' (1991) concept of the public sphere, a "network of communication", in which individuals within that realm regulate their behaviors and interactions based on their perceived notions of acceptable behavior in that environment. Within that realm exists a hierarchy of "identity building" based on how the individuals wish to be viewed and how they adjust their behavior according to those objectives. The internet is identified as a public sphere that impacts identity building and "agenda setting" in the context of individuals' self-presentation. The degree to which individuals police their behavior within an online environment, as with any other setting, depends on their cognizance of their roles within that setting and their awareness regarding how hierarchies of expectations within that setting operate. The behaviors and choices of participants in e-Learning environments likely function no differently. However, significant differences may exist in students' level of awareness of themselves as members of an e-Learning environment and their subsequent roles within that realm as opposed to their roles and expectations within a face-to-face classroom environment. Furthermore, categorical issues may come into play. An e-Learning platform is, after all, the internet. Individuals who operate in other online environments such as social media platforms with degrees of comfort and familiarity may have similar assumptions about how to conduct themselves within an e-Learning environment. Different online environments may be perceived as similar by individuals operating within those environments despite fundamental differences existing among them.

2. E-LEARNING: BENEFITS AND DRAWBACKS

The use of data tracking and surveillance in e-Learning environments is increasing, partly due to the use of tools highlighting such features as "learning guidance" and "assessment" in efforts to ensure an online course contributes adequately to a high-quality education (May & George, 2011). This access to data sets a precedent unique to the online classroom. In a traditional, face-to-face course, information about the student's study habits or engagement within the course is restricted to what is observable in the classroom and information the student voluntarily provides. In contrast, e-Learning systems foster an environment of surveillance inconceivable through an in-person course format. All online activity pertaining to a course, as long as it is funneled through the e-Learning platform, is recorded automatically and can subsequently be audited. An instructor can see a student's attempted logins, views of recorded lectures or other URLs posted in the platform, downloads of course materials, length of time the student spent in the platform, and even the IP address from which the student accessed the course.

Many e-Learning platforms provide canned reports of student activity supplemented by visualizations such as informative and accessible charts and graphs. A savvy instructor can use these data to assess student behaviors and even make predictions or assumptions about students based on their level of activity in the platform. An instructor may be less inclined toward lenient grading with students who are enrolled in online sections due to the increased accessibility of course content in conjunction with whatever observations the instructor might make based on the students' online activity recorded in the platform. This places the instructor at a distinct advantage.

Conversely, the e-Learning environment may create potential liabilities instructors are unlikely to encounter within traditional classroom settings. While the Department of Education has established that recording students in online classroom settings is not a violation of FERPA (2020), recordings still produce some degree of vulnerability to participants. The number of participants in a traditional classroom is generally restricted, if not to enrolled students then at least by room capacity. Potentially, recordings can last indefinitely and access to those recordings may be allocated to other than sanctioned participants. Unless restrictions are set in place preemptively, "unfettered access" (DeNeui & Dodge, 2006) to recorded lectures could have a much wider and potentially unregulated audience than intended, which may have intellectual property, privacy and liability implications.

Accessibility to lectures via recordings, especially if not adequately restricted, may also create a precedent that inhibits discourse in the virtual classroom. Any classroom setting, whether it be face-to-face or virtual, is public. Participants in a classroom would be expected to be aware of this and censor their communication to some degree regardless of the mode of course delivery. However, a recorded lecture can be saved indefinitely and replayed, and therefore presents unique implications that are less likely to manifest in a traditional classroom setting. Thus, willingness of participants to contribute to meaningful discussion within the classroom may be affected, as might course content. For example, students in a face-to-face classroom might not be as likely to fixate on semantics or potentially take innocuous comments out of context as they could with access to a lecture they can save and re-visit and subsequently overanalyze. It is possible instructors sensitive to this phenomenon might adjust the content of their lectures accordingly to discourage misinterpretation or unwanted controversy.

May and George (2011) advocate a three-fold "system of transparency" to ensure students and other users of e-Learning platforms are adequately protected within a surveilled e-Learning environment: 1. Informing users of any tracking process in place whenever accessing any online learning platform; 2. Acquiring approval from users that such tracking may occur; and 3. Allowing users "full control" of their tracking data and the power to make their data accessible or inaccessible to others. Whether this is feasible in all e-Learning platforms or within existing university data governance policies should at least be examined.

3. CASE STUDIES & ASSESSMENT

Despite the potential issues associated with e-Learning described above, self-awareness and subsequent self-presentation of some students as they engage within learning management platforms appears to be limited. Several anecdotal cases support this suggestion. Multiple seasoned instructors of both synchronous and asynchronous courses described encounters with students over many semesters. Many students were seemingly unaware their online activity within the platform was recorded and auditable, or, in some cases, observed at all.

In one case study, an online asynchronous undergraduate student who performed poorly in a business course attempted to negotiate with the professor to elevate the student's grade. The instructor requested an audit of the student's activity and the teaching assistant and IT support staff compared it to the activity of other students in the course who scored higher on the exam. The data gleaned from user activity reports within the eLearning platform illustrated that not only had the student failed to view nearly all of the recorded lectures, the student also displayed significantly less online activity than other students in the course who had performed better. These tools allowed the instructor to parry further negotiations or excuses preemptively. The activity data gleaned from the platform reports were also used constructively to suggest the student increase activity in the course.

Electronic delivery of materials in conjunction with software designed to check plagiarism also renders cheating relatively easy to catch, although some students persist in engaging in such activities. Another case study involves a business instructor who described several students who turned in identical assignments, only to be shocked when they were caught. In another particularly provocative case, an online sociology instructor received a submission of a paper only to recognize some of the content presented in the submitted assignment as the instructor's own writing.

The final case illustrating students' compromised self-presentation is a professor of business who described students in a synchronous online business course who made an appearance at the initial start of class only to disappear mid-lecture, turning off their cameras and failing to respond to the instructor's attendance checks in the online chat feature embedded in the course. Upon conclusion of the lecture, the students (or their Zoom screens, rather) lingered idly in class, their representatives clearly still away from their computers.

These behaviors and the dichotomy of this phenomenon are perplexing. The current generation of traditional undergraduate students represented in e-Learning courses is considered to be the best-educated and most technologically-savvy generation (Bradshaw, 2019; Parker & Igielnik, 2020). Many students, however, demonstrate a troubling lack of awareness (or apathy) that their behavior is observed by others as well as every aspect of their online activity is recorded and saved and can be retrieved. According to a 2016 Gallup poll, Millennials are more apt than previous generations to be comfortable with organizations (institutions of higher education were not listed in this survey) accessing their personal data and 80% reported they trusted businesses to keep their information secure (Alton, 2017). Fleming and Adkins (2016) theorize this trust may be the result of growing up while under constant surveillance by technology that blurs the boundaries between public and private.

Some students have expressed concerns about their privacy and voiced reluctance to being surveilled by their institutions but these objections seem to occur more frequently when they are actively made aware of being surveilled and some physical action on their part is required, such as being compelled to use tracking devices or a camera or face recognition software to discourage cheating during exams (Mangan, 2021). It appears that if the surveillance is "out of sight" it is also "out of mind". Surveillance and data collection within an e-Learning platform likely does not enter a student's consciousness unless the data are actively retrieved under circumstances described in the case studies.

4. CONCLUSION

The student behavior described in these case studies could be explained by a limited awareness of their roles within an e-Learning environment as well as difficulties identifying it as another social environment possessing a set of expectations and rules. Factors that contribute to this phenomenon may include generational characteristics of enrolled students and their relationship with technology. It is also possible the e-Learning environment, being relatively new and dynamic, with rules that are not always clearly defined, sends mixed messages to the participants, resulting in behaviors that appear contradictory or careless. Many students likely have never participated in e-Learning until entering college, and their ability to identify expectations within that environment and implications of their behavior within it may be limited. These challenges might not be restricted to student participants and may also apply somewhat to the instructors of online courses as well, who, as participants in a new and evolving arena, are still learning what the rules are and developing their own self-presentation.

Universities must carefully construct technological and business process measures that adequately restrict access to recorded lectures. Enforcement of security measures in e-Learning is vital to encourage participation as well as confidence in the online method of delivery. Such measures may include, but are not limited to, restricting the amount of time recorded lectures are available online and ensuring they are delivered in formats that are not downloadable; utilizing a single sign on (SSO) to limit access to course content; or simply requiring students to view online lectures synchronously and not providing recordings of lectures at all. While all universities have general policies in place to ensure student data are protected and restrict access to student data, these protections do not explicitly examine how these data are being used internally. Universities should take steps to encourage a culture of data awareness for all participants in e-Learning platforms that addresses the unique issues associated with engaging within those environments.

5. LIMITATIONS

The onset of institution-wide mandatory remote learning in response to COVID-19 resulted in a large number of new (and sometimes reluctant) participants. Explanations for the behaviors observed in the case studies described in this paper are primarily speculative. If such behavior adjustments are indeed occurring, it is not known how directly or consciously they are being made. It is hypothesized, but not known, that those recently introduced to e-Learning environments may behave differently from their counterparts who are accustomed to operating within such realms. Further research is needed to ascertain whether a relationship exists between individuals' familiarity with e-Learning environments and their behavior and whether those individuals consciously adjust their behavior in response to their perceived roles within the e-Learning environment.

REFERENCES

Alton, L. (2017, December 1). *How Millennials Think Differently About Online Security.* Forbes. https://www.forbes.com/sites/larryalton/2017/12/01/how-millennials-think-differently-about-online-security/?sh=93d5d33705f3

Baumeister, R. F., & Vohs, K. D. (Eds.) (2007). *Encyclopedia of social psychology.* SAGE Publications, Inc., https://www.doi.org/10.4135/9781412956253

Bradshaw, J. (2019, March 13). *What's Different About Generation Z Tech Talent?* Forbes. https://www.forbes.com/sites/forbestechcouncil/2019/03/13/whats-different-about-generation-z-tech-talent/?sh=50fdb4cb1f50

DeNeui, D., & Dodge, T. L. (2006). Asynchronous Learning Networks and Student Outcomes: The Utility of Online Learning Components in Hybrid Courses. *Journal of Instructional Psychology, 33*(4), p256-259.

FERPA and virtual learning. (2020, March). Protecting Student Privacy | U.S. Department of Education.
https://studentprivacy.ed.gov/resources/ferpa-and-virtual-learning

Fleming, J., & Adkins, A. (2016, June 9). *Data Security: Not a Big Concern for Millennials.* Gallup Business Journal. https://news.gallup.com/businessjournal/192401/data-security-not-big-concern-millennials.aspx

Habermas, J. (1991). The structural transformation of the public sphere: An inquiry into a category of bourgeois society. Cambridge, MA: MIT Press.

Mahlouly, D. (2014). Rational criticism, ideological sustainability and intellectual leadership in the digital public sphere. *International Journal of E-Politics, 5*(1), 78-90. https://doi.org/10.4018/ijep.2014010105

Mangan, K. (2021). *The Surveilled student.* Chronicle of Higher Education. https://www.chronicle.com/article/the-surveilled-student

May, M., & George, S. (2011). Privacy concerns in E-learning: Is Using Tracking Systems a Threat? *International Journal of Information and Education Technology*, 1-8. https://doi.org/10.7763/ijiet.2011.v1.1

O'Callaghan, F. V., Neumann, D. L., Jones, L. (2017). The use of lecture recordings in higher education: A review of institutional, student, and lecturer issues. *Education and Information Technologies* 22, 399–415 https://doi.org/10.1007/s10639-015-9451-z

Parker, K., & Igielnik, R. (2020, May 14). *On the Cusp of Adulthood and Facing an Uncertain Future: What we know about Gen Z so far.* Pew Research Center's Social & Demographic Trends Project. https://www.pewresearch.org/social-trends/2020/05/14/on-the-cusp-of-adulthood-and-facing-an-uncertain-future-what-we-know-about-gen-z-so-far-2

Rauchfleisch, A., & Kovic, M. (2016). The Internet and Generalized Functions of the Public Sphere: Transformative Potentials from a Comparative Perspective. *Social Media + Society.* https://doi.org/10.1177/2056305116646393

von Konsky, B. R., Ivins, J., & Gribble, S. J. (2009). Lecture attendance and web-based lecture technologies: A comparison of student perceptions and usage patterns. *Australasian Journal of Educational Technology, 25*(4). https://doi.org/10.14742/ajet.1130

AUTHOR INDEX